MW00343958

# Comparative Mythology, Cultural and Social Studies and The Cultural Category- Factor Correlation Method

# A New Approach to Comparative Cultural, Religious and Mythological Studies with its Application

By
Dr. Muata Ashby

# Comparative Mythology, Cultural and Social Studies

Sema Institute/Cruzian Mystic Books
P.O.Box 570459
Miami, Florida, 33257
(305) 378-6253 Fax: (305) 378-6253

The author is available for group lectures and individual counseling. For further information contact the publisher.

Ashby, Muata
Comparative Mythology, Cultural and Social Studies and The Cultural Category- Factor Correlation Method: A New Approach to Comparative Cultural, Religious and Mythological Studies
ISBN: 1-884564-72-0

Library of Congress Cataloging in Publication Data

## Other books by Muata Ashby

*See back section for more listings*

# Table of Contents

## *Chapter 3: Cultural Expressions and Folklore Differences and how they Manifest Over Universal Principles of Human Nature* ............ *93*

## *Chapter 4: Cultural Category - Factor Correlation Method of Classifying, Studying and Comparing Categories and Factors of Cultural Expression* ...... *123*

**What is Reality? And Why is It Important For Society to be Guided by Reality when Constructing and Maintaining its Societal Philosophy?** ...................................................................................... **147**

# List of Tables

# Table of Figures

# Introduction to Comparative Cultural, Religious and Mythological Studies

My hope is that a comparative elucidation may contribute to the perhaps not-quite desperate cause of those forces that are working in the present world for unification, not in the name of some ecclesiastical or political empire, but in the sense of human mutual understanding. As we are told in the Vedas: "Truth is one, the sages speak of it by many names."

—Joseph Campbell
June 10, 1948

As one can ascend to the top of a house by means of a ladder or a tree or a staircase or a rope, so diverse is the ways and means to approach God, and every religion in the world shows one of these ways.

—Paramahamsa Ramakrishna (1836-1886)
(Indian Sage)

There is no more important knowledge to a people than their history and culture. If they do not know this they are lost in the world.

—Cicero, Roman Philosopher (106-43 BC)

# The Basis for the Study of Comparative Religions and Mythologies

This volume is the exposition of a method for studying and comparing cultures, myths and social aspects of a society. It is an expansion on the Cultural Category Factor Correlation method that was originally introduced in the book AFRICAN ORIGINS OF CIVILIZATION, RELIGION, YOGA MYSTICAL SPIRITUALITY, ETHICS PHILOSOPHY. This volume contains an expanded treatment as well as several refinements along with examples of the application of the method.

The first section of this volume introduces the most important questions that will shape the context of as well as the manner in which we will explore the themes presented. Therefore, it is prudent to establish, as it were, a common basis for our study, and present the parameters which we will use to conduct our study and look at evidences to determine social interrelationships and the interconnectedness of certain cultures. The following questions are vital to our study. The implications of the answers will be a prominent aspect of this first section, but will also be a central theme throughout the entire book.

**Question:** What is Humanity and how is the origin and history of humanity classified by scholars?

**Question:** What is "Culture"? What are the characteristics of culture? How important is culture in studying a people, their customs and traditions?

**Question:** What is "Civilization"?

**Question:** Where did Civilization begin?

**Questions:** Can the common basis of cultural expressions, concepts and doctrines between cultures be determined? If so, what are the criteria or factors to be examined and compared for such a study, and what is the methodology to be applied to those criteria to reveal their similarity or disparity? Can a scientific procedure be applied to those criteria in order to systematically arrive at a conclusive determination and thereby allow a researcher to ascertain the existence or non-existence of a

13

relationship between the cultures, and possibly also the nature of such a relationship?

**Question:** If it is possible to answer the questions above might it also be possible to rediscover and perhaps even reconstruct and authentic history and description of ancient African culture or other cultures so as to repair or reconstruct African civilization, Religion and Philosophy?

The Cultural Category- Factor Correlation Method may be used for comparative studies to determine the meaning of cultural manifestations. It can also be used to determine cultural relations and correlations. If we compare two cultural factors from two cultures we can discover the meaning of an object, ritual, philosophical tenet, etc. by comparing various aspects of its significance in the two cultures. This is perhaps the most important reason to conduct the comparative studies. It is useful in reconstructing cultural practices, histories or wisdom teachings.

The Cultural Category- Factor Correlation Method may be used for comparative studies to determine the relationships between cultures or between certain of their artifacts (factors of cultural expression). This is useful in understanding how cultures interacted or currently interact and how they related or currently relate to each other.

# Chapter 1: The Origins of Creation, Culture, Humanity, Religion and Philosophy

# The Origins of Humankind

In order to begin our journey of comparative studies, we will need a reference point. Science offers a useful reference point to understand the origins of life, classifying the evolution of human life on earth. However, as we will see, science does not provide all of the answers about history. Therefore, we will eventually need to move beyond the confining ideas of evolution and scientific thinking. The Stone Age is a period that is regarded as being early in the development of human cultures. The Stone Age refers to the period before the use of metals. The artifacts used by people as tools and weapons were made of stone. The dates given for the Stone Age differ greatly for different parts of the world due to varying rates of development among societies and also due to the limitations of science. In Europe, Asia, and Africa, it is thought to have begun about two million years ago and to have ended in most parts of Northeast Africa (Ancient Egypt), Southwest Asia (Middle East) and Southeast Asia, by about 6000 B.C.E. It is also thought to have lingered in Europe, the rest of Asia, and other parts of Africa until 4,000 B.C.E. or later. However, the remarkable new evidence surrounding the Ancient Egyptian Sphinx shows that Ancient Egypt has a much older history than was previously thought and therefore, did not experience the ages of time as did the rest of the world. The Stone Age has been divided into three periods: Paleolithic, Mesolithic, and Neolithic.

**Figure 1: The World**

15

The Paleolithic Age lasted from two million years ago to the end of the last ice age, which was about 13,000 B.C.E. Agricultural villages began to develop by the year 8,000 B.C.E. By the year 6,000 B.C.E. pottery began to appear in the regions of the ancient Middle East, and the use of copper began for the first time in some regions. The Mesolithic or Middle Stone Age followed the Paleolithic Age. It is thought to have begun about 10,000 B.C.E. in Europe. In the Neolithic Age or New Stone Age which followed the Mesolithic Age, human beings first lived in settled villages, bred and domesticated animals, cultivated grain crops, and practiced pottery, flint-mining, and weaving.

**Figure 2:The Ancient Egyptian *Horemakhet* (Sphinx)**

The theories about the origins of humanity are not firm because much of the evidence of the evolutionary development of human beings has been swept away by the active nature of the planet. Volcanoes, storms, floods, etc., eventually wipe away all remnants of everything that happens on the surface of the earth as they recycle matter to bring forth life sustaining conditions again. For example, by the time it was rediscovered the city of Rome was buried in several feet of dust, ash and other natural particles, which eventually claim the surface of the earth through the action of wind and other natural phenomena of weather. Further, new scientific evidence compels scientists to revise their estimates to account for the new findings. One important example in this area relates to the Ancient Egyptian Sphinx, in the area today known as Giza, in Egypt. The Great Sphinx was once known as *Horemakhet* or "Heru in the Horizon." It was later known by the Greeks as Harmachis. New discoveries show the Ancient Egyptian Sphinx to be much older than previously thought. The importance of this discovery is that it

16

places advanced civilization first in northeast Africa (Ancient Egypt), at the time when Europe, Mesopotamia[1] and the rest of Asia were just coming out of the Paleolithic Age. Thus, when Ancient Egypt had already created the Sphinx, the Temple complexes and the Great Pyramids, the rest of the world was just beginning to learn how to practice farming and to use sleds, boats and other elementary instruments which were just being invented there. The new findings related to the Sphinx, which are supported by many ancient writings, are leading us to realize the true depths of human origins and the starting point for civilization. This means that we must begin to open up to expand our present concepts of reality, history and religion beyond the limitations of antiquated beliefs in order to discover the secrets of existence. Creation myths and the Mystical philosophy related to religious traditions can add to our knowledge of the origin and destiny of humankind from a philosophical point of view that can be compared and which can be used to reconstruct a more complete picture of human existence.

## Cultural Correlations in The Ancient Creation Myths

The creation stories of Ancient Egypt, the Bible, Cabalism (Jewish Mysticism) and the Hindu-Vedantic tradition are remarkably similar in the notion of the existence of a primeval formlessness which subsequently gave rise to different forms resulting in the differentiation and objectification of matter.

Ancient Egyptian Shabaka Inscription:

"Ptah conceived in his heart (reasoning consciousness) all that would exist and at his utterance (the word - will, power to make manifest), created Nun, the primeval waters (unformed matter-energy).

Then, not having a place to sit Ptah causes Nun to emerge from the primeval waters as the Primeval Hill so that he may have a place to sit. Atom (Atum) then emerges and sits upon Ptah. Then came out of the waters four pairs of Gods, the Ogdoad (eight Gods)...

In the Ancient Egyptian creation story involving the Asarian Mysteries, The Supreme Being (Nebertcher, Neberdjer) assumes the role of Asar and creates the universe in the form of Khepra (Khepera) and Tem:

"Neb-er-djer saith, I am the creator of what hath come into being, and I myself came into being under the form of the god Khepra (Khepera), and I came into being in primeval time. I had union with my hand, and I embraced my shadow in a love embrace; I poured seed into my own mouth, and I sent forth from myself issue in the form of the gods Shu (air) and Tefnut (moisture)."

"I came into being in the form of Khepera, and I was the creator of what came into being, I formed myself out of the primeval matter, and I formed myself in the primeval matter. My name is Ausares (Asar).

---

[1] Mesopotamia (from a Greek term meaning "between rivers") lies between the Tigris and Euphrates rivers, a region that is part of modern Iraq[75]

I was alone, for the gods were not yet born, and I had emitted from myself neither Shu nor Tefnut. I brought into my own mouth, *hekau* (utterance – the word), and I forthwith came into being under the form of things which were created under the form of Khepera."

Genesis 1 (Bible)
1. In the beginning God created the heaven and the earth.
2 And the earth was without form, and void; and darkness [was] upon the face of the deep. And the Spirit of God moved upon the face of the waters.

From the Sepher (Sefir) Yezirah (Cabalism):
These are the ten spheres of existence, which came out of nothing. From the spirit of the Living God emanated air, from the air water, from the water, fire or ether, from the ether, the height and the depth, the East and the West, the North and the South.

From the Zohar (Cabalism):
Before God manifested Himself, when all things were still hidden in him... He began by forming an imperceptible point; this was His own thought. With this thought He then began to construct a mysterious and holy form...the Universe.

From the Laws of Manu (Indian):
Manu is a Sage-Creator God of Indian Hindu-Vedic tradition who recounts the process of Creation wherein the *Self Existent Spirit* (God) felt desire. Wishing to create all things from his own body, God created the primeval waters (Nara) and threw a seed into it. From the seed came the golden cosmic egg. The Self-Existent Spirit (Narayana) developed in the egg into Brahma (Purusha, God) and after a year of meditation, divided into two parts (male and female).

## Correlations in the Mystic Philosophy relating to the Creation

When we think of our body, we don't differentiate between the lips and the face, or the fingers and the arm, etc. In a mysterious way we consider all of the parts as a whole and call this "me" or "my body." In the same way, in the state of Enlightenment, Christhood (Horushood, Buddhahood, etc.), the entire universe is understood as "me." This is the state wherein the Kingdom of Heaven is experienced. A psychological understanding of consciousness in terms of Christian Gnostic philosophy would render Jesus as the ego within us and Christ as the underlying source of consciousness, which supports and transcends the ego. Thus, Jesus' journey was to go from being Jesus, an ordinary human being, to Christ, a human being who is aware of the grander reality beyond the body and is one with God. The attainment of his Christhood occurred as a result of his movement towards enlightenment through his practices of Yoga (virtue, meditation, communion with God). This is what is supposed to be the goal of every Christian, to become Christ-like while alive, and not just after death, by following the teachings of Jesus Christ (Christian Yoga). According to the mystical philosophy, the consciousness of every human being is essentially pure, deep down (Christ-like), until the mind associates with the ego. Then the Christ

Consciousness becomes submerged. When this occurs, multiplicity and duality appear to exist, but as the following Cabalistic passage explains, the multiplicity of creation is merely the forms which energy takes on as it moves and interacts in different polarities or the pairs of opposites. This same concept of vibrations being the underlying cause of the phenomenal world existed prior to Cabalism within the Shabaka Inscription (above) and the Ancient Egyptian metaphysical text, *Kybalion* (below). This teaching is equivalent to the concept of *Ying and Yang* of Taoism which holds that Creation is composed of two opposite but complementary forces which balance each other and form a transcendental harmony.

From the Kabbalah (Cabala):

Polarity is the principle that runs through the whole of creation, and is in fact, the basis of manifestation. Polarity really means the flowing of force from a sphere of high pressure to a sphere of low pressure, high and low being always relative terms. Every sphere of energy needs to receive the stimulus of an influx of energy at higher pressure, and to have an output into a sphere of lower pressure. The source of all energy is the Great Unmanifest (God), and it makes its own way down the levels, changing its form from one to the other, till it is finally "earthed" in matter.

The pure impulse of dynamic creation is formless; and being formless, the creation it gives rise to can assume any and every form.

The following passage comes from *Lao-Tzu*, the classical Taoist writer who popularized Taoism in China at the same time that *Buddha* and *Mahavira* developed Buddhism and Jainism in India, respectively. He further illustrates the idea of undifferentiated versus differentiated consciousness.

There was something undifferentiated and yet complete, which existed before heaven and earth.
Soundless and formless, it depends on nothing and does not change.
It operates everywhere and is free from danger.
It may be considered the mother of the universe.

The same idea of *"formlessness"* or *"undifferentiated"* matter occurs in the *Rig* (Rik) *Veda*, the Upanishads and the Bhagavad Gita from India as well. The only difference between the following texts is that the Gita applies all of the attributes of the manifest and unmanifest nature of divinity and incorporates them in the anthropomorphic personality of Krishna.

From the Rig Veda:

There was neither non-existence nor existence then; there was neither the realm of space nor the sky beyond.
There was no distinguishing sign of night nor of day...

Desire came upon that one in the beginning; that was the first seed of mind.

From the Upanishads:

There are, assuredly, two forms of the Eternal: the formed and the formless, the mortal and the immortal, the stationary and the moving, the actual and the yon (that one or those yonder).

Gita: Chapter 9:17

I am the Father of the universe; I am the Mother, the sustainer, as well as the Grandfather. I am the goal of Vedic knowledge, I am the sacred Om, and I am verily the Vedas in the form of Rik, Yaju and Sama.

The following passages from the Kybalion, an Ancient Egyptian metaphysical text which contains the same idea of energy in different levels of manifestation and show how this knowledge may be applied to control one's mind:

"To change your mood or mental state, change your vibration."

"Mastery of self consists not in abnormal dreams, visions and fantastic imaginings or living, but in using the higher forces against the lower thus escaping the pains of the lower by vibrating on the higher."

"Mind, as matter, may be transmuted from state to state, degree to degree, condition to condition, pole to pole; and vibration to vibration. Transmutation is a Mental Art."

"To destroy an undesirable rate of mental vibration, concentrate on the opposite vibration to the one to be suppressed."

"The wise ones serve the higher planes and rule the lower, in this way one operates the laws instead being a slave to them."

"Those who may come to understand the law of vibrations will hold the scepter of power in their hand."

"Nothing rests, everything moves; everything vibrates."

"Gender is in everything; everything has its Masculine and Feminine Principles; Gender manifests on all planes."

"Everything is dual; everything has poles; everything has its pair of opposites; like and unlike are the same; opposites are identical in nature, but different in degree; extremes meet; all truths are but half- truths; all paradoxes may be reconciled."

"Everything flows out and in; everything has its tides; all things rise and fall; the pendulum-swing manifests in everything; the measure of the swing to the right is the measure to the left; rhythm compensates."

"Every cause has its Effect; every Effect has its Cause; everything happens according to Law; Chance is a name for Law unrecognized; there are many planes of causation, but nothing escapes the Law."

# The Cultural Category Factor Correlation Method
## New Discoveries and How they Affect the Understanding of Cultures and their Interactions

Having fascinated scholars ever since their discovery in 1945, the 52 Gnostic texts found at Nag Hammadi, Egypt constitute an extremely important discovery relating to the understanding of early Christianity. Nag Hammadi is a modern name for a town which is located in east central Egypt, and 48 km (about 30 mi.) south of Qina. These texts which date back to the time of the biblical Jesus have redefined the manner in which the social climate and history during the time of Jesus are being viewed. Up to the time of their discovery, it was known that many sects of Christian groups existed. These groups were considered to be outcasts and heretics by the Orthodox Roman Catholic groups. It was also known that the early councils of the Roman Catholic Bishops had altered, edited and even omitted from the Bible, many existing scriptures of the time claimed to be inspired by Jesus. By the time the Roman Catholic Church had compiled and canonized the scriptures which would make up the present day Christian Bible, these works had undergone many revisions and changes. The term *Gnostic* is derived from the Greek word *gnostikos*, meaning "one who knows," which is based on a word for "knowledge," *gnosis*. In Gnostic Christianity, Jesus Christ is only the revealer of knowledge. Gnosis means knowledge gained from the source, referring to Christhood itself as the ultimate source, superseding even the scriptures (Bible, Gospels, etc.) themselves. Knowledge is of two types, information and experience. The Gnostic form of knowledge relates to having experience of the Divine as opposed to just simply having information about the Divine from scriptures, wisdom teachings and other such texts. This is the difference between someone describing to you what ice cream tastes like (information) as opposed to your actually tasting it for yourself (gnosis, experience).

In 1769, the first Gnostic texts turned up in modern times when a Scottish tourist purchased a Coptic (Late Ancient Egyptian) manuscript near Thebes (Waset) in Upper Egypt. It contained a record of Jesus' teachings to his disciples, a group composed of both men and women. In 1773 a collector discovered another Coptic text which contained a conversation on the "mysteries" between Jesus and his disciples. In 1896, a German Egyptologist purchased manuscripts in Cairo, Egypt, which contained the *Gospel of Mary* (Magdalene) and the *Apocryphon* (secret book) *of John* (which was also found at Nag Hammadi in 1945).

By the time of the translation of the *Essene Gospel of Peace* in 1929, a Gnostic Christian text written by the Essenes, it became evident that many of those ancient Gnostic (knowing) texts survived. The Essenes were a group of Jewish ascetic communities which had cultural and religious ties to Ancient Egypt and the Near East. The Essenes, along with the *Therapeuts,* another Jewish sect of Egypt that did not follow the established Jewish authorities, claimed to follow the true teachings of their leader, whose title was "Teacher of Righteousness. *"*

The entire group of texts discovered at Nag Hammadi are referred to as the *Nag Hammadi Library.* Some of the texts are Christian in nature, while others have no mention of a person called Jesus. However, they all deal with the same theme as other Gnostic texts, that is, knowing the mystery of life within oneself. Among the texts discovered at Nag Hammadi are: *The Gospel of Thomas, The*

*Gospel of Philip, The Gospel of Truth, The Gospel to the Egyptians, The Secret Book of James, The Apocalypse of Paul, The Letter of Peter to Philip,* and *The Apocalypse of Peter.*

The discoveries in Egypt in 1945 coupled with the discovery of the Dead Sea Scrolls in Qumran (Palestine) in 1947 have been the source of controversy as well as speculation into the true nature of Christianity and Judaism, respectively, as to their origins and teachings. Consequently, many scholarly studies have been undertaken to completely catalogue and translate the texts and to attempt to ascertain the meanings intended by them. While the discovery of the *Dead Sea Scrolls* received much publicity, the discovery of the *Nag Hammadi Library* was shrouded in secrecy by the authorities. It was not until several years after the discovery that they were fully translated and made available to the world. This extraordinary discovery was finally published and translated into English in 1977 as 'The Nag Hammadi Library.' As one begins to see their importance, it becomes clear why modern day officials of the church and government would be apprehensive about releasing information related to ancient literary works that might completely revolutionize the current understanding of the teachings which so many people have held for over fifteen hundred years. One in particular, *The Gospel of Thomas,* opens with: *"These are the secret words which the living Jesus spoke, and which the twin, Judas Thomas, wrote down."* It contains many of the sayings from the New Testament but in different contexts from the Bible gospel versions. The new perspective from the newly found texts is fueling the speculation and controversy over the teachings of Christianity as they have been given by the mainstream biblical tradition, the Roman Catholic Church as well as the other Christian churches that emerged after.

For example, some texts like *The Gospel of Thomas* seem to suggest that Jesus had a twin and that he gave secret teachings to his disciples. The Roman Catholic Bible itself establishes the idea that there is a secret or inner teaching through the following statement, but does not elaborate on it further. It simply suggests that there is a secret understanding but does not tell us what it is.

> Mark 4:11
> And he said to them, "To you it is given to know the mystery of the Kingdom of God: but to them that are outside, all [these] things are done in parables..."

*The Gospel of Philip* states that the companion of Jesus was Mary Magdalene, that he kissed her on the mouth and that he loved her more than the other disciples. Other Gnostic texts strongly refute the Catholic view of bodily resurrection and the virgin birth, calling these notions ridiculous and misunderstood by the orthodox community. The following excerpt from the Gnostic *Gospel of Phillip* brings home this point.

> "Those who say that the Lord died first and then rose up are in error, for he rose up and then died. We are to receive the resurrection while we live."

# The Cultural Category Factor Correlation Method

Gnosticism developed during a period of time (600 B.C.E - 100 C.E) when the whole world was undergoing a renaissance (if not revolution) in the way in which religion, social justice, and the nature of existence were viewed throughout the entire ancient world from Egypt, Africa in the South to Rome in the West, and China and India in the East.

During the sixth century B.C.E. there was a special age in human history, which some authors have termed "Axial age" due to its role in history that may be likened to an axis upon which many events turned. However, that period may be better described as a religious *"Counter-Reversion Era."* The name Counter-Reversion Era was chosen because it describes a time when the religious philosophy of the past [time before that era] was in decline due to the emergence of barbarism. Certain mystical/Gnostic type religious movements emerged to counter that decline and revert back to the original *perennial philosophy[2]* of religion. During that time, there were several wars of conquest in which several nations in the Middle East developed into conquering forces. Some examples include the Persians and the Assyrians. That period marked a time when the power of Ancient Egypt, which had previously controlled the land areas from present day Sudan to India at one time in the past, reached its lowest state. Ancient Egypt was under constant siege during that period. However, Egypt did not experience a religious *Counter-Reversion Era.* The Ancient Egyptian religion was a purveyor of the perennial philosophy, the religious tradition of henotheism and panentheism that continued to be practiced openly until the 5th century A.C.E. [1,000 years later] when the Roman Orthodox Christians closed the last Egyptian temples by force.[3] Ancient Egypt had been the beacon of learning and science as well as spiritual wisdom. This is why the ancient pre-Judaic, pre-Christian and pre-Islamic religions had many areas of compatibility with Ancient Egyptian religion and some even included Ancient Egyptian gods and goddesses in their pantheon of divinities. The time prior to the *Counter-Reversion Era* was marked by the practice of *henotheism[4]* and in a more developed format, *pantheism.[5]*

---

[2] The Perennial Philosophy (Latin philosophia perennis) is the idea that a universal set of truths common to all people and cultures exists. The term was first used by the German mathematician and philosopher Gottfried Leibniz to designate the common, eternal philosophy that underlies all religious movements, in particular the mystical streams within them. The term was later popularized by Aldous Huxley in his 1945 book The Perennial Philosophy. The term "perennial philosophy" has also been used to translate the concept of the "eternal or perennial truth" in the Sanskrit Sanatana Dharma.
The concept of perennial philosophy is the fundamental tenet of the Traditionalist School, formalized in the writings of 20th century metaphysicians René Guénon and Frithjof Schuon. The Indian scholar and writer Ananda Coomaraswamy, associated with the Traditionalists, also wrote extensively about the perennial philosophy.
http://en.wikipedia.org/wiki/Perennial_philosophy

[3] African Origins of Civilization, by Muata Ashby, Mystical Journey From Jesus to Christ, by Muata Ashby

[4] {In philosophy and religion, is a term coined by Max Müller, which means devotion to a single God while accepting the existence of other Gods.}

In the East, *Buddha* and *Mahavira* emerged in India with new views on a philosophy of self-knowledge based on the oneness of creation and humankind. During the same time, farther East in China, Confucius and Lao-Tsu emerged with basically the same philosophy. By contrast, in Persia, Zoroaster became a proponent of a dualistic philosophy of creation which saw good and evil in everything as well as rigid religious rules that must be followed in order to live according to "God's will." It is notable that in later times the Judeo-Christian-Islamic orthodox traditions developed a dualistic view of nature, God, and humanity, being influenced by Zoroastrianism and Aristotelian rationalism rather than the "Monistic" and "Panentheistic" traditions (Ancient Egyptian religion, Gnosticism, Eastern Philosophy) which originally gave birth to them and influenced their early development. Monism is the belief that all reality comes from and exists in one source. Panentheism is the belief that all existence is a manifestation of (one) God, but also that God is more than the phenomenal universe. A major reason for this fundamental change in the basic concepts of the philosophy lies in the development of Christianity, Islam and Judaism in Western civilization. As we move through our study of comparative religion and culture, we discover the points in history where the original philosophies of Western civilization diverged from their common origins with African and Eastern religions and we are able to see how these diverging views branched off into seemingly new doctrines. With this insight we will be able to work back from the present in order to discover the ancient meaning of the teachings in the past original tradition.

As the Ancient Egyptian society and government organizations deteriorated after more than 5,000 years of high civilization, the early Greek philosophers such as *Thales* and *Pythagoras* began their studies in the Egyptian temples.[6] Later on, when the Druids, Therapeuts and others left Egypt, this same philosophy which was originally espoused in Ancient Egypt became masked under the local folklore and customs of individual tribes and religious groups in Europe and the Middle East.[7]

---

[5] {a doctrine identifying the Deity with the universe and its phenomena; belief in and
  worship of all gods and goddesses as manifestations of the one Supreme Being}
  and panentheism {the Creator is creation and transcends creation}.[5]
[6] *"Stolen Legacy"* by George G.M. James
[7] *"Egyptian Yoga: The Philosophy of Enlightenment"* by Reginald Muata Ashby

# The Common Ancestry of Humanity According to the Bible and the myth of race and racism

This essay illustrates how perceptions through religion are important because they shape perspectives in cultural comparison studies. People often look through the prisms of their own mental socializations, ideas, illusions of misconceptions as they evaluate the world around them. Thus we will take some time to examine a few as we prepare to follow a path to promote more objective examination of cultures and their constituent elements.

The Bible, like other books considered as "Holy" by peoples around the world, is not a book of history but rather a book of myth. It seeks to explain the most important question of humanity, where the world came from. This knowledge provides a reference point to understand how everything came into existence. The next question is more profound. When you look around you see a world of multiplicity and seemingly endless variety, how did this come about and why is it so? These question and its misunderstanding has been the greatest cause of strife among people throughout history, because people also see themselves as they see nature, as separate and different elements in competition for survival. However, an in depth study of the Bible reveals the insights into the most divisive issue of modern times, the question of race, the origin of humanity and the relationship between all human beings.

Acts 17
> 26 And hath made of one blood all nations of men to dwell on all the face of the earth, and hath determined the times before appointed, and the bounds of their habitation...

There are some very important Bible texts found in the books of Acts and Corinthians, which illuminate and clarify the question of race. In Acts 17: 26 we are told that God made only one blood out of which all nations emerged (Nations: i.e. Africans, Europeans, Asiatics, Native Americans, etc.). This means that all human beings share one common physiology, that there is no difference between human beings from different parts of the world. According to Strong's Concordance of ancient Hebrew, blood also has a deeper meaning than just the medium which carries oxygen throughout the body. It is the seat of life itself, the essence of life which sustains a human being.

1 Corinthians 15
> 39 All flesh [is] not the same flesh: but [there is] one [kind of] flesh of men, another flesh of beasts, another of fishes, [and] another of fowls.

1 Corinthians 15
> 44 It is sown a natural body; it is raised a spiritual body. There is a natural body, and there is a spiritual body.

In 1 Corinthians 15, we learn that all living beings are classified according to their physiology. The word used in the Bible is "flesh." It relates to the outer appearance of a living being as well as the group it belongs to exclusively. The word flesh in the Bible may be likened to the modern term "species." According to the American Heritage Dictionary, species means *1. a. A fundamental category of taxonomic classification consisting of organisms capable of interbreeding. 1. b. an organism belonging to such a category. 2. A kind, variety, or type.* We are to understand that while every species is unique within its own group, there is no such thing as different species within the human populations of the world. All human beings belong to the same "flesh," i.e. species. Also, there is no such thing as racial difference within the human population. All human beings can interbreed and produce offspring. All human beings can bleed and feel the same pain. All human beings desire the same thing, happiness. The body of every human being is constructed in basically the same way. Even distinctions based on gender are not reliable for distinguishing human beings. The spirit is beyond the body. This is the lesson from 1 Corinthians 15: 44. So gender is only a superficial difference, as is skin color. Therefore, all human beings are members of one single group, regardless of their physical appearance. It is interesting that all dogs are referred to as dogs regardless of the breed,[8] but some human beings are classified as "different" than others. The fallacy of racial distinctions is self-evident for the discerning and honest student of life and the scriptures of the Bible. This is exactly the same teaching presented in the Ancient Egyptian Hymns of Amun and the Asarian Resurrection Myth:

> "Thou makest the color of the skin of one race to be different from that of another, but however many may be the varieties of mankind, it is thou that makes them all to live."
> -Ancient Egyptian Proverb from *The Hymns of Amun*

> "Souls, Heru, son, are of the self-same nature, since they came from the same place where the Creator modeled them; nor male nor female are they. Sex is a thing of bodies, not of Souls."
> -Ancient Egyptian Proverb from *The Asarian Resurrection*

Romans 12
> 3 For, through the grace given to me, I say, to every man that is among you, not to think [of himself] more highly than he ought to think; but to think soberly, according as God hath dealt to every man the measure of faith. {Soberly: Gr. to sobriety}
> 4 For as we have many members in one body, and all members have not the same office:

---

[8] **breed** *n.* **1.** A group of organisms having common ancestors and certain distinguishable characteristics, especially a group within a species developed by artificial selection and maintained by controlled propagation.

5 So we, [being] many, are one body in Christ, and every one members one of another.

The message of Romans 12: 3-5 is that human beings should not engage in self-important and egoistic acts or thoughts. In light of the other teachings, this would be ridiculous. Egoism is like a spark which can ignite the greatest fires of human conflict if it is not checked before it gets out of control. Ignorance as to the true origins of humanity is one of the most important contributing sources of strife between nations. Therefore, the study of the teachings along with the insights of modern science pave the way to harmony in society and spiritual enlightenment for every human being. The differences in abilities such as artistic capacity or intellectual capacity cannot be ascribed to groups of people since there are intelligent individuals as well as less intelligent individuals in all ethnic groups. The gifts given to each human being by God, or their genetic heritage are for the purpose of allowing every individual to fulfill their own special mission in life, and to fulfill the needs of the society into which they are born. One individual may need to work as an engineer while another as a storekeeper. Through these tasks they both assist society and grow through the unique experiences that each opportunity affords, and neither should look down on the other. Imagine all the garbage that would pile up in the streets and in your home if there were no garbage persons. It would not serve society well to have everyone be a doctor or an engineer. However, at the time of death all people go to the grave, the crematorium, etc., i.e., the same death state. Therefore, the higher reality is that a human being needs to affirm the higher essence of life instead of concentrating on the transient and unpredictable occurrences of life. The higher reality of life is constant while the aberrations are variable; while the apparent differences among human beings and their cultures may provide "spice" to life, by stimulating entertaining interactions and varieties of manifestation, they are not abiding and therefore should not be used as a basis for determining what reality is or what the correct nature for human cultural interaction should be. So all human beings, while working in different areas of society, are all the same when it comes to their spiritual essence and destiny. They are part of a single body, a common root and a common fate. If this higher understanding is affirmed, there is less room for ignorance and the destructive ego to have an effect. This should be the higher goal of the church policies and the governments of all countries who claim to follow Christian spiritual or Yogic values. Until this ideal is fulfilled by affirmation in the church doctrines, teachings and community works, those who would claim to be in the church and followers of Christianity's central tenets cannot claim to uphold Christianity in its truest and most powerful form; the same applies to any other religion or belief system. Indeed, a person who claims to be a Christian but does not uphold these principles cannot in good conscience consider himself or herself to be a follower of Christianity as Jesus and the writers of the New Testaments conceptualized it. The idea that God created some human beings who are inherently inferior and others who are inherently superior would point to the concept of God as either cruel and evil if this was done purposely, or limited and imperfect if it was done by mistake.

## Comparative Mythology, Cultural and Social Studies
## Conclusion: One World, One Humanity, One Destiny

The animosity and hatred of modern times, caused by the ignorance of the true teachings of the Bible, has led to a situation where social problems have rendered many practitioners of what they consider to be the correct teaching s of their religion incapable of reaching a higher level of spiritual understanding. Many people in modern society are caught up in the degraded level of disputes and wars in an attempt to support ideas, which are in reality absurd and destructive in reference to the doctrines of religion. Ironically, the inability of leaders in the church, synagogue, mosque or secular society to accept the truth about the origins of humanity comes from their fear of losing control over their followers. Now that modern science is showing that all human beings originated from the same source, in Africa, and that racial distinctions are at least erroneous and misleading, it means that those who have perpetrated and sustained racism can no longer use science or biblical teachings to support their evil and ignorant designs. They have no leg to stand on. The following exert was taken from Encarta Encyclopedia 1994, and is typical of the modern scientific understanding of the question of human genetics and race issues.

> The concept of race has often been misapplied. One of the most telling arguments against classifying people into races is that persons in various cultures have often mistakenly acted as if one race were superior to another. Although, with social disadvantages eliminated, it is possible that one human group or another might have some genetic advantages in response to such factors as climate, altitude, and specific food availability, these differences are small. There are no differences in native intelligence or mental capacity that cannot be explained by environmental circumstances. Rather than using racial classifications to study human variability, anthropologists today define geographic or social groups by geographic or social criteria. They then study the nature of the genetic attributes of these groups and seek to understand the causes of changes in their genetic makeup. Contributed by: Gabriel W. Laser "Races, Classification of," Microsoft (R) Encarta. Copyright (c) 1994

One of the major problems in society and in the church is that the teachings and scientific evidence presented here has not been taught to the world population at large. Most people grow up accepting the ignorance of their parents who received the erroneous information from their own parents, and so on. Racism, sexism and other scourges of society are not genetically transmitted. They are transmitted by ignorant family members who pass on their prejudices and bigotry's to their children, and so on down through the generations. The cycle of ignorance and strife is thus carried on from one generation to another. A child cannot live in a family and believe in a certain way and act in a certain way if the parents do not allow it. In the same way, the masses of people are like children and the church and government leaders are like the parents. If racism, sexism and other injustices exist, it is because the leaders are not making an effort to lead the masses towards truth and righteousness. Leaders lead in three ways, by example, by words and by influence. The values of truth and righteousness must be part of every aspect of teaching, otherwise they are not good leaders and society will go astray. The leaders of society as well as the leaders of the church must make a concerted effort to engage the struggle against misunderstanding and unrighteousness. Then they will be able to lead society to an enlightened way of relating to other ethnic groups and thereby provide real hope of creating harmony in the human community. Through this harmony it would be easier to cope with the struggles of life and thereby achieve a greater insight into the mystical teachings of Christianity or any other religious path. Anger, hatred, greed and animosity have an adverse effect on the mind. Therefore, those who engage in racism as well as those who do not know how to deal with racists will have a much more difficult time in trying to achieve the kind of mental control and peace which is necessary to progress on the spiritual path. The Bible itself speaks out against any and all forms of egoism, and racism is perhaps the most blatant and destructive form of egoism. In Romans 12:3, above, the followers of Christianity are admonished to take control of egoistic tendencies and to practice humility instead of thinking of oneself as superior to others. Instead one must learn to look at others as having been given the same spark of divinity and therefore, all human beings deserve equal treatment, love and compassion. This teaching applies directly to those who try to impose themselves on others (racists, sexists, tyrants, capitalists, etc.). Those who have enough courage to face their fears, prejudices and to approach the scriptures with honesty instead of delusions of superiority and greed will discover forgiveness and inner peace, as well as the true meaning of the scriptural teachings.

## DNA and The Spirit

DNA is an abbreviation for "Deoxyribonucleic acid." It is a complex giant molecule that contains the information needed for every cell of a living creature to create its physical features (hair, skin, bones, eyes, legs, etc., as well as their texture, coloration, their efficient functioning, etc.). All of this is contained in a chemically coded form. The Life Force of the Soul or Spirit engenders the impetus in the DNA to function. This in turn leads to the creation of the physical aspect of all living beings (human beings, animals, insects, microorganisms, etc.)

**Figure 3: Strand of DNA**

The DNA is what determines if two living beings are compatible with each other for the purpose of mating and producing offspring. If they are not compatible, then they are considered to be different species. All human beings are compatible with each other, therefore, they are members of a single species, i.e. one human race.

Therefore, DNA is an instrument of the Spirit, which it uses to create the body and thereby avail itself of physical existence and experiences. According to mystical philosophy, the soul chooses the particular world, country, and family in which to incarnate in order to have the kind of experiences it wants to experience. This is all expressed in the physical plane through the miracle of DNA.[126]

# Chapter 2: Principles of Cultural Expression

## What is Culture?

The concept of culture will be an extremely important if not the most important aspect of humanity in our study and so it will be a developing theme throughout our study. The following principles are offered as a standard for understanding what culture is, how it manifests in the world, and how that manifestation affects other cultures. Let's begin with a dictionary definition of culture.

> cul·ture (kŭl'chər) *n.* **1.a.** The totality of
> socially transmitted behavior patterns,
> arts, beliefs, institutions, and all other
> products of human work and thought.
> -American Heritage Dictionary

## Purpose of Culture:

Culture can have the function of promoting the cohesion and stabilization of society. It can also express a society's world view. There may also be subcultures within a larger overall cultural perspective of a given society. Among the most important functions of culture, the following may be considered as foremost.

- Culture is a people's window on whatever they perceive as reality (to understand the world around them) and their concept of self.

- Culture is a conditioning process, necessary for the early development of a human being.

- Culture defines the agenda of a society (government, economics, religion). Religion is the most powerful force driving culture.

31

# The Study of Culture

**Cultural Anthropology** is the study concerned with depicting the character of various cultures, and the similarities and differences between them. This branch of anthropology is concerned with all cultures whether simple or complex and its methodology entails a holistic view, field work, comparative analysis (both within the society and cross-culturally), and a tendency to base theoretical models on empirical data rather than vice versa.[9]

**Ethnology**, is the comparative study of cultures. Using ethnographic material from two or more societies, ethnology can attempt to cover their whole cultural range or concentrate on a single cultural trait. Ethnology was originally a term covering the whole of anthropology, toward the end of the 19th century historical ethnology was developed in an attempt to trace cultural diffusion. Now ethnologists concentrate on cross-cultural studies, using statistical methods of analysis.[10]

While this work may be considered as a form of cultural anthropology and ethnology, it will also serve as an overview of the mythological (Comparative mythology) and theological (comparative theology) principles espoused by the cultures in question. The techniques used in this book to compare cultures will lay heavy emphasis on iconographical and philosophical factors as well as historical evidences, as opposed to only statistical methods of analysis. It is possible to focus on the apparent differences between cultures and religious philosophies. This has been the predominant form of philosophical discourse and study of Western scholarship. The seeming differences between religions have led to innumerable conflicts between the groups throughout history, all because of the outer expression of religion. However, throughout this work I will attempt to focus on the syncretic aspects of the philosophies and religions in question because it is in the similarities wherein harmony is to be found; harmony in the form of concurrence in ideas and meaning. In light of this idea of harmony, it is possible to look at the folklore of cultural traditions throughout the world and see the same "psycho-mythological" message being espoused through the various cultural masks. They are all referring to the same Supreme Being. While giving commentary and adding notes,

---

[9] Random House Encyclopedia Copyright (C) 1983,1990
[10] ibid.

which I feel will be helpful to the understanding of the texts which I will compare, I have endeavored to use the actual texts wherever possible so that you, the reader, may see for yourself and make your own judgment about their comparability and the meaning that those comparisons represent.

Culture is everything a human being learns from living in a society including language, history, values and religion, etc. However, the outer learning masks an inner experience. Spirituality is that movement to transcend culture and discover the essence of humanity. This Ultimate Truth, known by many names, such as God, Goddess, Supreme Being, and their varied names in all of the world's cultures, is revered by all peoples, though culture and folk differences color the expression of that reverence. This is what is called the *folk expressions of religion based on culture and local traditions*. For example, the same Ultimate Reality is expressed by Christians based on European culture and traditions, as God or the Kingdom of Heaven. The same Ultimate Reality is expressed by Muslims based on Arab culture and traditions as Allah. The same Ultimate and Transcendental Reality is worshipped by Jews based on Hebrew culture and traditions. The same Ultimate and Transcendental Reality is worshipped by the Chinese based on Chinese culture and traditions, etc. If people who practice religion stay at the outer levels (basing their religious practice and wisdom on their culture, myths and traditions), they will always see differences between faiths.

As introduced earlier, religion has three aspects, myth, ritual and mysticism. Myth and ritual relate to the folk expression of religion, whereas mysticism relates to that movement of self-discovery that transcends all worldly concepts. Mysticism allows any person in any religion to discover that the same Supreme Being is being worshipped by all under different names and forms, and by different means. It is the worship itself and the object of that worship that underlies the human movement. Therefore, the task of all true mystics (spiritual seekers) is to go beyond the veil of the outer forms of religion, including the symbols, but more importantly, the doctrines, rituals and traditions (see model below).

**Figure 4: Below: The Culture-Myth Model, showing how the innate human desire for meaning manifests through culture, based on folk myth expressions of religion dedicated to revealing the ultimate reality.**

# The Cultural Category Factor Correlation Method

In studying and comparing diverse groups of peoples, we are essentially comparing their cultures. Culture includes all activities and manners of manifestation, which a group of peoples have developed over the period of their existence. Cultural expressions are composed of cultural elements or aspects of cultural activity, therefore, they may fall under the following categories. An important theme to understand throughout this study is that the underlying principle purpose or function of culture in a given society may be equal to that of another culture, but the mode of manifestation will invariably be unique. The exception to this is when there is contact between the cultures. Some coincidental similarities may be found between two cultures that have never been in contact with each other, but the frequency and quality of those correlations belies the superficiality of the contact or random nature of the correlation. Similarities and commonalties pointing to a strong interrelationship between the cultures can be expected when comparing two apparently different cultures if the cultures in question have sustained some form of contact or emerged from a common origin. The degree of parallelism and harmony between varied cultures can be measured by the nature and frequency of synchronicity or concordance of the factors from each culture being compared.

In the study of the theology[11] of the varied religious traditions of the world (comparative religious studies), it is very possible to encounter similar general points of philosophical conceptualization in reference to the institutions for the worship of a spiritual being or divinities. In other words, the existence of religion itself (not necessarily its forms) is a point of commonality in all cultures and all historical periods. The basic common ideas manifested by cultures in and of themselves cannot be used as justification for concluding that there is a common origin or common cultural concept being expressed by two different religions. So just because two religions espouse the idea that there is a Supreme Being or that Supreme Being is one, a scholar cannot conclude that the religions have a common origin or that their concept in reference to the entity being worshipped is compatible. The factor of theology is there in both cultures, but the mode of expression may be different, and even if it is not different, it may have been arrived at by different means. That is, the myth-plot system of the religion may contain various episodes which are not synchronous, thus expressing a divergent theological idea even though it may ultimately lead to the same philosophical realization. The forms of iconography may show depictions of the divinities in different situations and engaged in different activities. The rituals and traditions related to the myths of the religions may be carried out in different ways and at different times. These deviating factors point to a different origin for the two cultures in question. On the other hand it is possible to have a common

---

[11] **the·ol·o·gy** (th¶-¼l"...-j¶) *n., pl.* **the·ol·o·gies.** *Abbr.* **theol. 1.** The study of the nature of God and religious truth; rational inquiry into religious questions. (American Heritage Dictionary)

origin and later observe some divergence from the original expression while the theme and plot of myth within the religion stays essentially the same. This finding may not only point to a common origin, but also to a divergent practice in later times. If two traditions are shown to have been in contact, and they are found to have common elements in the basis of their espoused philosophy, as well as the manifestation of that philosophy through iconography, artifacts, rituals, traditions, myth-plots, etc., then this determination suggests a strong correlation in the origin, and or contact throughout the development of the cultures in question. In order to make such a judgment, it is necessary to identify and match several essential specific criteria or factors confirming the commonality or convergence indicating a communal[12] origin and or common cultural factor.

---

[12] *com·mu·nal (k...-my› "n...l, k¼m"y...-) adj. 1. Of or relating to a commune. 2. Of or relating to a community. 3.a. Of, belonging to, or shared by the people of a community; public. b. Marked by collective ownership and control of goods and property.* (American Heritage Dictionary)

# The Cultural Category Factor Correlation Method

## Table 1: Categories of Cultural Expression and Factors of Cultural Expression

### Categories of Cultural Expression

1. Art: design (lay out), composition-style, and pattern
2. Artifacts - tools
3. Customs and Traditions – non-secular
4. Customs and Traditions - secular
5. Ethnicity
6. Folklore - legend
7. Form –Architecture
8. Language
9. Music and Performing arts – Theater
10. Philosophy
    a. Social
        i. Economics
        ii. Legal system
        iii. Government
10. Religion-Spirituality

### Factors of Cultural Expression

These categories can be correlated by matches in the following features (elements of the categories):

### Myth and Religion Related Correlation Methods

1. Gender concordance[13]
2. Iconography
    a. Conventional
    b. Naturalistic
    c. Stylized
3. Myth-
    a. Plot
    b. Motif[14]
    c. Theme
4. Rituals and or Traditions

---

[13] Gender of characters in the myth
[14] Myth and Mythological motif (subject matter)

**Comparative Mythology, Cultural and Social Studies**

a. Myth and Mythological motif
b. Customs and Traditions - Ritual
c. Mystical philosophy

    a. Function
    b. Actions performed

5. Scriptural Synchronicity
6. Form
    a. Architecture
    b. Artifacts
7. Function – usage -purpose
    a. Architecture
    b. Artifacts
8. Grammar
    a. Phonetics
    b. Linguistics
9. Historical Events
    c. Common origins of the Genesis of the Cultures
    d. Concurrent events throughout the history of the cultures
10. Genetics
11. Nationality
12. Political systems
13. Level of civilization (civilization or Barbarism)
14. calendar celebrations

# Factors of Cultural Expression as Artifacts with Intent

The Cultural Category Factor Method of comparing aspects of cultures relates to breaking down cultures into their constituent elements, Categories of Cultural Expression and then breaking those categories down further into their elementary parts, the *Factors of Categories of Cultural Expression*. Those factors are actually *artifacts*. An artifact is anything created by human culture as an expression of culture. An artifact can be a tool, a mythic character, a language, architecture, an amulet, a scroll, an icon, a poem, a speech, an article of clothing, a book, etc. Reading (determining the meaning and import of) an artifacts requires allowing the artifact to come to life in its own context. Having read it the artifact once again comes to life. A useful method to "read" an artifact was presented in a manuscript by Dominick A. Iorio, and Laurence L. Murphy.[15]

> Just as we must "open" the book to read it, we must open the artifact to read it, and suspend time to allow the artifact to take place, to occur, to be an event for us in time as a creative act. If we only see a book as a volume (an object) sitting on a shelf, none of this will take place. The act of reading the book restores its active element which is a part of our own active consciousness. This is the "value" of the book, not its situation as an object on a shelf. This is also why, when we participate in the activity of an artwork, and appreciate it, we wish to go back and "read the book again," "or see the movie one more time," or hear the music performed "live," or once again "attend" a performance. We are longing for the artifact to take place for us all over again.
>
> To allow the artifact to appear as an active event, we must do away with the presupposition that a book is just an object sitting on a shelf. We must allow the volume to show itself on its own terms. This is not as easy as it may first appear, however, because the traditional appearance of an Artifact may actually conceal it. Suspending the Artifact in time-space allows the work to show itself, to not just be another volume on a shelf, but to create its own context and stand out. This is the same thing that a story does for us. By focusing on the actions, demeanors, attitudes and behavior of its characters, the story lets those characters stand out and capture our attention. Otherwise, the characters are merely just more faces in a crowd.

So an artifact should be opened. Then we should experience its usage, its context, its feel. An artifact has an intention, a purpose. It is created by an agent (the person or the culture) for a reason. That reason informs us about the culture that created it, its way of thinking, acting, feeling and finally being. That intention

---

[15] *Self, Identity and Time*.

may be derived from the usage of the artifact. For example, an electric generator informs us that the creator intended to produce electricity. There are artifacts created by nature and animals. However, human created artifacts have a special quality in that they are dedicated to interaction with other humans. What about the "intentionality" of the human agency? The following statement outlines this aspect of human actions culture relating to agency and intention.

> By the time we reach human Agency, the intentions may even be toward what is not apparent in the physical world: the realms of death, the cosmic mysteries, the forces of nature, and an infinite dimension of "inner worlds," concepts, emotions, even visions. If the Agency acts upon these intentions, there is a good chance it may express it as an Artifact.

> We can attempt to read these intentions by observing the artifact. Thus our intention becomes the Project of reading what the Artifact has to say to us. Clearly, the artifact itself had an intention of expressing what it was trying to say. Consequently, the line of Intentionality between Noesis and Noema is bi-directional and appears thus:

> Noesis <-----------------------> Noema

> The Intentionality between the two poles is thus reciprocal. The problem is that the direction of this Intentionality is interactive and is not flowing from one pole to the other and back again, but is occurring simultaneously, just as when looking at another person, both glances occur at once even though they are directed at the other. I look at you as you look at me as I look at you. There is an interactive element to the glance. The line of Intentionality is here like a rope tied to two poles which, once it is waved, waves back and forth simultaneously through both poles. Metaphorically, the Intentionality is a bi-directional energy of Projection. If one pole "acts" upon another this projection becomes Project.[16]

---

[16] ibid

# Definitions of the Categories of Cultural Expression and Factors of Cultural Expression method of Cultural Anthropology

The following definitions are clarifications so as to have a common basis of understanding in which the items treated throughout are to be understood within the context of this book. The following are general designations to describe the dominant cultures or world views being explored in this volume. These do not include all the cultures of the world.

**Definition:** *Western Culture* = For the purpose of this study, "Western Culture" constitutes the traditions, beliefs and productions of those people who have developed societies in the western part of the continent of Asia (Europe), and who see this part of the world as their homeland or view the world from the perspective of the traditions (including religion) and norms of that region (Eurocentric). This includes the United States of America, Canada, as well as other countries which have societies that were founded by and or dominated by descendants from the European colonial rulers, and which control the governments of the former colonies (including Australia, New Zealand, etc.). Also included are countries where the political, social and or economic order is supported or enforced (neocolonialism or capitalistic globalism) by the Western countries. In a broad sense, Western Culture is a way of thinking that has spread far a field and now includes all who adopt the philosophies, norms and customs of that region, including secularism and religions that are predominantly Christian, followed by the Jewish and Islamic.

**Definition:** *Arab Culture* = For the purpose of this study, "Arab Culture" constitutes the traditions, beliefs and productions of those people who have developed societies in the south-western part of the continent of Asia (Arabia, Mesopotamia and now also north Africa), and who see this part of the world as their homeland or view the world from the perspective of the traditions (including religion) and norms of that region. In a broad sense, Arab Culture is a way of thinking that has spread far a field and now includes all who adopt the philosophies, norms and customs of that region.

**Definition:** *Eastern Culture* = For the purpose of this study, "Eastern Culture" constitutes the traditions, beliefs and productions of those people who have developed societies in the Eastern part of the continent of Asia (India, China) and who see this part of the world as their homeland or view the world from the perspective of the traditions (including religion) and norms of that region (Indocentric). In a broad sense, Eastern Culture is a way of thinking that includes all who adopt the philosophies, norms and customs of that region.

**Definition:** *African Culture* = For the purpose of this study, "African Culture" or "Southern Culture" constitutes the traditions, beliefs and productions of those people who have developed societies in the continent of Africa (Sub-Saharan countries) and who see this part of the world as their homeland or view the world from the perspective of the native traditions (including religion) and norms of that region (Africentric {Africentric}). In a broad sense, African Culture is a way of thinking that includes all who adopt the philosophies, norms and customs of that region.

The following definitions are the two simple keys to understanding the Categories of Cultural Expression and Factors of Cultural Expression system of Cultural Anthropology.

**Definition:** *Categories of Cultural Expression* = Broad areas whereby a culture expresses itself in the world. Exp. Religion is a broad category of cultural expression. All cultures may have a religion, however, those religions are not necessarily the same. What are the differences? How can these differences be classified and compared?

**Definition:** *Factors of Cultural Expression* = methods or means by which a culture expresses its categories. Exp. Myth is a factor of religion by which a religion is expressed in a unique way by a particular culture. In determining the common elements of different religions, there are several factors which can be used as criteria to determine whether or not cultures had common origins. If cultures are related, they will use common stories or other common factors or patterns to express the main doctrines of the religion or spiritual path, social philosophy, etc. These are listed below. The following section introduces the categories of cultural expression as well as factors or aspects of the Categories which reflect the unique forms of manifestation within a given culture.

The following definitions are of selected Categories of Cultural Expression and Factors of Cultural Expression. These may be expanded in other parts of this text.

# Linguistics

**Linguistics** – Spelling, grammar and script symbols

> *linguistics* (**a.** Of or relating to the synchronic[17] typological[18] comparison of languages)

**Phonetics** – Sound of the words

> *phonetics* (**2.** *The system of sounds of a particular language.*)[19]

## Using Linguistics as a Cultural Factor for Correlation Purposes

There are some possible problems in trying to use linguistics for comparative studies for ascertaining dates of cultures.[20] However there is some usefulness in using linguistics for discerning meanings and relationships between cultures that use the same language family. There are even more difficulties in trying to use linguistics for intercultural comparative studies. For example, there have been some scholars who have attempted to show a connection between Yoruba and Ancient Egypt based on linguistic correlations. While some correlations have been demonstrated, this form of criteria is based on a mechanical interpretation of human interaction and evolutionary interaction. In other words, the idea that there needs to be a direct linguistic connection between two cultures in order to show a cultural, social or ethnic relationship is based on linear thinking rather than a scientific study of the manner in which human beings interact and influence each other. While a linguistic correlation (direct word borrowings or evolutions from one language to another) may be present, the absence of such factors should not preclude research into other forms of connection. For example, Dr. Cheikh Anta Diop discovered many connections between the Ancient Egyptian language and the Wolof

---

[17] **syn·chro·ny** (sᴵng"kr…-n¶, sᴵn"-) *n., pl.* **syn·chro·nies.** Simultaneous occurrence; synchronism. (American Heritage Dictionary)

[18] **ty·pog·ra·phy** (tº-p¼g"r…-f¶) *n., pl.* **ty·pog·ra·phies.** *Abbr.* **typ., typo.** *Printing* **2.** The arrangement and appearance of printed matter. (American Heritage Dictionary)

[19] American Heritage Dictionary

[20] The Aryan Culture, the Indus Culture and the Origins of Civilization in the book *The African Origins of Civilization* by Muata Ashby

language of West Africa.[21] As introduced earlier, while a linguistic correlations (direct word borrowings or evolutions from one language to another) may be present, the absence of such factors should not preclude research into other forms of connection. Therefore, phonetic connections may or be not present and in and of themselves offer only a superficial or theoretical basis to establish a connection, but if present along with correlations in other related factors of cultural expression, such as meaning (definition), grammar, or etymology, as well as factors in other categories beyond Language, then this kind of linguistic evidence carries more weight. This is what professor Cheikh Anta Diop demonstrated. What is remarkable in these numerous cited examples is that we have not only grammatical and phonetic correlations, but also meaning (sense-connotation) correlations as well.

In using linguistics as a factor for determining the common elements between two religions, the following should be noted. The existence or lack thereof of commonality in the use of language spelling or script symbols to describe objects, deities and or spiritual philosophy of a culture in and of itself cannot be used to conclude that there is or is not a common basis, origin or concept between the cultures in question. It is possible that these (language, spelling or script symbols to describe objects and deities) may have developed independently over a period of time after the initial contact; the meaning may be the same while the language developed independently.

The comparison of the phonetics as opposed to linguistics, for example, the names used to describe deities or philosophies is a better factor to compare since in ancient times, before the movements to standardize spellings and script symbols, script forms tended to change while name sounds remained more constant. The impetus in society to standardize and stabilize language only began in the $18^{th}$ to the $19^{th}$ centuries (A.C.E.).[22] Therefore, it is possible to find name sounds and uses for the name that are alike in two different cultures, while their spellings or script forms may be different. Therefore, the requirement of the presence of a logical sequence of grammatical relationships between the languages of the two cultures need not be present in order to establish a relationship. The common basis in this case can be confirmed by the evidence of contact and the usage of the name and can be further confirmed by the form or gender related to the name.

Many people have been led to believe that the Ancient Egyptian language pronunciations are not certain. Modern Egyptological and

---

[21] *Civilization or Barbarism*
[22] Random House Encyclopedia Copyright (C) 1983,1990

linguistic scholarship has reconstituted hundreds of words by means of extrapolation from the last major manifestation of the Ancient Egyptian language, the Coptic language, as well as the Ancient Greek translations of Ancient Egyptian words. However, there has been a reluctance to look at other sources for comparison and extrapolation. The language could be even further reconstituted if even more comparative work was undertaken to study the Ancient Egyptian language in light of other African languages where there is documented evidence of contact, including those of the Dogon ethnic group of Mali, the Wolof[23] ethnic group of Senegal, and as we will see, also the Indian Bengali language. A few scholars have taken up this work in the past 44 years, but still to date there is no comprehensive work which takes all the factors into account, making them available to all Egyptologists and Indologists.

Further, the Ancient Egyptian language is special in many ways because it reflects many universal cosmic principles of sound. An example of this is the Ancient Egyptian word *"mut."* Mut means mother and it is reflected in "mata" of the Hindu language, "madre" of Spanish, "mother" in English, etc. The "m" sound is a universal "seed sound" principle of motherhood. However, this is not an absolute rule because other words can and are used in other languages as well. The use of names in the Ancient Egyptian language is important because they act as keys to unlocking the mysteries of life, but this is true only for those initiated into the philosophy. In Ancient Egyptian philosophy, words are seen as abstract representatives of phenomenal reality. Since the mind is the only reality, and the external world only reflects a conceptualized form based on an idea in the mind of the Supreme Being, words are a higher reality when compared to the physical world. All Ancient Egyptian words are names for objects and/or concepts. In fact, in Ancient Egyptian and other mystical philosophies, Creation is viewed as a concept given a name and not an absolute, abiding reality in and of itself.

Thus, by studying the phonetic and pictorial (Ancient Egyptian language is not only phonetic, but also illustrative) etymology (the origin and development of a linguistic form) and etiology (the study of causes or origins) of names and applying the initiatic philosophy (of the spiritual culture), it is possible to decipher the mysteries of Creation by discovering the teachings embedded in the language by the Sages of Ancient Egypt.

Moreover, in the Ancient Egyptian language as in others such as the ancient Greek, Hebrew, and Sanskrit, where the pronunciations and meanings of some words are not known with certainty or at all, the meaning of many more words and terms are known with exactness. So, while a time traveler who has studied the Ancient Egyptian language in modern times might have some difficulty speaking to an Ancient Egyptian

---

[23] *The African Origin of Civilization*, *Civilization or Barbarism,* Cheikh Anta Diop

person, they would have less trouble communicating in the written form of the language. This means that the philosophy and myth can be understood even if the pronunciation of some words is uncertain. Therefore, the philosophy and myth of the Ancient Egyptian culture can be a pathway to understanding the Ancient Egyptian language and also, comparisons can be made between the philosophy of the Ancient Egyptian culture and that of others. This also means that philosophy is a legitimate and viable means to compare mythologies as a factor in determining the contact and communication between cultures and their relationship, if any.

## Form

> **form** *(fôrm) n. 1.a. The shape and structure of an object. b. The body or outward appearance of a person or an animal considered separately from the face or head; figure.)* [24]

The form of an object is related to its name and function. Thus, correlations based on form will often be noted in conjunction with the other related factors. As we saw earlier, language (name) is merely a symbol of concept, which is itself a representation of truth. However, the concept of something which exists at the level of the unconscious mind will be compatible even if at the conscious level of mind of people who speak different languages. Aspects of human activity such as concept, intent, desire, etc., can be alike, while the manifestation is variable. Again, if the concepts, intents, desires, etc., are alike, but there is an absence of manifestations (language, artifacts, myths, etc.) that can be compared in order to confirm this likeness at the conscious level, the case is hard to make that there is a commonality or contact between the two cultures. The specificity of form in ritual objects, architecture, artifacts, myths, etc. makes them excellent factors to compare within different traditions within the same culture or between cultures of different countries or geographically **separated societies** in order to determine their synchronism or nonconformity. However, the unconscious psychological principles being conveyed through the medium of the forms of the objects, iconographies, rituals, etc. are to be compared along with the external forms used to symbolize those principles.

---

[24] American Heritage Dictionary

# Architecture

**ar·chi·tec·ture** (är"k¹-tμk"ch...r) *n. Abbr.* **archit., arch. 1.** The art and science of designing and erecting buildings. **2.** Buildings and other large structures. **3.** A style and method of design and construction.

Architecture is the conscious creation of buildings and dwellings which the culture may use to promote its existence. The implementation of architecture signifies the existence of organized culture because architecture requires the orderly and systematic application of mathematics, geometry, the organization of labor, resources, etc. Architecture invariably reflects the philosophical and/or spiritual outlook of a culture, and thus is distinctive. Some cultures have created architecture that supports war (castles, fortresses, etc.), others have created architecture that supports commerce, while others have created architecture that seeks to reflect spiritual principles. For example, Islamic architecture reflects Islamic culture and Islamic beliefs. Modern American architecture reflects modern American culture and beliefs. In the same manner, Ancient Egyptian architecture reflects Ancient Egyptian culture and religious beliefs, and includes art and iconography which give insights into the values and beliefs of the Ancient Egyptians that may be compared to the values and beliefs of other cultures.

Ancient Egyptian architecture exhibits one additional aspect which is not found in most cultures. In Ancient Egypt, architecture was used to express a concretized coming into being of the spiritual myth and to reflect the nature of the cosmos. This is to say, the architecture was created in such a way as to express the religious philosophy of a myth in a concrete form. For example, the placing of a winged sundisk above the Temple entrances follows the decree given by the God Djehuti in the myth of the Asarian Resurrection to do so. This factor of mythological expression in architecture is also found in other spiritual traditions.

# Function – Usage

*(**1.a.** The act, manner, or amount of using; use.)*[25]

The usage of an artifact, particularly a ritual object, is important when considering their origins. There are some important artifacts which are central to the rituals of the religions and they, therefore, constitute "mythological anchors" or focal points for the practice of the religion or spiritual tradition. These objects remain constant throughout the history of the culture while items of lesser importance may come into and out of

---

[25] American Heritage Dictionary

existence over periods of time, being created with the same general form and having the same ritual function. This constitutes an important key in determining the congruence of the religious traditions in question, as it may support other forms of congruent factors such as the symmetry between the myths and or plots in religious stories (myths) being compared.

## Rituals and Traditions

**rit·u·al** (rĭch′ōō-əl) *n.* **1.a.** The prescribed order of a religious ceremony. **b.** The body of ceremonies or rites used in a place of worship. [26]

**tra·di·tion** (trə-dĭsh′ən) *n.* **1.** The passing down of elements of a culture from generation to generation, especially by oral communication. **2.a.** A mode of thought or behavior followed by a people continuously from generation to generation; a custom or usage. **b.** A set of such customs and usages viewed as a coherent body of precedents influencing the present. **3.** A body of unwritten religious precepts. **4.** A time-honored practice or set of such practices.[27]

Rituals, ritual objects and traditions (implying observances, festivals, holidays, etc., related to the myths) are used by a society as tangible symbols of the myth. Traditions, in this context, may be understood as a legacy of rituals performed at an earlier point in history and handed down to the descendants of a mythological-religious-spiritual heritage to which a particular culture adheres. As such they are instruments to facilitate the remembrance, practice and identification with the key elements of a myth. This function of rituals and traditions is more significant than just being a social link to the past generations of a culture. When the identification of a practitioner of a myth with the protagonist of the myth is advanced, the practitioner of the rituals and traditions of the myth partakes in the myth and thus becomes one with the passion of the deity of the myth and in so doing, attains a communion with that divinity. This advanced practice of rituals and traditions constitutes the third level of religion, the metaphysics or mystical level, which will be explained in the following section.

## Myth and its Origins, and Elements

Since the study of myth and mythic symbolism in ancient scriptures, iconography, etc., forms an integral part of the comparison of cultures, we must first begin by gaining a deeper understanding of what myth is, and its

---

[26] American Heritage Dictionary
[27] American Heritage Dictionary

purpose. We will begin with some historical background about myth and some popular definitions of the term.

> The word *myth* comes from Ancient Greek language: μυθολογία "story-telling", from μῦθος *muthos*, "story, legend", and λόγος *logos*, "account , speech". The word μῦθος itself is of unknown origin.
>
> The term *mythology* has been in use since the 15th century, and means "an exposition of myths". The current meaning of "body of myths" itself dates to 1781 (Oxford English Dictionary (OED)).[28] The adjective *mythical* dates to 1678.
>
> *Myth* in general use is often interchangeable with legend or allegory, but some scholars strictly distinguish the terms. The term has been used in English since the 19th century. The newest edition of the OED distinguishes the meanings.[29]
>
>> 1a. "A traditional story, typically involving supernatural beings or forces, which embodies and provides an explanation, aetiology, or justification for something such as the early history of a society, a religious belief or ritual, or a natural phenomenon", citing the Westminster Review of 1830 as the first English attestation[30]
>> 1b. "As a mass noun: such stories collectively or as a genre." (1840)
>> 2a. "A widespread but untrue or erroneous story or belief" (1849)
>> 2b. "A person or thing held in awe or generally referred to with near reverential admiration on the basis of popularly repeated stories (whether real or fictitious)." (1853)
>> 2c. "A popular conception of a person or thing which exaggerates or idealizes the truth." (1928)

---

[28] In extended use, the word can also refer to collective or personal ideological or socially constructed received wisdon, as in "At least since Tocqueville compared American society to 'a vast lottery', our mythology of business has celebrated risk-taking." (2000 *The New Republic*, 29 May 2000)

[29] *Mythology,* Wikipedia Encyclopedia

[30] Earlier editions of the OED also present this quote as the earliest attestation of *myth*, but consider it an example of the definition corresponding to definition 2.

## The Ancient Egyptian Concept of Myth and its Purpose

Many of the Ancient Greek philosophers[31] who developed Greek Philosophy were students of the Ancient Egypt Egyptian Sages. In Ancient Egypt the purpose and importance of ritual in the religious process was an important aspect of the religious teaching. In Ancient Egyptian language and philosophy a prototype for the Greek word, muthos, can be discerned. If we look at religious practice as a three part process including three levels: myth, ritual, and mysticism (philosophy and metaphysics) we find the following Ancient Egyptian hieroglyphic terms.

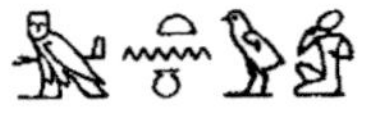 *Matnu* -the Myth: - legend, story, myth,

 *Aru* - ritual – ceremony.

 *Shetaut Neter*- the Mystical.

As in other African religions, which use the role and practice of *griot*, in Ancient Egyptian religion the Matnu (myth) is given through *Sdjedt*  - story telling (to speak proverbs, to speak tales). In the myth stage the *Shemsu.* , followers of a religion learn about its story. This story is not historical although it may have historical elements embedded in it, such as names of places or objects or people. However, the historic period and setting should not be confused with the historicity of a religion. That is to say, just because the name Asar, or Jesus, or Krishna are used in their respective religions, does not mean that everything they are described as doing was actually done in physical terms. Myth is not exclusive. It does not apply only to those who lived in ancient times. Rather, it relates to recurrent themes in human culture as well as common psycho-mystical aspects of the human psyche that have to do with the primal need to evolve and expand in consciousness and common forms of

---

[31] "This is also confirmed by the most learned of Greeks such as Solon, Thales, Plato, Eudoxus, Pythagoras, and as some say, even Lycurgus going to Egypt and conversing with the priests; of whom they say Euxodus was a hearer of Chonuphis of Memphis,* Solon of Sonchis of Sais,* and Pythagoras of Oenuphis of Heliopolis.*"

-Plutarch, Morals, 10
(c. 46-120 AD), Greek author/Initiate of the temple of Isis
*(Greek names for cities in Ancient Egypt)

experience in all humanity. Therefore, human beings alive today are not different from those who lived thousands of years ago. They have the same desires, the same concerns and the same yearning to discover and experience immortality and transcendental consciousness. Myth is a special language that relates to the higher aspect of spirit, the transcendent, in all things. Therefore, the myth is metaphorical, relating to truths that cannot all be expressed in physical terms and yet uses physical terminology, similes and parables to point the mind in the direction of the transcendent. Thus, myth uses the phenomenological conceptual language of the mind because the mind is limited and gross, in comparison to the transcendent. The *maut* -is the moral of the myth, the most important teaching in the myth that is to be remembered.

Ritual is the next stage of religion, after myth, because it takes aspects of the myth and allows a follower to perform certain *Ari* actions related to the myth and in so doing to come closer to the divinity of the myth through ritual actions. In Ancient Egyptian religious ritual-theater the actors (participants in the reenactment of the myth) assume the role of a character in the myth. The actor is to adopt the image *tut* (form-image) of the divine character of the myth they are portraying. They are also to adopt the words *djedeti* words to be said. There needs to be *Djed medu* - reciting words of power – *Hekau* or , that is, the words of the teaching, the *Medu-Neter* - writings. As the ritual is intensified the participant is to begin to think and feel like that character of the myth and thereby they become one with that divine principle. This process leads to a ritual identification wherein the follower becomes *Nuk pu Nuk Asar Neter* (I am that I am) "identified with the divinity" and thereby also becomes divine.

# On Myth, Truth and Literalism

Definitions 2a and 2c are noteworthy in that they reflect the development in western culture that associates myth with something "untrue" or false or "exaggerated"; in other words, it is not real and by extrapolation the implication is that myth is a concoction or fabrication based on imagination or nonsense. While myth may or may not have historical elements or personalities in it, it is not primarily a historical treatise. Myth is not a vehicle of literal information such as historical documents. Myth has a metaphorical reality as well as allegorical insights into philosophical teachings of legends and stories that explain the origins and values of a society.

> *Myth* in this sense does not imply that a story is either objectively false or true, it rather refers to a spiritual, psychological or symbolical notion of *truth* unrelated to materialist or objectivist notions… Literalism refers to the attitude of some adherents of modern dominant religions that regards the traditions surrounding the origin and development of their faith as literal historic accounts.[32]

The American Heritage Dictionary defines *Myth* as follows:

1. A traditional story presenting supernatural beings, ancestors, or heroes that serve as primordial types in a primitive view of the world.
2. A fictitious or imaginary story, person, or thing.
3. A false belief.

The American Heritage Dictionary defines *Myth* as follows:

1. A body of myths about the origin and history of a people.

The Random House Encyclopedia defines *Myth* as follows:

> Myth, a body of myths or traditional stories dealing with gods and legendary heroes. The myths of a people serves to present their world view, their explanations of natural phenomena, their religious and other beliefs. Mythological literature includes the Greek *Iliad* and *Odyssey*, the Scandinavian *Edda*, the Indian *Ramayana*, and the Babylonian *Gilgamesh*, among others. Various interpretations of myth have been made by anthropologists

---

[32] *Religion and mythology*, Wikipedia Encyclopedia

such as Sir James Frazer and Claude Lévi-Strauss. In literature, myth has been used as the basis for poetry, stories, plays, and other writings.

Excerpted from *Compton's Interactive Encyclopedia*:

> **MYTHOLOGY.** The origin of the universe can be explained by modern astronomers and astrophysicists, while archaeologists and historians try to clarify the origin of human societies. In the distant past, however, before any sciences existed, the beginnings of the world and of society were explained by mythology.
>
> The word myth is often mistakenly understood to mean fiction something that never happened, a made-up story or fanciful tale. Myth is really a way of thinking about the past. Mircea Eliade, a historian of religions, once stated: "Myths tell only of that which really happened." This does not mean that myths correctly explain what literally happened. It does suggest, however, that behind the explanation there is a reality that cannot be seen and examined.

Myth-ology is the study or science (ology) of myths and their deeper implications for the values and belief systems of a society. In relation to mythology, the term epic is also used. The American Heritage Dictionary defines an *Epic* as:

> 1. A long narrative poem that celebrates episodes of a people's heroic tradition.

The Encarta/Funk & Wagnall's Encyclopedia defines an Epic as:

> "A long narrative poem, majestic both in theme and style. Epics deal with legendary or historical events of national or universal significance, involving action of broad sweep and grandeur. Most epics deal with the exploits of a single individual, thereby giving unity to the composition. Typically, an epic involves the introduction of supernatural forces that shape the action, conflict in the form of battles or other physical combat, and certain stylistic conventions: an invocation to the Muse, a formal statement of the theme, long lists of the protagonists involved, and set speeches couched in elevated language. Commonplace details of everyday life may appear, but they serve as background for the story, and are described in the same lofty style as the rest of the poem."

These definitions have been included here to provide a reference as to what society at large, especially in the West, has accepted as the definition and purpose of mythological and epic literature. Now we will explore the yogic-mystical meaning of *Myth*. First however, one more definition is required. We need to understand what a Metaphor is. The American Heritage Dictionary defines *Metaphor* as follows:

> "A figure of speech in which a term that ordinarily designates an object or idea is used to designate a dissimilar object or idea in order to suggest comparison or analogy, as in the phrase *evening of life*."

## A Universal Vision for Comparative Mythology

In the book *Comparative Mythology,* the author, Jaan Puhvel, traces the term "myth" to the writings of Homer (900 B.C.E.), with the usage *épos kai muthos* 'word and speech.' In the writings of Homer and the ancient Greek writers of tragic plays, Jaan Puhvel also sees that the term can mean "tale, story, narrative," and that this story or tale can be without reference to truth content.[33] Truth content here implies a historical or real relationship to time and space events or realities. In the writings of the later Greek authors such as Herodotus, Puhvel sees a different meaning in the term Mûthos, that of fictive "narrative," "tall tale," and "legend." It is felt that Herodotus spoke of Mûthos as those items he himself found incredulous, and used the term *logos* for that information which he felt was more or less based on truth or facts. Further, with the writings of Plato, a new interpretation of the terms emerge, as Mûthos takes on a different character in relation to logos. Mûthos (myth) is more of a non-rational basis for understanding existence while logos is seen as the rational basis. In Western Culture, the term "logos" has come to be associated with absolute knowledge and logical thinking and analysis. In terms of mysticism, it is understood as the Divine intelligence, consciousness, which permeates and enlivens matter, time and space. In later times logos came to be known as 'the Word' or inner, esoteric spiritual knowledge, and in early Christianity, Jesus became 'the word (logos) made flesh.' From these origins and many deprecating arguments from the church and western scientists, through the middle and dark ages and into the renaissance period of Western Culture, the meaning of the word "myth" in modern times, perhaps in an effort to contrast it (myth) from the supposed "historical" and "real" western religion, has come to be understood primarily as a colloquialism to refer to anything devoid of a basis in truth or reality. Saying "it's a myth" has come to be understood by most people as a reference to something that does not contain even a fragment of truth.

---

[33] *Comparative Mythology,* Jaan Puhvel

# The Cultural Category Factor Correlation Method

Myth has come to be thought of in terms of being neurotic expressions of ancient religions, movie ideas spinning out of Hollywood, governments telling myths (lies) or Madison Avenue advertising (the "myth-makers"), etc., in other words, something without any truth or factual basis. In ancient times, Plato referred to the term 'mythologia' as meaning "myth-telling," as opposed to storytelling. Modern scholars refer to this term as mythology (the study of myth), which, until recently, primarily meant Greek Mythology. The body of ancient Greek narratives relating to the legends and traditions connected to the gods and goddesses of Greece are referred to as the mythological narratives.

Thus, mythology is the study of myths. Myths (mythos) are stories which relate human consciousness to the transcendental essence of reality. This work is essentially a study in comparative mythology. It seeks to discover the common elements in two or more systems of mythos in order to understand their deeper meaning and develop the larger picture as they are fitted into the overall patchwork of traditions throughout history. In effect, this work attempts to show a connection and continuity between traditions that will enable the comprehension of them as a flow of the one primordial and recurrent theme of self-discovery. In such a study, there are always some who object, maintaining that differences are the overriding defining factors in any aspect of life. But this way of thinking is incongruous in the face of all the scientific evidence pointing to a common origin for all humanity as well as the discoveries of quantum physics that demonstrate the common basis and interconnectedness of all matter in Creation itself. Therefore, it seems that the movement to understand our common bonds as human beings should as well move into to the arena of the mythology and psychology. In this manner we may discover that what binds us is greater than that which tears us apart, for when we examine the arguments and concepts used to separate, they are inevitably derived from emotion, politics, misconception or superficialities based on ignorance. These lead to major controversies, debates, refutations and egoistic opinions founded on nothing but faith in rumors, conjectures and speculation, and not on first hand examination of the traditions from the point of view of a practitioner. Joseph Campbell summed up this issue as follows.

> "Perhaps it will be objected that in bringing out the correspondences I have overlooked the differences between the various Oriental and Occidental, modern, ancient, and primitive traditions. The same objection might be brought, however, against any textbook or chart of anatomy, where the physiological variations of race are disregarded in the interest of a basic general understanding of the human physique. There are of course differences between the numerous mythologies and religions of mankind, but this is a book about the similarities; and

once these are understood the differences will be found to be much less great than is popularly (and politically) supposed. My hope is that a comparative elucidation may contribute to the perhaps not-quite desperate cause of those forces that are working in the present world for unification, not in the name of some ecclesiastical or political empire, but in the sense of human mutual understanding. As we are told in the Vedas: "Truth is one, the sages speak of it by many names."

J.C.<br>
New York City<br>
June 10, 1948

In *Comparative Mythology,* Puhvel underscored the importance of myth and the operation of myth as an integral, organic component of human existence. It is a defining aspect of social order in which human existence is guided to discover the "sacred" and "timeless" nature of self and Creation. He also discusses how the "historical landscape" becomes "littered with the husks of desiccated myths" even as "societies pass and religious systems change," remaining submerged in the traditions and epics of modern times.

"Myth in the technical sense is a serious object of study, because true myth is by definition deadly serious to its originating environment. In myth are expressed the thought patterns by which a group formulates self-cognition and self-realization, attains self-knowledge and self-confidence, explains its own source and being and that of its surroundings, and sometimes tries to chart its destinies. By myth man has lived, died, and-all too often-killed. Myth operates by bringing a sacred (and hence essentially and paradoxically "timeless") past to bear preemptively on the present and inferentially on the future ("as it was in the beginning, is now, and ever shall be"). Yet in the course of human events societies pass and religious systems change; the historical landscape gets littered with the husks of desiccated myths. These are valuable nonmaterial fossils of mankind's recorded history, especially if still embedded in layers of embalmed religion, as part of a stratum of tradition complete with cult, liturgy, and ritual. Yet equally important is the next level of transmission, in which the sacred narrative has already been secularized, myth has been turned into saga, sacred time into heroic past, gods into heroes, and mythical action into "historical" plot. Many genuine "national epics" constitute repositories of tradition where the mythical underpinnings have been submerged via such literary transposition. Old chronicles can turn out to be "prose epics" where the probing modem mythologist can uncover otherwise lost mythical traditions. Such survival is quite apart from, or wholly incidental to, the conscious exploitative use of myth in literature, as raw material of fiction, something that Western civilization has practiced since artful verbal creativity began."[34]

The key element in myth is its metaphorical purpose in that its stories and characters are designed to provide a reference towards an etiological, moral or spiritual message that transcends the story itself. This means that there is an exoteric meaning which refers to the events and circumstances in the story, which may or may not have a basis in fact, and also an esoteric or mystical meaning which refers to a deeper teaching or message which transcends the boundaries of the events in the story. This message is spiritual in nature when the myth is religious. Through the myth many ideas which are not easily explained in rational, logical terms can be freely explored and elucidated in imaginative and colorful ways. Mystical myths are particularly important because their purpose is to point to where the answers to the most important questions of every individual may be found. Everyone is searching for answers to questions like "Who am I really?" "Is this all that I am?" "Where do I come from?" "What is death?" and "What is my purpose in life?" Through myths, the teachings of Sages and Saints can take full flight, free of the constraints of normal grammatical or thematic boundaries. Therefore, myths are an ideal way to impart spiritual truths which transcend ordinary human experiences and ordinary human concepts of rationality.

The question of the similarities between myths, rituals and traditions has been explored in the book *"The Mythic Image,"* where the late world renowned mythologist, Joseph Campbell, explained the concepts surrounding the treatment of equivalent elements and symbols that can be seen in myths from apparently separate cultures.

One explanation that has been proposed to account for the appearance of homologous structures and often even identical motifs in the myths and rites of widely separate cultures is psychological: namely, to cite a formula of James G. Frazer in *The Golden Bough,* that such occurrences are most likely *"the effect of similar causes acting alike on the similar constitution of the human mind in different countries and under different skies."*
There are, however, instances that cannot be accounted for in this way, and then suggest the need for another

---

[34] *Comparative Mythology,* Jaan Puhvel

interpretation: for example, in India the number of years assigned to an eon[35] is 4,320,000; whereas in the Icelandic *Poetic Edda* it is declared that in Othin's warrior hall, Valhall, there are 540 doors, through each of which, on the "day of the war of the wolf,"[36] 800 battle-ready warriors will pass to engage the antigods in combat.' But 540 times 800 equals 432,000!

Moreover, a Chaldean[37] priest, Berossos, writing in Greek ca. 289 B.C., reported that according to Mesopotamian belief 432,000 years elapsed between the crowning of the first earthly king and the coming of the deluge.

No one, I should think, would wish to argue that these figures could have arisen independently in India, Iceland, and Babylon.[38]

Campbell explains that there is a view that the commonalties observed in myth, symbolism, etc., are a factor of psychological forces that are common to all human beings. One example of this concept is that every human being on earth feels the desire for happiness. Therefore, when we see people from different places (*"different countries and under different skies"*), who have never met each other, pursuing happiness in similar ways, we should not be surprised. However, Campbell makes the point that some coincidences go beyond the nature of conformity due to a primal urge. Those concurrences can only be explained by a closer relationship, because the uniformity of "structure" or configuration of the myths as well as the usage of the exact same symbols and rites could only occur when there is an intimate relationship between the cultures. In other words, the two pursuers of happiness can be explained by the theory of common urges, however, the pursuit of happiness using the same procedures (rites or rituals), the same way of defining happiness, the same philosophy of how to go about looking for happiness, idealizing happiness in the same way (myth), representing happiness the same way (symbolism), etc., are signs that the cultures have had a common origin, upbringing, socialization, indoctrination, contact, etc. This occurs when a culture "diffuses" some new technology, philosophy or cultural element to another culture. Campbell continues:

---

[35] A "Great Cycle" *(Mahayuga)* of cosmic time.

[36] i.e., at the ending of the cosmic eon, Wagner's *Götterdämmerung.*

[37] According to the Egyptians, Diodorus reports, the Chaldaens were *"a colony of their priests that Belus had transported on the Euphrates and organized on the model of the mother-caste, and this colony continues to cultivate the knowledge of the stars, knowledge that it brought from the homeland."*

[38] *The Mythic Image*, Joseph Campbell

A second approach to interpretation has therefore been proposed, based on the observation that at certain identifiable times, in identifiable places, epochal transformations of culture have occurred, the effects of which have been diffused to the quarters of the earth; and that along with these there have traveled constellations of associated mythological systems and motifs.[39]

Thus, Campbell introduces another way to understand the commonalties observed in separate cultures that cannot be explained by the theory of similar forces operating on the minds of separate individuals. There are milestones in history wherein major social events or advancements in culture affect humanity as if like a ripple of water caused by a stone being dropped into a calm lake. The resulting undulations of powerful concepts, and technologies move along the trade and communication routs, the arteries of human communication and interaction, spreading (diffusing) the advanced knowledge in waves across the cultural ocean of humanity throughout the world. Like a surfer, being carried along with the force of the wave, so too the concepts and symbols move across the human landscape being empowered by the innate human desire to achieve higher understanding and the intellectual capacity to recognize something better or a new way to express the same treasured truths. This important principle related to the transference of ideas and symbols between cultures was seminal to Campbell's groundbreaking work as a teacher of comparative mythology in the West.

## Psychomythology

*Psychomythology* is the study of the *psychomyth* of a culture. Mystical teaching holds that the essence of Creation and therefore, of each individual human being, is transcendental; it transcends the ordinary bounds of mental perception and understanding. However, all human experiences occur in and through the mind. Therefore, the heart of all human experiences, be they painful or pleasurable, is rooted in the mind. The purpose of myth is to bridge the gap between the limited human mind and its conscious, worldly level and that which transcends all physicality as well as the mind and senses. Thus, religious myths must be understood in the light of their psychological and mystical (transcending body, mind and senses) implications. We will refer to this concept by a new term: "*psychomyth*". "*Psycho-Mythology*" is the study of myths as psychological, spiritual and mythic artifacts or aspects of culture.

The term "*psycho,*" as it is used here, must be understood as far more than simply that which refers to the mind in the worldly sense. The term

---

[39] *The Mythic Image*, Joseph Campbell

"psycho" must be understood to mean everything that constitutes human consciousness in all of its stages and states, but most importantly, the subconscious and unconscious levels of mind wherein understanding about self and the universe occurs. *"Mythology"* here refers to the study of the codes, messages, ideas, directives, stories, culture, beliefs, etc., that affect the personality through the conscious, subconscious and unconscious aspects of the mind of an individual, specifically those effects which result in psycho-spiritual transformation, that is, a transpersonal or transcendental change in the personality of an individual which leads to the discovery of the transcendental reality behind all existence.

As a rule, generally, myth should never be understood literally even though some of its origins may involve actual events or actions, otherwise one will miss the transcendental message being related through the metaphor. This would be like going to a theater to see a fictional movie or reading a fantasy novel, and believing it to be real. However, as a movie or novel may be based on unreal events and yet carry an important message which is imparted through the medium of actors, a plot and so on, mystical myths are not to be understood as being completely baseless nor as having been put together purely for entertainment purposes nor should they be seen as "primitive mumbo-jumbo." Myths constitute a symbolic language that speaks to people in psycho-symbolic ways, satisfying their conscious need for entertainment, but also affecting the subconscious and unconscious mind and its need for spiritual evolution. This psychological language of myths can lead people to understand and experience the transcendental truths of existence, which cannot be easily expressed in words.

Myth is the first stage of religion and the reenactment of the myth constitutes the second level of religion: Ritual.[40] Myths constitute the heart and soul of rituals. Myth is a mystical language for transmitting and teaching the principles of life and creation. Rituals are the medium through which the myths are practiced, lived and realized.

The study of religious mythical stories is important to gain insight into the *"Psycho-Mythology"* or psychological implications of myth for the spiritual transformation of the individual which leads to the attainment of Enlightenment. Enlightenment implies the attainment of an expanded state of consciousness, termed as *"awet ab,"* dilation (expansion) of the heart in Ancient Egyptian Mystical Philosophy, in which there is a full and perfect awareness of one's existence beyond the mind and body. Thus, when you delve into a myth, you must expect more than just entertainment. You should be equipped with the knowledge which will allow you to decipher the hidden meanings in the story so that you may also begin to experience and benefit from them on a personal level, that is to say. live the myth and

---

[40] *African Religion Vol. 4: Asarian Theology*, Muata Ashby, 1997

nlightenment. Only then will a person be
nation in their life which will lead them to
as well as contentment. This is the third
nystical or metaphysical level.

## The Keys to Reading and Understanding a Myth

*Religion without myth not only fails to work, it also fails to offer man the promise of unity with the transpersonal and eternal.*

—C. G. Jung (1875-1961)

## Key #1: Myths (Religious/Mystical) are relevant to our lives in the present.

The first and most important key to understanding a myth is to comprehend that the myth is not talking about some ancient personality or story which occurred a long time ago and which has no relevance to the present. In fact, the myth is speaking about you. It is a story about human life, its origins, its destiny, its plight and the correct action, in the present, which is based on the same principles of the past, for leading a truly successful life which paves the way to Enlightenment and true happiness.

## Key #2: Myth is a journey of spiritual transformation.

The second key to understanding a myth is comprehending that it is usually written in the form of a journey in which the subject must learn about himself or herself and transcend the ordinary human consciousness, thereby discovering a greater essence of self. In this movement there are experiences of happiness, sorrow, struggle and learning. It is a movement from ignorance and darkness towards light, wisdom and ultimately, to spiritual Enlightenment.

## Key #3: Myths are to be lived in order to understand their true meaning.

The third key to understanding a myth is that comprehension comes from living the myth. Living a myth does not mean simply reading a myth, being able to recount the events with perfect memory or simply practicing the rituals of a myth without a deeper understanding of their implications and purpose. It means making the essence of the teaching being conveyed through the myth an integral part of one's life. If this practice is not implemented, the teachings remain at the intellectual level and the deeper truths of the myth are not revealed. One lives with dry intellectualism or blind faith, the former leading to a superficial and therefore frustrated spiritual life, and the latter leading to dogmatism, ritualism and emotional frustration. Therefore, one must resolve to discover the myth in every facet of your life, and in so doing, you will be triumphant as the hero(ine) of the myth.

## Key #4: Myth points the way to victory in life.

Myths show us our heritage as a culture as well as the legacy we are to receive. They give human beings a place in the scheme of things as well as a purpose in life and the means to achieve the fulfillment of that purpose. The ultimate purpose is to achieve victory in the battle of life, to defeat the forces of ignorance within oneself which lead to adversity and frustration and thereby become masters of life here and in the hereafter, discovering undifferentiated peace, love and joy...Enlightenment.

> "God is a metaphor for a mystery that transcends all human categories of thought...It depends on how much you want to think about it, whether or not it's doing you any good, whether it's putting you in touch with the mystery which is the ground of your own being."
> —Joseph Campbell

Thus, when comparing the myths of different cultures for the purpose of religious studies, it is necessary to understand their respective metaphorical aspects as well as their attendant underlying philosophies along with their apparent iconographical forms and artistic intent (ex. naturalistic[41] or stylized[42]).

## Other Aspects of Myth

**Plot** refers to the plan of events or main story in a narrative or drama.[43]
The synchronicity in the situations presented in myths can be used as a factor in discerning the communal nature of two myths. This congruence must be specific, involving characters of similar age group, gender and genealogy or provenance, experiencing similar situations in the same or similar ways.

---

[41] Imitating or producing the effect or appearance of nature.
[42] To restrict or make conform to a particular style. **2.** To represent conventionally; conventionalize.
[43] American Heritage Dictionary

# The Cultural Category Factor Correlation Method

**Theme** *—noun*
1. a subject of discourse, discussion, meditation, or composition; topic: *The need for world peace was the theme of the meeting.*
2. a unifying or dominant idea, motif, etc., as in a work of art.

In comparing myths, there are several important concerns. The purpose of myth, the language of myth and the levels of myth must be understood prior to making a comparison. *Myth is a language*[44] by which sages and saints transmit the basic elements of culture through a "common story" for all within a society to believe in as well as draw answers to the basic questions of life such as, Where do I come from?, To which group do I belong? What is the purpose of life? and How do I fulfill that purpose? This is all conveyed through the story, plot and theme of the myth and their inherent teachings of social order as well as their spiritual morals.

Most religions and spiritual philosophies tend to be *deistic* at the elementary levels. *Deism*, as a religious belief or form of theism (belief in the existence of a Supreme Being or gods) holds that the Supreme Being's action was restricted to an initial act of creation, after which He/She retired (separated) to contemplate the majesty of His/Her work. Deists hold that the natural creation is regulated by laws put in place by the Supreme Being at the time of creation which are supposed to be inscribed with perfect moral principles. Therefore, deism is closely related to the exoteric or personal but also outer (phenomenal) and dogmatic and conventional understanding of the Divinity.

Two approaches to myth dominate the intellectual landscape during the first half of the twentieth century: the ritualistic and the psychoanalytic. The former, epitomized by the "myth and ritual" or Cambridge school beholden to the Oxonian E. B. Tylor's *Primitive Culture* (1871) and with James G. Frazer's *Golden Bough* as its central talisman, owes its theoretical underpinnings to Jane E. Harrison's *Prolegomena to the Study of Greek Religion* (1903) and *Themis* (1912). Harrison provided a strikingly simple and exclusionary definition of myth: myth is nothing but the verbalization of ritual, "the spoken correlative of the acted rite" *(Themis,* P. 328), *ta legomena* 'what is said' accompanying *ta dromena* 'what is being done', myth and ritual being accordingly but two sides of the same religious coin; thus in principle there can be no

---

[44] *The Power of Myth,* Joseph Campbell

myth without ritual, although time may have obliterated the act and left the narrative free to survive as myth or its debased subspecies (saga, legend, folktale, etc.). [45]

An assumption adopted by many comparative mythology scholars is the idea that myth is a means of explaining ritual. This idea is often predicated upon the concept that "primitive" cultures developed myth as a means of coping with the mysteries of life and Creation due to the lack of "scientific" knowledge. Supposedly, in the absence of science, ritual and superstition were substituted in order to allay the fears caused by the unknown. Further, this theory therefore holds that myth developed as an emanation of the actions of the practitioners of the rituals to justify those rituals. While this theory may accurately describe aspects of some societies whose practitioners who are ignorant as to the reason behind the rituals of their religion, it is wholly incorrect when considering cultures possessing mystical philosophy. In those cultures the sacred writings of their religions present models of rituals as expressions of myth, and myth as expressions of philosophy or mysticism. Ritual is therefore a means to make a myth effective and not just legend, in order to understand myth, and the realization of myth is a means to attain spiritual enlightenment. The erroneous concept is evident not only in modern scholarship, but also in ancient cultures which adopted symbols and myths from other cultures without fully understanding their purpose or the philosophy behind them. The following example given by Count Goblet D' Alviella provides an insight into the process called "iconological mythology."

> Sometimes, in similar cases, the new owners of the image will endeavor to explain it by a more or less ingenious interpretation, and in this manner they will restore to it a symbolical import, though applied to a new conception.
>
> The rising sun has often been compared to a new-born child. Amongst the Egyptians, this comparison led to Horus being represented as an infant sucking its finger. The Greeks imagined that he placed his finger on his lips to enjoin secrecy on the initiated, and they made him the image of Harpocrates, the god of silence. [46]
>
> This is what M. Clermont-Ganneau has very happily termed *iconological mythology*; it is here no longer the myth which gives rise to the image, but the image which gives rise to the myth.

---

[45] *Comparative Mythology,* Jaan Puhvel
[46] G. Lafaye. *Historie des divinités d'Alexandrie hors de l' Egypte.* Paris, 18984, p.259

We may further quote, as an interpretation of the same kind, the legend related by Hygin, which made the Caduceus originate in Hermes throwing his wand between two serpents fighting. It is evident that, here also, this hypothesis, soon to be transformed into a myth by the popular imagination, was due to a desire, unconscious perhaps, to explain the Caduceus.

Most frequently it is a conception pre-existent in the local traditions which we think we find amongst the products of foreign imagery.[47]

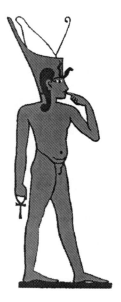

**Figure 5: The Ancient Egyptian God Heru pointing to his mouth**

Another case in point is the relationship between Ancient Egypt and Greece. The Greeks adopted what they could understand of Ancient Egyptian philosophy, but did not adopt the culture or social philosophy. The Greeks made some changes in what they learned. Therefore, Greek culture cannot be claimed as an African (Ancient Egyptian) heritage. The problem was so severe that the Sages of Ancient Egypt felt the need to reprimand and denounce the Greek distortions. They indicted Greek culture as the culprit leading to the way of speech (communication and relation) which was of a "loose," "disdainful" and "confusing" character.

---

[47] _The Migration of Symbols,_ Count Goblet D' Alviella, 1894

"The Greek tongue is a noise of words, a language of argument and confusion."

"Keep this teaching from translation in order that such mighty Mysteries might not come to the Greeks and to the disdainful speech of Greece, with all its looseness and its surface beauty, taking all the strength out of the solemn and the strong - the energetic speech of Names."

"Unto those who come across these words, their composition will seem most simple and clear; but on the contrary, as this is unclear, and has the true meaning of its words concealed, it will be still unclear, when, afterwards, the Greeks will want to turn our tongue into their own - for this will be a very great distorting and obscuring of even what has heretofore been written. Turned into our own native tongue, the teachings keepeth clear the meaning of the words. For that its very quality of sound, the very power of Ancient Egyptian names, have in themselves the bringing into act of what is said."

## Myth in Orthodox Religion

# Myth ➔ Ritual ➔ Mysticism

As previously discussed, in its complete form, religion is composed of three aspects, *mythological, ritual* and *metaphysical* (or the *mystical experience* (mysticism - mystical philosophy)). Mystical philosophy is the basis of myth. It is expressed in ritual and experienced in the metaphysics (spiritual disciplines, yoga) of the given religion. While many religions contain rituals, traditions, metaphors and myths, there are few professionals trained in understanding their deeper aspects and psychological implications (metaphysics and mystical). Thus, there is disappointment, frustration and disillusionment among many followers as well as leaders within many religions, particularly in the Western Hemisphere, because it is difficult to evolve spiritually without the proper spiritual guidance. Through introspection and spiritual research, it is possible to discover mythological vistas within religion which can rekindle the light of spirituality and at the same time increase the possibility of gaining a fuller experience of life. The exoteric (outer, ritualistic) forms of religion with which most people are familiar is only the tip of an iceberg so to speak; it is only a beginning, an invitation or prompting to seek a deeper (esoteric) discovery of the transcendental truths of existence.

While on the surface it seems that there are many differences between the religious philosophies, upon closer reflection there is only one major division, that of belief (theist) or non-belief (atheist). Among the believers there are differences of opinion as to how to believe. This is the source of much the trouble between religions and spiritual groups; One reason for this is because ordinary religion is deistic, based on traditions and customs which are themselves based on culture. Since culture varies from place to place and from one time in history to another, there will always be some variation in spiritual traditions. These differences will occur not only between cultures but also even within the same culture. An example of this is orthodox Christianity with its myriad of denominations and fundamental changes over the period of its existence.

An important theme, in the study of comparative mythology and cultural comparison studies, is the understanding of complete religion, that is, in its three aspects, *mythological, ritual* and *metaphysical* or the *mystical experience.* At the first level, a human being learns the stories and traditions of the religion. At the second level, rituals are learned and practiced. At the third level the practitioner, now called a spiritual aspirant, is led to actually go beyond myths and rituals and to attain the ultimate goal of religion. This is an important principle, because many religions present different aspects of philosophy at different levels, and an uninformed onlooker may label it as primitive or idolatrous, etc., without understanding what is going on. For example, Hinduism[48] and Ancient Egyptian religion present what appear to be polytheism and duality at the first two levels of religious practice. However, at the third level, mysticism, the practitioner is made to understand that all of the gods and goddesses being worshipped do not exist in fact, but are in reality aspects of the single, transcendental Supreme Self. This means that at the mystical level of religious practice the concept of religion and its attendant symbols must also be left behind, that is to say, transcended. The mystical disciplines constitute the technology or means by which the myth and ritual of religion, and the spiritual philosophy can be developed to its highest level.

In contrast, orthodox religions present images as if they are in fact mundane realities as well as transcendental reality. By definition, idolatry is the presentation of an image of the divine as if it is a reality. Therefore, by this understanding it is the orthodox traditions that are the true

---

[48] The word "Hinduism" is a Western term. The religion called Hinduism is actually referred to by the Hindus themselves as "Sanatana-Dharma," which means "the eternal law" or "the path or righteous actions or way of life." The major religion of the Indian subcontinent is Hinduism. The word derives from an ancient Sanskrit term meaning "dwellers by the Indus River," a reference to the location of India's earliest known civilization in what is now Pakistan. (*Feuerstein, Georg, The Shambhala Encyclopedia of Yoga* 1997 and *Compton's Interactive Encyclopedia.* Copyright (c) 1994, 1995 Compton's NewMedia, Inc. All Rights Reserved) .

idolaters. The mystical religions, since they do not ascribe absolute or abiding qualities to their images, are not idolatrous.

Some view religion as an outgrowth of an ethnic or "racial" development, thereby conflating the concept of ethnicity or the erroneous notion of race with religious philosophy, thereby also facilitating the flawed concept that there is a particular ethnic group or "race" that has a true or correct religion while others are of course incorrect or simply false. Those who cling to the idea that religion has to be related to a particular culture and its specific practices or rituals will always have some difference with someone else's conception. This point of view may be considered as "dogmatic"[49] or "orthodox."[50] In the three stages of religion, *Myth, Ritual* and *Mysticism,* culture belongs to the myth and ritual stages of religious practice, the most elementary levels.

## Changes in Religious Practices Over Time

Along with the levels or stages of religious practice, it is important to be aware of changes in religious practices and beliefs over time. Two forms of religious practice in two societies could appear to be different in the present but could have had the same origin in the past. The following chart illustrates such an example of changes in the religious doctrines of the Christian tradition. Some changes within other religious traditions, like those in Indian religion may be considered in many ways even more startling.[51]

---

[49] **dog·ma** (dôg"m…, d¼g"-) *n., pl.* **dog·mas** or **dog·ma·ta** (-m…-t…). **1.** *Theology.* A doctrine or a corpus of doctrines relating to matters such as morality and faith, set forth in an authoritative manner by a church.

[50] **or·tho·dox** (ôr"th…-d¼ks") *adj.* **1.** Adhering to the accepted or traditional and established faith, especially in religion.

[51] *Changes in Indian religion from Ancient to Modern Times, Contrasts With Ancient Egyptian Religion, The African Origins of Civilization, Religion, Yoga Mystical Spirituality and Ethics Philosophy.* Sema Institute of Yoga, 2002. *Muata Ashby*

# The Cultural Category Factor Correlation Method

## Table 2: Changes in Doctrines affect Cultural Comparisons

Changes in Doctrines and how care must be taken to be aware of those changes so as not to miss correlating two cultures that may have been compatible at one time in the past or correlate doctrines that appear to be compatible but may have differing intents, or meaning due to different origins, different political or other changes in the culture over time that are unrelated to the other culture being compared to it.

| DOCTRINE | EARLY CHURCH DOCTRINE | LATER CHURCH DOCTRINE |
|---|---|---|
| Who is Jesus Christ | The Savior | Son of God |
| When is Christ returning? | Any time now | No one knows for sure |
| What is the Christian Church? | Those who are preparing for the return of Christ | Those receiving the teachings of Christianity |
| Who can be part of the church? | Only the Jews | Gentiles as well as Jews |
| What is the correct way of Christian worship? | In Synagogues and through Jewish temple services | The Christian church and the Christian rituals |
| Reincarnation | Reincarnation is a reality | Reincarnation is false |

## Myth: The Fluid Language of the Unconscious Mind

Myth is a fluid language. It is the language of concepts, which are represented through the symbols, themes, legends, traditions, heritage and philosophy contained in the myth. Myths are representations of the higher transcendental spiritual experience. These representations are manifestations of intuitional truths that are mirrored in the unconscious mind as the transcendent spirit projects into time and space. As it relates to something otherworldly, the language of myth is necessarily free from the encumbrance of historicity, race, politics, economics, gender, or even culture. Thus, the cultural manifestation of spiritual concepts are not the meaning or essence of the myth, but rather its mode of manifestation within that particular culture. Accordingly, myth is highly interchangeable in a way that the written word is not. This is why concepts are more easily communicated between people who speak a different language than translated words; concept is closer to reality (the mental ideal, not the physical reality) than words. The more a concept is concretized, codified, interpreted as historical events or made into dogmatic teachings and imposed on culture, their power to communicate the transcendental nature of self is subverted. Then myth becomes a whipping tool to use against political, religious or social enemies. At this level, true religion cannot be practiced. Here the myth degrades to the level of dogmatism which expresses as narrow-mindedness, social pride, nationalism, sexism, prejudice, intolerance, and racism. Consequently, it is important and at times, a matter of life (peace) and death (war), to understand the deeper psychological and spiritual nature and purpose of myth.

### More Working Definitions

Before proceeding with the main body of this work, it would be helpful to establish some working definitions for the disciplines which will be discussed in order to provide a common basis for understanding the journey we will undertake. These terms will be further defined and explored throughout the course of this work.

# Philosophy

**Philosophy** is the discipline concerned with the questions of how one should live (<u>ethics</u>); what sorts of things exist and what are their essential natures (<u>metaphysics</u>); what

counts as genuine knowledge (<u>epistemology</u>); and what are the correct principles of reasoning (<u>logic</u>).[52]
The word itself is of <u>Greek</u> origin: φιλοσοφία (*philosophía*) is a compound of φίλος (*phílos*: friend, or lover) and σοφία (*sophía*: wisdom).[53/54]

**phi·los·o·phy** [fi-**los**-*uh*-fee][55]
—*noun, plural* -**phies.**
1. the rational investigation of the truths and principles of being, knowledge, or conduct.
2. any of the three branches, namely natural philosophy, moral philosophy, and metaphysical philosophy, that are accepted as composing this study.
3. a system of philosophical doctrine: *the philosophy of Spinoza.*
4. the critical study of the basic principles and concepts of a particular branch of knowledge, esp. with a view to improving or reconstituting them: *the philosophy of science.*
5. a system of principles for guidance in practical affairs.

While the concept of philosophy has been known since before the time of Classical Greece, having been practiced in Ancient Egypt in the temples as part of the religion of the Egyptian Mysteries, the discipline which was originally dedicated to discovering the nature of self and Creation was transformed to something else as Western culture adopted. The word "philosophy" and concept of it was present in Ancient Egyptian culture. The Ancient Greeks learned much of what they knew about philosophy from the Ancient Egyptians, beginning with the first Greek philosopher, Thales, to Pythagoras and Plato, all of whom studied in Ancient Egypt.

In Ancient Egypt the *Sbai* is the Spiritual Preceptor, one who espouses mystical philosophy, the Divine Mysteries- Shetaut Neter. The *Sbaiu* are Spiritual Preceptors, or teachers of the high mysteries. The term *Sbai* (Sebai) also means "philosopher." The *Sbai* teaches the *Shetaut Neter* (Egyptian Mysteries)

---

[52] Quinton, Anthony; ed. Ted Honderich (1996). *"Philosophy"*. *The Oxford Companion to Philosophy.*
[53] "But philosophy has been both the seeking of wisdom and the wisdom sought." Dagobert D. Runes. *Dictionary of Philosophy.* Kessinger Publishing. ISBN 1428613102
[54] The definition of philosophy is: "1.orig., love of, or the search for, wisdom or knowledge 2.theory or logical analysis of the principles underlying conduct, thought, knowledge, and the nature of the universe." *Webster's New World Dictionary*, Second College.
[55] *Unabridged (v 1.1) Based on the Random House Unabridged Dictionary,* © *Random House, Inc. 2006.*

but in this context the teaching is referred to as *Sbait* 𓈖𓏤𓂋𓏏𓍯𓂝 - "spiritual philosophy", instruction, teaching and education. This Shetaut (mysteries- rituals, wisdom, philosophy) about the Neter (Supreme Being) are related in the ⌂⌂𓏤𓏤𓏤 *Shetitu* or writings related to the hidden teaching. And those writings are referred to as 𓎛𓃭𓂋𓏤 *Medu Neter* or "Divine Speech," the writings of the god Djehuti (Ancient Egyptian god of the divine word- known to the Greeks as Thoth/Hermes) – also refers to any hieroglyphic texts or inscriptions generally. The term Medu Neter makes use of a special hieroglyph, 𓌃, which means *"medu"* or "staff - walking stick-speech." This means that speech is the support for the Divine, 𓂝. Thus, just as the staff supports an elderly person, the hieroglyphic writing (the word) is a prop (staff) which sustains the Divine in the realm of time and space. That is, the Divine writings contain the wisdom which enlightens us about to the "Hidden" (Shetaut) Divine (Neter), 𓊝𓂧𓃭𓂝𓏤𓅱 *Shetaut Neter* (Egyptian Mysteries = Ancient Egyptian Religion).

Prior to the advent of Western culture, after the fall of ancient Greece, the *Epistemology* of Western Philosophy, its concern with the nature and scope of knowledge, and whether knowledge is possible, tended to become associated with a phenomenological outlook; in the middle ages, perhaps due to its association with the Catholic Church, which prevented researches into anything that could challenge the Biblical version of knowledge, and later with its association with the mechanistic viewpoint of science itself, Western Philosophy tended towards logical thinking and the exclusion of myth or idealistic or inferential (inferring wisdom implied in mythic texts) thinking because it was likened to illogic or irrationality. Also, Western Philosophy has been strongly affected by the Western concept of the *scientific method*, which precludes evidences that cannot be physically observed and measured. Western culture has been challenged by *skepticism* which is the idea that all our thoughts and beliefs can be illusory or mistaken somehow. Western Philosophy has developed a different outlook from the rest of the world's philosophies. Eastern and African philosophies, for example, are related to religion and myth while philosophy and religion have been separated in western scholarship. Thus, even though the dictionary definition of philosophy states that philosophy is: *the rational investigation of the truths and principles of being, knowledge, or conduct,* in reality that investigation is modified and circumscribed by a conventional viewpoint that excludes spirituality or *esotericism*. This factor alone would seem to invalidate Western Philosophy's capacity to investigate myth since virtually all the great myths of the world are intimately related to a spiritual or mystical outlook. The definition of philosophy as *a system of principles for guidance in practical affairs* fits into our concept of *societal philosophy*, which will be explained later.

In the post Greco-Roman era of Western Philosophy we have the *Medieval philosophy,* of the middle ages, *Early modern philosophy* (c. 1600 - c. 1800), including personalities such as Montaigne, Descartes, Locke, Spinoza, Berkeley, Leibniz, Hume, and Kant.; Later modern philosophy (c. 1800 - c. 1960) including *German idealists*, such as Hegel, Peirce and William James introduced *pragmatism*, Husserl introduced *phenomenology*, Kierkegaard and Nietzsche introduced *existentialism*, Frege's worked in logic and that work was used in early *analytic philosophy*, Mill's *utilitarianism* and Marx & Engels' Marxism overshadowed political philosophy until the late 20th century with Rawls' 1971 work *A Theory of Justice*. Then we have *Contemporary philosophy* (c. 1960 - present).

Western Philosophy has struggled through several abstract and some possibly illusory forms of thought processes that have been arranged by the intellectual mind (mind not balanced with intellect and feeling) that may have detrimentally conditioned the thought processes in western academia in philosophy studies into a form that is less capable of approaching mysticism and religious philosophies as legitimate areas of human activity. In other words, Western Philosophy is impaired in its capacity to explore the first dictionary deffinition of its concern, *the rational investigation of the truths and principles of being, knowledge, or conduct. Idealism* is the concept that there are some things that have real existence outside of the mind. *Realism* has sometimes been seen as the opposite position (18th-century). Idealism is considered to be the opposite of *nominalism*, which views universal or abstract terms as words only, or that they only denote mental states such as beliefs, ideas or intentions. Due to the dominance of western culture over the rest of the world, the viewpoints of Western Philosophy have affected the philosophical concepts of other countries and how the peoples from other countries, who tend to value western culture even over their own, sometimes adopt the western philosophical views and then try to institute them in their own non-western countries.

Philosophy has been defined as the speculative inquiry concerning the source and nature of human knowledge and a system of ideas based on such thinking. In this work, the idea of philosophy will be confined to the modes of thinking employed for the purpose of discovering the meaning of life by transforming the human mind, leading it to achieve transpersonal states of consciousness {transpersonal psychology, psycho-mythology, psycho-spirituality through mystical awakening (mysticism)}. In its original sense philosophy is a mental discipline for leading a person to enlightenment. In modern times this lofty notion of philosophy has come to be regarded as unscientific speculation or even as an opinion or belief of one person or group versus another. Specifically, we will look at Christianity as a philosophy of psychological transformation.

"Never forget, the words are not the reality, only reality is reality; picture symbols are the idea, words are confusion."[56]

One caveat which any true philosophy must follow is the understanding that words in themselves cannot capture the ultimate essence of reality. Words can be a trap to the highly developed intellect. Therefore, we must always keep in mind that words and philosophical discourse can only point the way to the truth. In order to discover the truth we must go beyond all words, all thoughts, and all of our mental concepts and philosophies because the truth, as *mystic* philosophy would say, can only be experienced; it cannot be encapsulated in any way, shape or form.

The study of philosophy in its highest form is to assist the student in understanding his/her own mind in order to be able to transcend it, and thus, experience the "transcendental" reality which lies beyond words, thoughts, concepts and mental notions. Mental conceptions are based on our own worldly experiences. They help us to understand the world as the senses perceive it. However, clinging to these experiences as the only reality precludes our discovery of other forms of reality or existence which lies beyond the capacity of the senses. A dog's olfactory sense and the vision of a hawk are much superior to that of the human being. The world of a dog or hawk is much different because they have an expanded range of sensitivity in their senses. Human beings use instruments such as telescopes and microscopes to expand the capability of the senses, but these are also limited and cannot capture reality as it truly is. If the human senses cannot even perceive the atoms which scientists tell us comprise all material objects in creation, how can they be expected to perceive that which is even subtler than the atom, the Spiritual realm?

**1** In the beginning God created the heavens and the earth.
**2** The earth was formless and void, and darkness was over

---

[56] Hermetic proverb.

the surface of the deep, and the Spirit of God was moving over the surface of the waters.[57]

However, the human has one advantage which is superior to all senses and scientific instruments, the intuitional mind when it is purified by the practice of Yoga philosophy and disciplines. Ancient mystical philosophical systems have as their main goal the destruction of the limited concepts and illusions of the mind. In essence, the philosophies related to understanding nature and a human being's place in it were the first disciplines which practiced what would today be called Transpersonal Psychology, that is, a system of psychology which assists us in going beyond the personal or ego-based aspects of the psyche in order to discover what lies beyond (trans) the personal (relating to the personality).

> 1. Let him who seeks go on seeking until he finds. When he finds he will become astonished {troubled}. When he becomes troubled, he will be awed and he will reign over the universe {all}.

> 98. He who seeks will find and whomever knocks will be let in.

> —Gospel of Thomas
> {Gnostic Christianity}

## Metaphysics

Metaphysics is the branch of philosophy that systematically investigates first causes of nature, the universe and ultimate reality. The term comes from the Greek "*meta physika*," meaning "after the things of nature." In Aristotle's works, he envisioned that the first philosophy came after the physics. Metaphysics has been divided into *ontology*, or the study of the essence of being or that which is or exists, and *cosmology*, the study of the structure and laws of the universe and the manner of its creation. From time immemorial, philosophers, such as those who wrote the Ancient Egyptian Creation myths, to Greek philosophers such as Plato and Aristotle, to more modern philosophers such as Whitehead and Kant, have written on metaphysics. Skeptics, however, have charged that speculation which cannot be verified by objective evidence is useless. However, these skeptics do not realize that what they consider as "objective reality" is not objective at all, since objectivity is based on the perceptions of the senses, and as just discussed, modern science itself has proven that the human senses cannot perceive the phenomenal universe as it really is. Further, the objective information that can be gathered by scientific instruments is only valid under certain conditions. This makes it relative and not absolute

---

[57] **Genesis 1:2, Bible, New American Standard** ©

information. Thus, what people ordinarily consider to be real and abiding is not. Einstein's proof of relativity confirms this. There must be something real beyond the phenomenal world which sustains it. The search for that higher essence is the purpose of philosophy and metaphysics. Therefore, the value of metaphysical and mystical philosophy studies is evident.

# Theology and Religious Studies

Theology is reasoned discourse concerning God (Greek θεος, *theos*, "God", + λογος, *logos*, "word" or "reason"). It can also refer to the study of other Theology is thus, the study of the discourse about God or the nature of spirituality as related by the different religious traditions. Religious studies, in western culture, is the multi-disciplinary, secular study of religion. It is distinct from theology and incorporates multiple disciplines and methodologies including the anthropology, sociology, psychology, philosophy, and history of religion in addition to comparative religion.[58] Religious studies in non-western disciplines tends to approach religion as including theology and philosophy.

Naturally, Theology and Religious studies are not necessarily distinct studies. However, from a scholarly perspectice, a theologian will express some aspects of theology through religious studies terminologies. The religious studies terminologies are also used frequently in comparative religious studies, comparing the teachings of varying religious traditions. This study will be presented from a combination of the historica, theological and religious studies perspectives. Some important religious studies terms are listed below:

**Ontology**
The branch of metaphysics that deals with the nature of being.

---

[58] From Wikipedia Encyclopedia

# Eschatology

1. The branch of theology that is concerned with the end of the world or of humankind.
2. A belief or a doctrine concerning the ultimate or final things, such as death, the destiny of humanity, the Second Coming, or the Last Judgment.

**Exegesis**. Critical explanation or analysis, especially of a text.

# Methodologies

A number of methodologies are used in Religious Studies. Methodologies are hermeneutics, or interpretive model, that provide a structure for the analysis of religious phenomena.

# Hermeneutics

a philosophical technique concerned with the interpretation and understanding of texts. It may be described as the theory of the interpretation and understanding of a text on the basis of the text itself. An interpretive agent is sometimes referred to as a *hermeneut*.

The concept of "text" has recently been extended beyond written documents to include, for example, speech, performances, works of art, and even events. Thus, one might speak of and interpret a "social text".

# Phenomenology

1. A philosophy or method of inquiry based on the premise that reality consists of objects and events as they are perceived or understood in human consciousness and not of anything independent of human consciousness.
2. A movement based on this, originated about 1905 by Edmund Husserl.

# Functionalism

Functionalism, in regard to religious studies, is the analysis of religions and their various communities of adherents using the functions of particular religious phenomena to interpret the structure of religious communities and their beliefs. A major criticism of functionalism is that it lends itself to teleological explanations. An example of a functionalist approach is understanding the dietary restrictions contained in the Pentateuch as having the function of promoting health or providing social identity (*i.e.* a sense of belonging though common practice).

## Soteriology

The term "Salvation" refers to the idea of "deliverance from an undesirable state or condition." In the study of religion, theology, the study or research on salvation teachings in different religions or sects of religions is called soteriology.

## Psychology

Psychology, as used by ordinary practitioners of the psychological disciplines in the West, has been defined as the study of the thought processes characteristic of an individual or group (mind, psyche, ethos, mentality). In this work we will focus on Christianity as a psychological discipline for understanding the human mind, its source, higher development and transformation. However, Mystical Psychology in reality does not relate only to the mind since a human being is composed of several complex aspects. The term personality, as it is used in Yoga, implies mind, body and spirit, as well as the conscious, subconscious and unconscious aspects of the mind. Therefore, the discipline of psychology must be expanded to include physical as well as spiritual dimensions. Once again, modern medical science has, within the last twenty years, acknowledged the understanding that health cannot be treated as a physical problem only, but as one which involves the mind, body and spirit. Likewise, spiritual teaching must be related as a discipline which involves not only the soul of an individual, but the mind and body as well – in other words, the entire human being.

## Yoga

The literal meaning of the word Yoga is to *"yoke"* or to *"link"* back; it has been defined as "union of the higher and lower self". The implication is to *link back* individual consciousness (human personality) to its original source, the original essence: Universal Consciousness. In a broad sense Yoga is any process which helps one to achieve liberation or freedom from bondage to the pain and spiritual ignorance of ordinary human existence. So whenever you engage in any activity with the goal of promoting the discovery of your true Self, be it studying the spiritual wisdom teachings, exercising, fasting, meditation, breath control, rituals, chanting, prayer, etc., you are practicing yoga. If the goal is to help you to discover your essential nature as one with God or the ultimate reality, or the Supreme Being, Higher Consciousness, etc. then it is Yoga.

Yoga (Sanskrit for "union") is a term used for a number of disciplines, the goal of each being to lead the practitioner to attain union with Universal Consciousness. While the practice of yoga disciplines and philosophical thought can be traced to Ancient Egypt,[59] present day Yoga philosophy is based on several Indian texts such as the *Upanishads, Bhagavad Gita* and the *Yoga-sutras* of Patañjali and several other Yoga treatises developed in India. The practice of Yoga generally involves meditation, moral restraints, and the awakening of energy centers (in the body) through specific postures (asanas) or physical exercises and breathing exercises. All Yoga disciplines are devoted to freeing the soul or individual self from worldly (mental) restraints. They have become popular in the West mostly as a means of self-control and relaxation.

Yoga, in all of its forms as the disciplines for spiritual development, was practiced in Ancient Egypt earlier than anywhere else in history. From here the teachings of Ancient Egyptian Religion and Yoga influenced the development of Christianity and other religions which survive to this day. The disciplines of Yoga fall under five major categories. These are: *Yoga of Wisdom, Yoga of Devotional Love, Yoga of Meditation, Tantric Yoga* and *Yoga of Selfless Action.* Within these categories there are subsidiary forms which are part of the main disciplines. The important point to remember is that all aspects of yoga can and should be used in an integral fashion to effect an efficient and harmonized spiritual movement in the practitioner. Therefore, while there may be an area of special interest to a person, other elements are bound to become part of the yoga program as needed. For example, while a yogin (practitioner of Yoga) may place emphasis on the yoga of wisdom, they may also practice devotional yoga and meditation yoga along with the wisdom studies.

While it is true that yogic practices may be found in religion, strictly speaking, yoga is neither a religion or a philosophy. It should be thought of more as spiritual a way of life or discipline for promoting greater fullness and experience of life, physically, mentally and spiritually. Yoga was developed at the dawn of history by those who wanted more out of life. These special men and women wanted to discover the true origins of creation and of themselves. Therefore, they set out to explore the vast reaches of consciousness within themselves. They are sometimes referred to as "Seers," "Sages," "Saints," etc. Awareness or consciousness can only be increased when the mind is in a state of peace and harmony. Thus, the

---

[59] See the Ancient Egyptian term Sema which means "union of the higher and lower self" in the book *Egyptian Yoga: The Philosophy of Enlightenment* by Muata Ashby

disciplines of devotion to the higher Self, meditation, right action and study of the wisdom teachings (which are all part of Yoga) are the primary means to controlling the mind and allowing the individual to mature psychologically and spiritually.

## Religion and Spirituality

All religions tend to be deistic at the elementary levels. Most often it manifests as an outgrowth of the cultural concepts of a people as they try to express the deeper feeling which they perceive, though not in its entirety. Thus, deism is based on limited spiritual knowledge. Deism, as a religious belief or form of theism, holds that God's action was restricted to an initial act of creation, after which he retired (separated) to contemplate the majesty of his work. Deists hold that the natural creation is regulated by laws put in place by God at the time of creation and inscribed with perfect moral principles. A deeper study of religion will reveal that in its original understanding, it seeks to reveal the deeper essential nature of creation, the human heart and their relation to God, which transcends the deistic model or doctrine. The term religion comes from the Latin *"Relegare"* which uses the word roots *"Re"* which means *"Back"* and *"Ligon"* which means *"to hold, to link, to bind"* in other words *"link back."* Therefore, the essence of true religion is the same as yoga, that is, of linking back, specifically, linking the soul of its follower back to its original source: God. So, although religion in its purest form is a Yoga system, incorporating the yoga disciplines within its teachings, the original intent and meaning of the religious scriptures are often misunderstood, if not distorted. This occurs because religions have developed in different geographic areas. As a result, the less advanced (complete) levels of religious practices which have become mixed with culture (historical accounts, stories and traditions) have developed independently, and thereby appear to be different from each other on the surface. This leads to confusion and animosity among people who are ignorant of the true process of religious movement. Religion consists of three levels: *myth, ritual and mystical experience.* If the first two levels are misunderstood or accepted literally, the spiritual movement will fail to proceed to the next higher level. In order for a religious experience to lead one to have a mystical experience, all three levels of religion must be completed. This process will be fully explained throughout the text of this volume.

## The Difference Between Religion and Spirituality

The way religion is practiced in modern times it is often not spiritual. From a political perspective it is often used as a tool to control others. In the field of religious studies many scholars approach religion from a spiritual activity without ultimate purpose besides a social pastime. Many practitioners of religion in the masses follow their religions as a faithful endeavor not requiring ethical conscience. As introduced earlier, the English term "religion" is derived from the Latin "relegare" ("re-link," or "link back"), meaning a process for human beings to rel-ink (reconnect) with God (a deity, divinity) or whatever a people consider to be a Supreme Being or cause behind existence. Theology is the study, "ology", of "theism" a belief in a divinity as opposed to atheism which is disbelief in the existence of a god, deity or divinity. In its full form religion has three steps: Mythology, Rituals and Metaphysics. Most people know something about the myth and rituals but not about their true meaning. This is when religion becomes degraded and loses its spirituality.

The Ancient Egyptian or Indian definition of religion refers to a process of reconnecting with the "Higher Self" the Supreme Being. However, while the Supreme Being concept of Western religion is monotheistic, and relating to a phenomenal[60] divinity, in other cultures, such as the African, East Asian, Native American cultures religion is based on a Henotheistic[61] conception. In the higher perspective of the African, Indian and Buddhist as well as Native American practice of religion the Supreme Divinity is not just a phenomenal personality as in Western monotheism, but rather a phenomenal and transcendental divinity; this means that God appears as a personality, as nature and also transcending forms and names, beyond Creation itself; so religion is a process for attaining spiritual development by re-linking one's soul with God, or the Divine. In Ancient Egyptian terminology, the term "Shetaut Neter" means "Hidden (mysterious) Divine Essence" this term has been rightly interpreted as the "religion" of the Ancient Egyptians. However, in the strict application of the grammatical meaning, the term "Shetaut Neter" is a known while the term religion is a known referring to a process. In Ancient Egyptian language the term "Shedy" is more applicable as it means: "process of penetrating the mysteries (i.e. the "Hidden (mysterious) Divine Essence").

The term "Spirituality" is defined as: "that which pertains to what is incorporeal or pertaining to the supernatural as distinguished from the physical nature": *a spiritual approach to life*. "Spiritology" is the study of the spiritual aspects of the soul and or of life (aspects that transcend the physical). However, in popular culture "spirituality" also has been applied to mean something pertaining to sacred things or matters; religious; devotional; the sacred or the spirit or soul. So the term religion specifically

---

[60] Existing in time and space and appearing with name and form
[61] There is a Supreme Divinity with lesser gods and goddesses that emanate from it.

relates to a theistic[62] perspective on spirituality: it relates to the soul and a Divinity. The term "spirituality" may or may not relate to a Divinity and may relate to incorporeal matters or concerns with non-physical matters. Religion without the three steps may be considered spirituality but in the strict interpretation it is not true religion. Thus, while true religion (religion that contains the three steps or levels of practice) will incorporate spirituality, we cannot say that all spirituality is religious, related to a Divinity (theistic) or even that it is enlightening. The term "mystical" is similarly misinterpreted by the popular culture just as the term "spiritual" is automatically confused with something sacred, altruistic, or even purer or sometimes even as a belief system or practice that is better than religion, etc. in the strictest terms we cannot say that a person worshipping a tree is practicing religion since religion is worshipping a Supreme Divinity unless that tree is an access point to the Higher Divinity. We cannot say that a person had a religious experience if they had an out of body experience. The OB experience may be spiritual but not specifically religious unless it relates the person to a conceptualized deity.

Mysticism relates to the achievement of consciousness wherein the individuality is evolved into universality, a oneness of soul with the Divine, like a drop with the ocean. So a person cannot say that they had a "mystical" experience by "going to a movie," "falling in love," "traveling," "seeing a celebrity" or "having a child," as is expressed often in modern culture, unless they are meaning that those experiences have led us to discover higher consciousness by transcending our physical reality, time and space and becoming one with the universe and what transcends it!

What is the proof that religion is a reality; in other words what is the substantiation that there is a god and that we are to reconnect with that divinity? If there is proof it lies in the experience of those who have reconnected (through the process enjoined by religion (myth, ritual, mysticism)) and who have reported about that reconnection to those who have not yet reconnected. However, disbelieving in religion (atheism) without engaging in the process enjoined by religion does not constitute proof of the invalidity of religion or non-existence of the Divine. Also, having faith in religion without engaging in the reconnection process does not constitute the authentic (complete) practice of religion. Faith in the existence of a divinity is not religion in and of itself, it is part of the myth aspect or stage of religion but alone may only be considered as theism or spirituality until the full course of a discipline to promote the reconnection

---

[62] Belief in a god or goddess

process is engaged (religion, Yoga, Mystical Philosophy, etc.). To be clear here, in order to be considered a religion, the discipline or tradition needs to incorporate as its goal the objective of reconnection of the soul to the high god or goddess, or supreme being or ultimate agency causing and sustaining existence; it is derived from the experience of those who have reconnected, that there is an ultimate agency or being that is responsible for the existence of souls and Creation and that there was an original connection between that being and the souls of human beings that was disconnected and needs to be reconnected so that a human being may find peace, contentment and completeness. Those practices that do not incorporate this goal may not be included as part of the definition of religion but would more aptly be included in the definition of spirituality.

## Mysticism

"Mysticism" is the philosophy, practices/disciplines and experiences that lead a person to attain a Mystical Union with the Ultimate Reality[63], generally referred to as The God, Goddess, The Absolute, Supreme Being, All-encompassing Divinity, etc.   Mysticism is a spiritual discipline for attaining union with the Divine through the practice of deep meditation or contemplation, and other spiritual disciplines such as austerity, detachment, renunciation, etc. The central idea of mysticism, the movement towards discovery and union with the Ultimate Reality, is extremely useful in our study because that movement is generally a common feature of the human psychology that acts as a catalyst promoting the creation of social systems such as religion, for the purpose of achieving the ultimate goal. Thus, in mysticism we have a motivating force that operates from outside the personality but which motivates it. It is that Ultimate Reality which calls on the soul to discover it and become one with it. Different religions may refer to it and even approach it differently but the idea of searching for some kind of Ultimate Reality, regardless of what it may be called, is the same.

Mystical philosophy, as well as the mystical writings and spiritual disciplines, are based on the experiences of mystics. Those mystics who have achieved such levels of consciousness as those promoted by the mystical disciplines have reported on their findings, namely that there is a transcendental reality beyond the phenomenal world of time and space. If this is so and it is also true that human existence transcends time and space then it is also true that the urge to religious movement is not just a mental

---

[63] Hinnells, John R. Facts on File Dictionary of Religions. Facts on File, 1984. 224-225.

fabrication of human beings, a delusion or error in thinking. Rather it is a natural and essential quest for the nature of reality which will bestow the peace and contentment that most people really are looking for in life.

## Dualism

Similar to Deism, Dualism is the belief that all things in nature are separate and real, and that they exist independently from any underlying essence or support. It is the belief in the pairs of opposites wherein everything has a polar counterpart. For example: male - female, here - there, hot - cold, etc. While these elements seem real and abiding to the human mind, mystical philosophers throughout history have been claiming that this is only an outer expression of the underlying essence from which they originate. In reality, the underlying essence of all things is non-dual and all-encompassing. It is the substratum of all that exists. Modern science has been confirming this view of matter. The latest experiments in quantum physics show that all matter is composed of energy. Most importantly for this study, dualism is a state of mind that occurs at an immature level of mental understanding of reality. It is akin to egoism and egoistic tendencies, a process of conditioning which tends to make a person see himself/herself as separate and distinct from the world and from other living beings. Through the study and practice of mystical spiritual teachings, dualism is replaced with non-dualism and salvation, spiritual enlightenment, then occurs. Therefore, salvation or resurrection is related to a non-dualistic view of existence and bondage and death are related to dualism and egoism.

A dualistic view of life can lead to agitation, suffering and even catastrophic events in human experience because the mind is trained to see either good or evil, acceptable or unacceptable, you or me, etc., and not the whole of creation composed of many parts. In the dualistic state of mind, the attitudes of separation and exclusion are exaggerated. These render the mind agitated. Mental agitation prevents the mind from achieving greater insights into the depths of spiritual teachings. Thus, agitated people are usually frustrated and unable to discover inner peace and spiritual fulfillment.

When societal institutions such as the church rationalize and even sanction dualism, then egoistic sentiments hold sway over the heart of human beings. In this sense, dualism and egoism go hand in hand. When universal love and humility are replaced by egoism and arrogance, then it becomes possible to hurt others and to hurt nature. When we forget our common origin and destiny, we easily fall into the vast pit of egoism. We see ourselves as an individual in a world of individuals, fighting a battle of survival for wealth in order to gain pleasures of the senses, rather than seeing ourselves as divine beings who are made in the same image, with the same frailties and potential. This degraded condition opens the doors to the deep-rooted fears and sense of inadequacy which translate into anger, resentment, hatred, greed and all negative tendencies in the human personality. The concept of dualism is the basis of the atrocities and injustices that have been committed in the history of the world. Under its control, human beings seek to control others and nature, and to satisfy their inner urges through violence because they cannot control themselves and express their deeper needs in constructive ways. In the Indian Vedantic tradition, duality or *dvaita* is seen as the greatest error of the human mind. For this reason all of the disciplines of Vedanta, Shetaut Neter, Yoga, Buddhism, Taoism and other forms of mystical (pantheistic/panentheistic) spirituality are directed toward developing a wholistic understanding of human existence. When the underlying unity behind the duality is discovered, there can be no violence or ill will against others. This is the basis of non-violence. Harmony and spiritual enlightenment then arise spontaneously. Egoism now gives way to universal love and peace.

**Spiritual Transformation**

Transformation here is to be understood as not merely a change in specific behavior patterns or a change in feeling based on temporary circumstances, but as a complete re-orientation of the psychology of the individual. This re-orientation will lead to permanent improvement in behavior and genuine metamorphosis of the innermost levels of the mind. Specifically, we will focus on spiritual systems such as religion, yoga, mysticism, etc. as cultural systems for psychological transformation wherein the individual ceases to be a limited individual, subject to the foibles and follies of human nature, and attains the state of transcendence of these failings.

**Mythology**

Most people hold the opinion that mythology is a lie, an illusion, fiction or fantasy. Mythology can be best understood as a language. However, it is a unique kind of language. An ordinary language is sometimes similar to another because it is a part of a family of languages. For example, Italian and Spanish words are similar. This similarity makes it possible for a person whose native language is Spanish to understand the meanings of some Italian words and somewhat follow along a conversation in Italian. Even so, mythology is much more intelligible than this. Mythology is more akin to music in its universality. If the key elements of this language of mythology are well understood, then it is possible to understand and relate any mythological system to another and thereby gain the understanding of the message being imparted through the myth.

## Enlightenment

Enlightenment is the central topic of our study and the coveted goal of all practitioners of Yoga and Religion. Enlightenment is the term used to describe the highest level of spiritual awakening. It means attaining such a level of spiritual awareness that one discovers the underlying unity of the entire universe as well as the fact that the source of all creation is the same source from which the innermost Self within every human heart arises.

All forms of spiritual practice are directed toward the goal of assisting every individual to discover the true essence of the universe both externally, in physical creation, and internally, within the human heart, as the very root of human consciousness. Thus, many terms are used to describe the attainment of the goal of spiritual knowledge and the eradication of spiritual ignorance. Some of these terms are: *Enlightenment, Resurrection, Salvation, The Kingdom of Heaven, Christ Consciousness, Cosmic Consciousness, Moksha or Liberation, Buddha Consciousness, One With The Tao, Self-realization, Know Thyself, Horushood, Nirvana, Sema, Yoga,* etc.

## Yoga Philosophy and the World Religious Philosophies Defined

Yoga philosophy and disciplines have developed independently as well as in conjunction with religious philosophies. It may be accurate to say that Yoga is a science unto itself which religions have used and incorporated into their religious philosophies and practices by relating the yogic principles to symbols such as deities, gods, goddesses, angels, saints, etc. The following is a brief description of yoga philosophy in comparison to the philosophies which developed along side it.

## Yoga Philosophy[64]

Human consciousness and universal consciousness are in reality one and the same. The appearance of separation is a mental illusion. Yoga is the mystical and mindful (thoughtful, aware, observant) union of individual and universal consciousness by integrating the aspects of

---

[64] "Egyptian Yoga: The Philosophy of Enlightenment" by Reginald Muata Ashby

individual personality, thereby allowing the personality to be purified so that it may behold its true essence.

## Monotheism[84]

Monotheism means the belief in the existence of a single God in the universe. Christianity, Judaism, and Islam are the major monotheistic religions. It must be noted here that the form of monotheism espoused by the major Western religions is that of an exclusive, personified deity who exists in fact and is separate from creation. In contrast, the monotheism of Ancient Egyptian, Hindu and Gnostic Christian traditions envisions a single Supreme Deity that is expressed as the Supreme Deity of all other traditions, as well as the phenomenal world; it is not exclusive, but universal.

## Polytheism[84]

Polytheism means the belief in or worship of many gods. Such gods usually have specific attributes or functions.

## Totemism[123]

Totemism is the belief in the idea that there is a relationship between kinship groups and specific animals and plants. Many scholars believe that religions which use these symbols are primitive because they are seen as worshipping those animals themselves. However, when the mythology behind the beliefs is examined more closely, the totems are understood as symbols of specific tutelary deities which relate the individuals to a group, but also to the greater workings of nature, and ultimately, to God.

## Pantheism[65]

1- Absolute Pantheism: Everything there is, is God. God and Creation are one.
2- Modified Pantheism: God is the reality or principle behind nature.

## Panentheism[66]

Term coined by KC F. Krause (1781-1832) to describe the doctrine that God is immanent in all things but also transcendent, so that every part of the universe has its existence in God, but He is more than the sum total of the parts.

---

[65] "Ferdmand's Handbook to the World's Religions"
[66] "Encyclopedia of Mysticism and Mystery Religions" by John Ferguson

## Shetaut Neter: Ancient Egyptian Philosophy - Egyptian Yoga[67]

1- Henotheism or Monotheistic Polytheism - Ancient Egyptian religion encompasses a single and absolute Supreme Deity that expresses as the cosmic forces (gods and goddesses), human beings and nature.

## Hinduism and Mahayana Buddhism

1-Henotheism or Monotheistic Polytheism.

## Vedanta Philosophy[68]

1- Absolute Monism: Only God is reality. All else is imagination.
2- Modified Monism: God is to nature as soul is to body.

While on the surface it seems that there are many differences between the philosophies, upon closer reflection there is only one major division, that of belief or non-belief. Among the believers there are differences of opinion as to how to believe. This is the source of much of the trouble between religions. This is because ordinary religion is deistic, based on traditions and customs which are themselves based on local folklore and cultural traditions, as we saw earlier. Since culture varies from place to place and from one time in history to another, there will always be some variation in spiritual traditions. These differences will occur not only between cultures, but even within the same culture. An example of this is Christianity with its myriad (hundreds) of denominations.

Therefore, those who cling to the idea that religion has to be related to a particular culture and its specific practices or rituals will always have some difference with someone else's conception. There are three stages of religion, Myth, Ritual and Mystical. Culture belongs to the myth and ritual stages of religious practice, the most elementary level.

# Myth →→ Ritual →→ Mysticism

As stated earlier, an important theme, which will be developed throughout this volume, is the complete practice of religion. In its complete form, religion is composed of three aspects, *mythology, ritual* and *metaphysical* or the *mystical experience* (mysticism - mystical philosophy). At the first level, myth, a human being learns the stories, legends and traditions of the religion. At the second level rituals are learned and practiced. At the third level a spiritual aspirant is led to

---

[67] "Egyptian Yoga: The Philosophy of Enlightenment" by Reginald Muata Ashby
[68] "Ferdmand's Handbook to the World's Religions"

actually go beyond myths and rituals and to attain the ultimate goal of religion. This is an important principle because many religions present different aspects of philosophy at different levels and an uninformed onlooker may label it as primitive or idolatrous, etc., without understanding what is going on. For example, Hinduism and Ancient Egyptian Religion present polytheism and duality at the first two levels of religious practice. However, at the third level, mysticism, the practitioner is made to understand that all of the gods and goddesses being worshipped do not exist in fact, as independent realities, but are in reality aspects of the single, transcendental Supreme Self.

In the area of Yoga Philosophy and the category of Monism, there are little, if any, differences. This is because these disciplines belong to the third level of religion wherein mysticism reaches its height. The goal of all mysticism is to transcend the phenomenal world and all mental concepts. Ordinary religion is a part of the world and the mental concepts of people, and must too be ultimately transcended.

## Selected Spiritual Philosophy Tenets Compared

This section presents a simple overview of the tenets or dogmas of selected spiritual traditions as a starting point for understanding general concepts expressed by the traditions. The deeper study is made on the elements or factors of the cultural manifestations of the philosophies in order to further determine comparative aspects if any.

The Sages of ancient times created philosophies through which it might be possible to explain the origins of creation, as we saw above. Then they set out to create disciplines which could lead a person to discover the spiritual truths of life for themselves, and thereby realize the higher reality which lies beyond the phenomenal world. These disciplines are referred to as religions and spiritual philosophies (mysticism-yoga). Below is a basic listing of world religious and spiritual philosophies. The following religious categories are presented so that the reader may gain a basis for comparing the varied forms of religious practice that are being discussed in this volume. The idea has been put forth that the varied religions exist so that varied personalities in human beings may be able to practice religion in accordance with their current desire and or psychological inclination, based on their level of spiritual development (maturity). Some of the religions may present features of more than one category.

The Cultural Category Factor Correlation Method

Table 3: Category: Religion and Religious Philosophy (A) & Some Folkloric Manifestations (B) (Factors of Cultural Expression)

| | Theism | Atheism | Ethicism | Ritualism | Monism | Polytheistic Monotheism | Pantheistic Monotheism | Mysticism |
|---|---|---|---|---|---|---|---|---|
| **A** | Belief in a God who will punish the sinners and save the faithful. | Salvation by doing what makes you happy. There is no God, only existence, which just happened on its own without any help. | Salvation by performing the right actions. | Salvation by performing the correct rituals. | Salvation by understanding that all is the Supreme Being and nothing else exists. | Salvation by approaching the Supreme Being by {his/her} manifestations Nature, cosmic forces, mystical experience). | Salvation by devotion to Supreme Being who manifests in All Things – leads to mystical union | Salvation by disciplines that lead to union with the Supreme Being |
| **B** | Example → Orthodox Christianity Orthodox Islam | Example → Epicureans Charvacas Atheists | Example → Zoroastrianism Jainism Confucianism Aristotelianism Taoism Gnosticism | Example → Brahmanism Priestcraft Shetaut Neter[70] | Example → Taoism Gnosticism Vedanta Shetaut Neter[71] Buddhism | Example → African Religions (including Shetaut Neter[73] | Example → Atonism (Akhnaton) Vaishnavites (Vishnu and Krishna) | Example → Yoga Shetaut Neter Sufism |

90

## The Cultural Category Factor Correlation Method

| Orthodox Judaism Zoroastrianism Brahmanism | Existentialists Stoics Humanists (western) | Vedanta Shetaut Neter[69] Buddhism Pythagoreanism Humanists (African religion, Eastern religion and Native American religion) Sanatana Dharma (Hinduism) Yoga | Sanatana Dharma (Hinduism) | Pythagoreanism Spinoza Cabalism Sufism Idealism Pythagoreanism Platonism Yoga[72] | Buddhism Sanatana Dharma (Hinduism) Native American | Shivaite (Shiva) Sufism Jainism Goddess | Vedanta Taoism Gnosticism |
|---|---|---|---|---|---|---|---|

[69] Ancient Egyptian religion.
[70] Ancient Egyptian religion.
[71] Ancient Egyptian religion.
[72] NOTE: Yoga is actually neither a religion nor a philosophy, but a way of life based on disciplines for spiritual evolution, and thus does not fit under any category. Yoga is rather, a set of disciplines that religions used to enhance the spiritual movement.
[73] Ancient Egyptian religion.

# Comparative Mythology, Cultural and Social Studies

## Table 4: **Major Mystical Religious Philosophies**

| Some Major Mystical Religious Philosophies | | | | |
|---|---|---|---|---|
| **Shetaut Neter** | **Vedanta** | **Samkhya** | **Buddhism** | **Yoga** |
| Non-dualist metaphysics. God manifests as nature and cosmic forces (neteru). Union with the Divine through wisdom, devotion and identification with the Divine. | Non-dualist metaphysics. God alone exists. Union with the Divine through wisdom, devotion and identification with the Divine. | Dualist Philosophy. Discipline of understanding what is real (God) from what is unreal (transient world of time and space). | Union with the Absolute through extinction of desire. | Mystical tradition: union of individual consciousness with the Absolute Consciousness (God) through cessation of mental activity by wisdom, devotion and identification with the Divine.<br><br>Example<br>→<br><br>Egyptian Yoga<br>Indian Yoga<br>Christian Yoga<br>Buddhist Yoga<br>Chinese (Taoist) Yoga |

# Chapter 3: Cultural Expressions and Folklore Differences and how they Manifest Over Universal Principles of Human Nature

> "Men and women are to become God-like through a life of virtue and the cultivation of the spirit through <u>scientific</u> knowledge, practice and bodily discipline."[74]
>
> Ancient Egyptian Proverb

Human beings, the world over, have innate needs, desires and expressive capacities. One such need is to discover a Supreme Being or "ultimate Reality". The impetus towards that discovery is impelled by a sense of incompleteness which leads to unrest, dissatisfaction with all situations of life, even if life seems to be abundant and or prosperous. From a mystical philosophical perspective, that need is there because the dualistic existence of humanity (male and female) and the agitation of life, cause a longing for a situation of peace and harmony, such as is experienced in the state of deep sleep, wherein there are no images, desires, or feelings of individuality. That state is perceived by the mystics as all-encompassing and transcendental, unitary and intelligent, beyond the mind and senses, and the ego. That state is referred to as "God" or the Supreme Being at the "folk" level of cultural expression. Thus, as the Ancient Egyptian Proverb describes, the goal of life is to become "Godlike".

Thus the purpose of religion, mysticism, yoga and other disciplines is to allow a human being to discover or reunite, reconnect with the "Ultimate Reality" from whence they came originally. That Ultimate Reality is referred to differently in different cultures through varied folk terms; it is called *Nehast* in Neterian (ancient Egyptian) Religion, *Moksha*[75] (liberation) as described in Hinduism, *Nirvana* (without desires) as described in Buddhism, and Kingdom of God/Heaven as described in Gnostic Christianity, and similarly as described in other religions.

That innate need or desire may be expressed in a virtually infinite variety of ways depending on the particular culture in which the human being develops within. Yet the innate need remains the same. However, just because that need may be the same or similar we cannot say that two cultures manifesting the need are related. We may say that they are

---

[74] Ashby, Muata. <u>Egyptian Proverbs</u>. Sema Institute, 1994 .
[75] Jyotirmayananda, Swami. Srimad Bhagavad Gita. Swami Lalitananda, 1986. p. 343

expressing similar needs and desires and those may be compared on that basis. The particular means through which this innate need manifests may be referred to as the "cultural folklore" of the particular culture in question. The elements of the folklore such as artifacts, rituals, myths, etc. may be compared and determinations may be made as to their similarities or differences. Yet though the elements (cultural factors) may be different we cannot say that from a human standpoint that the human beings practicing them are different but only their cultures are; since we know that all human beings originated from the same source (Africa) and are all related genetically.

If religion is a way of seeking for the "ultimate truth," God, and if that ultimate reality is revered by all peoples, we may correctly assume that the culture and folk differences "color" the expressions of those varied forms of reverence which in reality relate or point towards the same goal. This feature of human cultural expression may be termed: *folk expression of religion based on culture and local traditions (folklore)*. For example, the same ultimate reality, God, is expressed by Christians based on European (Western) culture and traditions. The same ultimate reality is expressed by Muslims based on Arab culture and traditions. The same ultimate and transcendental reality is worshipped by Jews based on Hebrew culture and traditions.

However, the act of seeking an "ultimate reality", which is common to all religions and therefore a "correlatable" cultural factor, should not be confused with the manner or philosophy upon which the seeking is based. The desire and volition to seek out an "ultimate reality" through religion may be compatible as an innate human expression of spiritual aspiration displayed through the particular cultural manifestations of a local form of religious practice. Nevertheless, even though we may recognize that people in different cultures are seeking the same goal that does not automatically translate to compatible forms of religious practice or cultural expressions because the cultural factors may differ, especially the philosophy about or understanding of the nature of and human relation to that "ultimate reality" in the religion of the given cultures. One culture may hold the doctrine that religion seeks the ultimate reality but their religious philosophy informs them that that "ultimate reality" is phenomenal (there is a physical heaven to go to one day) rather than mystical (becoming one with God, the transcendental existence-nonphysical). They could see themselves as different from those who hold the mystical perspective. Also, different cultures may not apply all of the levels (myth-ritual-mysticism) of religious practice and may therefore not progress to hold a mystical perspective, an outlook that recognizes the transcendental goal of spirituality, to attain liberation, enlightenment, mystic union with the Divine. We may view that goal of mystic union as manifestations of the highest expression of virtually all major pre Judaic ancient religions and present day mystical religions. Nevertheless, if people who practice religion stay at the outer (or lower) levels of religious practice, the culture, myths and traditions levels, they will always see differences between faiths. Any religion that practices mysticism allows any person to discover that the same Supreme Being is being worshipped by all under different names and forms, albeit perhaps in limited or advanced ways. Therefore, the task of a student of cultural comparative studies is to go beyond the veil of the outer forms of cultural manifestation, especially in religion and mythology studies, including the symbols, but more importantly, the doctrines, rituals and traditions (see model below).

It is possible to focus on the apparent differences between cultures and religious philosophies. This has been the predominant form of philosophical discourse and study of Western scholarship. The seeming differences between religions have led to innumerable conflicts between the groups throughout history, all because of the outer expression of religion. However, throughout this work we will focus on the more (syncretic) syncretism aspects of the cultures, philosophies and religions in question because it is in the similarities wherein harmony is to be found, harmony in the form of concurrence in ideas and meaning which reflect principles which are more abiding and therefore more reliable as reflections of reality and authenticity human meaning. In light of this idea of harmony it is possible to look at the folklore of cultural traditions throughout the world and see the same psycho-mythological message being espoused through the various cultural masks. They are all referring to the same Supreme Being. While giving commentary and adding notes which I feel will be helpful to the understanding of the texts which I will compare, I have endeavored to use the actual texts wherever possible.

**Figure 6: The Culture-Myth Model, showing how the folk expression of religion is based on culture and local traditions.**

The Cultural Category Factor Correlation Method

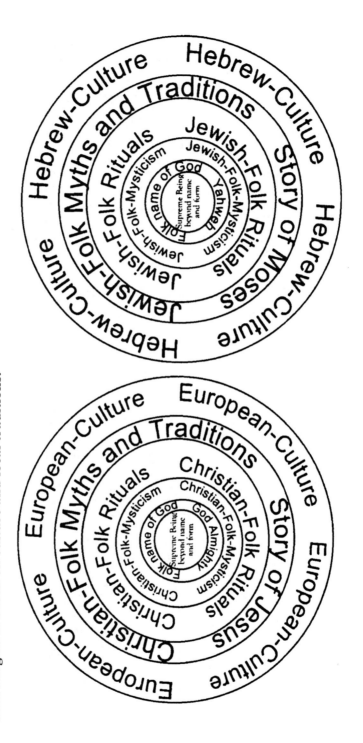

Figure 7: The Culture-Myth Models of four world spiritual systems, showing how the folk expression of each religion is based on culture and local traditions.

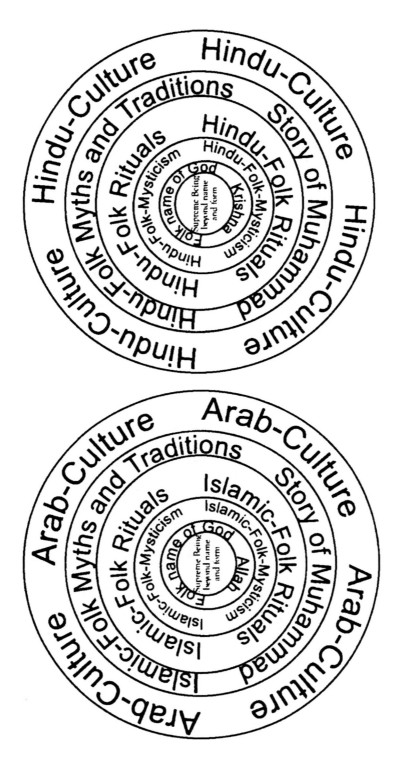

Keeping the preceding in mind, another important task of this study is to focus on the psycho-spiritual significance of the mythology, symbols and rituals, rather than their historical or ethnic features.[76] This psycho-mythical[77] point of view, when applied to Christianity, is supported by the Gnostic Christian texts. It is evident that many of the traditional Biblical texts originated from or were inspired by the Gnostic understanding, but were at some point edited or toned down, as it were, to a form which became ambiguous and which placed greater importance on historicity rather than on the mystical significance of the scriptures. For example, the idea of self-salvation through the practice of the teachings which was held by pre-Roman Catholic Christians was transformed into the idea of salvation through the church by later Orthodox Catholic Church authorities.

Below are two corresponding verses, first as it is presented in the Gnostic Christian text, and then as it appears in the Bible (Orthodox Christianity). The statement which appears in the Bible not only falls short of providing a deeper meaning, but it also turns the meaning away from the individual interpretation for every Christian follower and transforms it into what might be called a church or group statement. Thus, from a psychological standpoint, we move to a sectarian understanding of the statement in the Orthodox Church version. So the Orthodox Church may be considered as the first denominational movement in Christianity since it sought to set itself apart from the other Christians. Therefore, it is not surprising that the sectarian orthodox movement in the development of Christianity opposed the Gnostic or psycho-mystical[78] movement which had its roots in the Ancient Egyptian, Yogic, Hindu, Taoist and Buddhist teachings which are themselves essentially psychological teachings designed for individual practice and self-transformation leading to a mystical spiritual awakening.

---

[76] The word "ethnic" may have originated from the Bible term "ethnos" meaning "of or pertaining to a group of people recognized as a class on the basis of certain distinctive characteristics, such as religion, language, ancestry, culture, or national origin."[124]

[77] psychological messages contained in the myth dedicated to promoting mental changes in those who study, live or practice it to promote their spiritual evolution.

[78] psychological messages contained in the mystic philosophy dedicated to promoting mental changes in those who study, live or practice it to promote their spiritual evolution.

Gnostic text from the *Gospel of Thomas* where Jesus is speaking to his disciples:

Now let's compare the previous statement to the traditional Bible text:

55. If they ask you, "Whence have you come from?" tell them "We have come from the Light, from the place whence the Light is produced of itself." If someone says to you: "What are you?" say, "We are the sons and we are the elect of the living Father."

John 8
14 Jesus answered and said to them, Though I testify concerning myself, [yet] my testimony is true: for I know from where I came, and where I go; but ye cannot tell from where I come, and where I go.

It is evident that the Gnostic statement which originally sought to impart specific knowledge as to the origin of the disciple has been transformed, in the Biblical text, into an ambiguous statement which relates the reader to a worldly form of thinking based on a connection to the church rather than to a transcendental reference which is to be experienced in the heart of the individual. In the Bible, the emphasis is on the personal, rather than the transpersonal Jesus of the Gnostic texts. Further, the Biblical statement takes the form of a riddle with respect to the origins and status of the disciples. The latter text also uses "I" rather than "you." Thus, the focus of attention is in the personality of Jesus as an entity outside and separate from ourselves rather than the inner or mystical self-application of the teaching as a psychological metaphor dedicated to inner transformation.

# The Origins of Civilization and the Classifications of Human Social Evolution

## The Ancient Origins of the Human Species

Generally, human beings are regarded by science as a species of beings that evolved from primitive forms to the more advanced form, known today as *Homo Sapien Sapien.* The term "Homo Sapien Sapien" means "the modern species of human beings, the only extant species of the primate family Hominidae."[79] Species means "a fundamental category of taxonomic classification, ranking below a genus or subgenus and consisting of related organisms capable of interbreeding."[80] Webster's encyclopedia describes the scholarly consensus on "the origins of human species" as follows:

> Evolution of humans from ancestral primates. The African apes (gorilla and chimpanzee) are shown by anatomical and molecular comparisons to be the closest living relatives of humans. Humans are distinguished from apes by the size of their brain and jaw, their bipedalism, and their elaborate culture. Molecular studies put the date of the split between the human and African ape lines at 5–10 million years ago. There are only fragmentary remains of ape and hominid (of the human group) fossils from this period. Bones of the earliest known human ancestor, a hominid named Australopithecus ramidus 1994, were found in Ethiopia and dated as 4.4 million years old.[81]

The Stone Age period of history is that span of time regarded as being early in the development of human cultures. The Stone Age refers to the period before the use of metals. The artifacts used by people as tools and weapons were made of stone. In the discipline of archaeology, the Stone Age has been divided into the following main periods: Eolithic, Paleolithic, Mesolithic and Neolithic. The ages were experienced at different times in different geographical areas of the world in accordance with the changes in climate conditions and or the particular culture's capacity for technological ingenuity or contact with other technologically advanced groups.

---

[79] American Heritage Dictionary
[80] ibid.
[81] Copyright © 1995 Helicon Publishing Ltd Encyclopedia

Following the Stone Age is the Metal Age. Three important ages follow which are marked by the use of metals. These are the Copper Age, Iron Age and the Bronze Age.

**Copper Age**, or Chalcolithic Age, is the time period in which man discovered how to extract copper by heating its ore with charcoal. This art was known in the Middle East before 3500 BC. A subsequent important development was the alloying of copper with tin to produce bronze. [82]

**Bronze Age,** period from the early fourth millennium BC onward, in which man learned to make bronze artifacts and to use the wheel and the ox-drawn plow which allowed agriculture to support a larger population. The resulting growth of technology and trade occasioned the rise of the first civilizations in Sumer and Egypt.[83] In the Bronze Age, copper and bronze became the first metals worked extensively and used for tools and weapons. It developed out of the Stone Age, preceded the Iron Age, and may be dated 5000–1200 BC in the Middle East and about 2000–500 BC in Europe. Recent discoveries in Thailand suggest that the Far East, rather than the Middle East, was the cradle of the Bronze Age.[84]

**Iron Age,** period succeeding the Bronze Age in which man learned to smelt iron. The Hittites probably developed the first important iron industry in Armenia soon after 2000 BC. Iron's superior strength and the widespread availability of its ore caused it gradually to supersede bronze.[85]

The theories about the early origins of humanity are not firm because much of the evidence of the evolutionary development of human beings has been swept away by the active nature of the planet. Volcanoes, storms,

---

[82] Copyright © 1995 Helicon Publishing Ltd Encyclopedia, Random House Encyclopedia Copyright (C) 1983,1990, Microsoft (R) Encarta Encyclopedia. Copyright (c) 1994

[83] Random House Encyclopedia Copyright (C) 1983,1990

[84] Copyright © 1995 Helicon Publishing Ltd Encyclopedia

[85] Copyright © 1995 Helicon Publishing Ltd Encyclopedia, Random House Encyclopedia Copyright (C) 1983,1990, Microsoft (R) Encarta Encyclopedia. Copyright (c) 1994

floods, etc., eventually wipe away all remnants of everything that happens on the surface of the earth as they recycle matter to bring forth life sustaining conditions again. For example, in later history, the city of Rome was buried in several feet of dust, ash and other natural particles, which eventually claimed the surface of the earth through the action of wind and other natural phenomena of planetary weather. The encroaching sands of North East Africa tend to erode and encroach on the monuments in Egypt. For example, the Sphinx enclosure can fill up and cover the Sphinx with sand due to winds and sandstorms in just 20 years or less. Complicating these factors is the modern urbanizing of archeological areas. People move in and actually live over important archeological sites, preventing their discovery. Also, there is the confirmed fact that entire cultures have been lost over time, leaving little more than a scarce trace of their existence. Further, new scientific evidence compels scientists to revise their estimates to account for the new findings. One important example in this subject relates to the Ancient Egyptian Sphinx, located in the area today known as Giza, in Egypt. The Great Sphinx was once known as *Horemakhet* or "Heru in the Horizon." It was later known by the Greeks as Harmachis. New discoveries show the Ancient Egyptian Sphinx to be much older than previously thought. The importance of this discovery is that it places advanced civilization first in northeast Africa (Ancient Egypt), at the time when Europe, Mesopotamia[86] and the rest of Asia were just coming out of the Paleolithic Age.

Thus, when Ancient Egyptians had already created the Sphinx monument, and its attendant massive temple and other structures that would have required multitudes of workers, food, organization, etc., the rest of the world was just beginning to learn how to practice farming and to use sleds, boats and other elementary instruments which were just being invented by them. The new findings related to the Sphinx, which are supported by many ancient writings, are leading us to realize the true depths of human origins and the starting point for civilization.

---

[86] Mesopotamia (from a Greek term meaning "between rivers") lies between the Tigris and Euphrates rivers, a region that is part of modern Iraq.

## What is Civilization, What is the Difference Between Civilization and Culture and What Causes the Rise and Fall of Civilizations?

Civilization and barbarism are forms of cultural expressions. In order to conduct qualitative and insightful comparative studies involving myth and culture we need to understand the origins of civilization, religion and mystical philosophy in order to have a foundation or reference point from which to collect data and make correct selections of cultural factors for comparisons.

Science offers, not an absolute, but a useful reference point to understand the progress towards human civilization and human evolution. It is important to understand the classifications of ancient societies as they are used in modern scholarship in order to better understand their meaning in context.

In anthropology, civilization is defined as an advanced socio-political stage of cultural evolution, whereby a centralized government (over a city, ceremonial center, or larger region called a state) is supported by the taxation of surplus production, and rules the agricultural, and often mercantile base. Those who do not produce food become specialists who govern, lead religious ritual, impose and collect taxes, record the past and present, plan and have executed monumental public works (irrigation systems, roads, bridges, buildings, tombs), and elaborate and formalize the style and traditions of the society. These institutions are based on the use of leisure time to develop writing, mathematics, the sciences, engineering, architecture, philosophy, and the arts. Archeological remains of cities and ceremonial centers are evaluated to determine the degree of civilization of that culture, based on the trappings of both style and content.[87] The American Heritage Dictionary defines civilization as:

> **civ·i·li·za·tion** *n.* **1.** An advanced state of intellectual, cultural, and material development in human society, marked by progress in the arts and sciences, the extensive use of writing, and the appearance of complex political and social institutions.

Strictly speaking, civilization is defined as a highly developed human society with structured division of labor,[88] an advanced state of intellectual, cultural, and material development, marked by progress in the arts and sciences, the extensive use of writing, and the appearance of

---

[87] Copyright © 1995 Helicon Publishing Ltd Encyclopedia
[88] Copyright © 1995 Helicon Publishing Ltd Encyclopedia

complex political and social institutions.[89] In simple terms, civilization means acting in a civil manner towards other people, which implies cooperation in the furtherance of community goals and the support and raising of the individuals within the civilization. The earliest "highly developed human societies" developed in ancient times out of Neolithic farming societies. These in turn developed out of Mesolithic societies, and these out of Paleolithic societies. Thus, civilization or the lack thereof, can be considered in many ways. Prior to the existence of farming, human beings were considered to be "hunter gatherers," primitive groups fending for food, territory and the right to mate, with little conception of what lies beyond the basic survival activities of life. In hunter gatherer or nomadic societies as well as societies that have to struggle for survival, since time is constantly spent in competition for food and warding off potential danger, there is little opportunity for the higher aspects of life such as art, religion or philosophy. At most these factors will not progress beyond a primitive level under such conditions.

It is thought that the development of pottery, which follows agriculture, which follows sedentism (opposite of hunter-gatherer nomadic society), signifies a major step towards the establishment of a civilized society.

Sedentism is the process by which human beings changed their lifestyle from being based on hunting and gathering and non-permanent settlements to farming and the development of a sedentary (permanent settlements. ) perspective for social existence. The development of farming allowed the process of sedentism to occur as it no longer became necessary to move around to different areas in order to find food. The river valley societies such as the ones which developed along the Indus, Nile and Tigris Euphrates had an advantage over other societies in that they were able to develop a relationship with a river that delivered needed water for subsistence. The Ancient Egyptian society, along the Nile river in north-eastern Africa, was able to develop a special relationship with a river that delivered regular annual waters, sufficient in quantity and nutritious enough to inundate much of the valley, requiring them only to plan and plant seeds at the proper time and then harvest the fruit of their work. This advantage would allow these societies to devote more attention to matters of social interaction and government as opposed to applying their time to moving constantly and worrying about finding food. Therefore, the hunter gatherer may be expected to be different from that of the farmer. For example, some Native American peoples who based their culture on hunting also had prayers for their prey while other sedentary Native American cultures may have prayers to the spirit that makes Maize grow.

---

[89] American Heritage Dictionary

Thus, a society may be sedentary or not an that factor affects its cultural development and expressions; that includes its myths, its social institutions and societal philosophy.

The invention of writing is regarded as a very high development of civilization. For many years it was thought that writing was first invented by the Sumerians, but the recent evidence demonstrates that the invention of Ancient Egyptian writing and Ancient Egyptian architecture predate Sumerian civilization. The following report by the British team excavating the Ancient Egyptian city of Abdu (modern Abydos) dispels the misconceptions related to the first origins of writing in history.

> "Until recently it was thought that the earliest writing system was invented by the Sumerians in Mesopotamia towards the end of the fourth millennium BC and that the idea was borrowed by the Egyptians at the beginning of the First Dynasty (c.3100 BC). However, recent discoveries at Abydos have shown that the Egyptians had an advanced system of writing even earlier than the Mesopotamians, some 150 years before Narmer. Remarkably, there is no evidence that this writing developed from a more primitive pictographic stage. Already, at the very beginning, it incorporated signs for sounds.
> Unlike Mesopotamian writing, which can be shown to have gradually evolved through a number of stages, beginning as an accounting system, Egyptian writing appears to have been deliberately invented in a more-or-less finished form, its underlying principles fully in place right from the outset. A parallel for such a process is known from more recent times: in AD 1444 the Korean script (still widely regarded as one of the world's most efficient) was invented by order of the king, who assembled a group of scholars for the purpose.
> In Egypt this invention corresponds with the birth of the Egyptian state, and its growing administrative and bureaucratic needs."[90]

However, the aforementioned criteria denoting the presence or absence of "civilization" relate mostly to technological developments and increased sociopolitical complexity. Complexity in society and highly advanced technology cannot in themselves be used to determine the presence of civilization, because many cultures in the past have had these and they have fallen into oblivion (forgetfulness, unconsciousness) nevertheless due

---

[90] *Egypt Uncovered*, Vivian Davies and Renée Friedman

to their own degradation. While they display elements of civilized culture, organization to promote the benefit of people, they succumb to their own degraded social tendencies such as barbarism, greed, lust for power, etc. Some examples of these are the Greek Empire, the Roman Empire, the Ottoman Empire, the British Empire, etc. Ancient Egyptian civilization experienced a downfall not because of its internal degradation but due to deterioration caused by attacks from peoples of Asia Minor and Europe.

If civilization is an advancement in society, then it would follow that the advanced civilization must be doing something better, more efficient, that would promote not only prosperity, but also its own longevity. So what were these "civilizations" missing that allowed them to fall? Where did they go wrong?

**Albert Schweitzer** (1875-1965), the German-born theologian, philosopher, musicologist, medical missionary, and Nobel laureate, was one of the first Western scholars to examine the issue of civilization and the causes for its downfall as well as the means for its maintenance. As a missionary doctor in Africa, prior to and after the First World War, he gained valuable experiences while treating the sick there. He would doubtless have had occasion to experience the misery imposed on Africans due to the colonial system, and also he would have experienced the African concept of Ubuntu (humanity) and caring for family.

From 1917-1918 Schweitzer, who was a German national, was incarcerated in France, which was at war with Germany. During this period he wrote two volumes which became a projected philosophical study of civilization called *The Decay and the Restoration of Civilization* and *Civilization and Ethics* (both 1923).[91] These volumes were concerned with ethical thought in history. Schweitzer maintained that modern civilization is in decay because it lacks the will to love. As a solution to this problem he suggested that society should develop a philosophy based on what he termed "reverence for life," embracing with compassion all forms of life.[92] It is interesting to note that Schweitzer's solution, a return to love, is the primary concept behind the African philosophies of *Ubuntu*

---

[91] His other works include the theological studies *Indian Thought and Its Development* (1935; trans. 1936), *The Kingdom of God and Primitive Christianity* (1967; trans. 1968), *The Mysticism of Paul the Apostle* (1930; trans. 1931) and the autobiographical *Out of My Life and Thought* (1931; trans. 1933).

[92] "Schweitzer, Albert," *Microsoft® Encarta® Encyclopedia 2000.* © 1993-1999 Microsoft Corporation. All rights reserved.

(caring for humanity) and *Maat* (righteousness in society and caring for humanity). He was also exposed to Eastern mysticism which also exhorts the necessity to develop the capacity for compassion and universal love in order to attain spiritual enlightenment. He attempted to discover the mystical love upon which Christianity is founded and to raise the awareness of this aspect of Christianity, as he saw the lack of such awareness in the Western practice of the Christian religion as contributing to Western Culture's inability to love humanity.

The problem of inability to love and care in a civilization develops when it is not managed or ceases to be managed by leaders with the capacity to care for others, to be compassionate to others. We may study this concept of the ability or inability of a society to move towards or away from civilized culture as a factor of its Societal Philosophy (will be discussed in more detail later). It is often not realized that the concept of the word civilization includes the term *Civility* which means 1. Courteous behavior; politeness. 2. A courteous act or utterance. *-American Heritage Dictionary*. This definition excludes belligerent, warlike or aggressive behaviors and cultural practices. Therefore a culture that may have civilized aspects but which maintains violent tendencies can not be considered as a fully civilized culture; it is still barbarous. Caring and compassion are expressions of ethical conscience, which may be considered as an outgrowth of a spiritual outlook on the world, an awareness of the interconnectedness of and Divinity in all. Therefore, mystical studies (spiritual perspective encompassing all humanity transcending religion (considered as a folkloric, parochial practice) are imperative for any society to move towards civilization and away from greed, power, war and pleasure seeking that lead to conflict in society and between societies. Such a society that does not overcome the barbarous tendencies will be eventually doomed to self-destruction because this way of life promotes degraded culture and selfishness instead of respect for life. Consequently, under these conditions, people develop the capacity to hurt each other to achieve their own material goals, perpetuating a cycle of vice, violence, mistrust and hatred, leading to war, disease, poverty and suffering. This of course cannot be called "civilization." It is a form of culture which is struggling to discover itself, struggling to leave behind the vestiges of barbarism.

So civilization means the coming together of a group of people to organize themselves and promote the general good. This they do by using establishing a social philosophy that promotes the benefit of all people. They then use technology to facilitate their activities, promote health and the perpetuation of life. What sustains civilization is an ethical social conscience. The ethical social conscience comes from an underlying spiritual basis that recognizes all life a sacred. The philosophical insight which allows a human being to realize that all life is sacred is the fact that the universe promotes the continuation of life in all respects, animal, vegetable and mineral. The spiritual consciousness is predicated upon the idea that even death is not the final reality. This can be proven through the experience of spiritual enlightenment.

The process of spiritual enlightenment is achieved when a human being discovers what lies beyond their physical mortal existence. African Religion, through its most advanced expression, Ancient Egyptian Religion, was the first to proclaim this discovery and the means for any human being to achieve its realization. This (spiritual enlightenment) is the authentic basis for civilization. Until a society achieves this general awareness so that it is promoted in its policies, inventions, technologies and activities, (its institutions) it cannot be considered to have achieved the status of "civilized." Philosophy is the most important factor influencing the development of a culture. The way of thinking (belief system-philosophy) of a culture dictates whether a culture will develop civilized institutions (promote life) or institutions that promote destruction, slavery, greed and other vices (Barbarism). Thus, "Civilization" is an outgrowth of a well ordered, ethical and spiritually based culture. A culture without a philosophy that affirms universal divinity cannot develop into a "civilization." Just as a mother expresses love for a child by taking care of the child the culture that takes care of people's (not just its own but all people's) social needs is a loving and civilized culture. The lack of awareness of a universal and interconnected spiritual basis for all life is due to a disconnect between a society's cultural manifestation and its understanding of the meaning and purpose of life as an expression of universal existence in which all partake and all are integral, a concept that logically means that all should be treated alike and none should be segregated nor should there be exclusive groups or racial typing, etc. The lack of a universal outlook[93] in the societal philosophy that a culture is guided by leads to the separation between the secular and non-secular aspects of culture as opposed to seeing culture as a manifestation of spiritual awareness.

---

[93] That there is an ultimate reality which is the substratum of all existence and which is common to all human beings is what is being referred to here.

# The Cultural Category Factor Correlation Method

## Table 5: How the Societal Philosophy that a society lives by determines its ultimate propensity for Civilization or Barbarism

The diagram above depicts the two main methods that a society develops a concept related to an ultimate reality and then applies that concept to create id social institutions and directs them either to civilized life or barbarous life or a mixture of the two. The society that develops an awareness of an ultimate reality (➔ Wisdom is accessible) as a universal truth develops towards moral and ethical conscience while a society that does not (⊠ the wisdom is blocked) develop the awareness develops in an atmosphere of amorality and barbarism.

# The Cultural Category Factor Correlation Method

## Table 6: The Disconnect in Modern Culture between the Secular and Non-Secular

| | NON-SECULAR PERSPECTIVE (N-S) | Culture | Institutions | Sustain / Degrade Life | END PRODUCT |
|---|---|---|---|---|---|
| *The culture developed by a society which has lost connection with the idea of a humanistic / mystical Ultimate Reality, and has developed extremes of abundance in technological development,* | **NON-SECULAR PERSPECTIVE (N-S)** The religious philosophy (tenets/dogmas) of the society develop towards orthodoxy, historicity and exclusivism instead towards mysticism, ecumenism and inclusion. Develops intolerance towards secular and other religions.[94] | **(N-S)** The religious culture develops away from pluralism and towards exclusion and that which is uncaring of anyone who disagrees with its outlook. | **(N-S)** The institutions develop towards hoarding of resources, political power which means creating and supporting an elite group that dictates to the rest. | **(N-S)** The outlook of sustaining life turns towards destroying life to save it from what the orthodox perspective sees as damnation and hell. | **(N-S)** Orthodoxy Faith-based Exclusivism Intolerance Hatred Conflict Self-destruction |
| Societal Philosophy→→ ☒ ☒ ☒ ☒ ☒    Ultimate Reality ☒ | Orthodox / Exclusive / Phenomenal    ← Awareness →    Secular / Phenomenal | Loving/Caring    ← Culture →    Selfish/Greed | Institutions →→→ | Sustain Life (Civilization)    Degrade Life (Barbarism) | END PRODUCT |
| *material abundance and dearth of spiritual awareness. As Joseph Campbell would say, this culture does not have a "myth to live by." It lives by consumer culture and or fanatical spirituality.* | **SECULAR PERSPECTIVE (S)** The political, economic and social outlook (philosophy) develops towards the extreme of worldly desires, outcomes and pursuits and disdain for the non-secular[95] | **(S)** The secular culture develops towards unethical extreme uncaring for people or nature in pursuit of worldly satisfactions. | **(S)** Institutions develop towards exclusion, hoarding resources - creating and supporting an elite group that dictates to the rest with force and violence. | **(S)** Partisan politics and economics of consumption and excess unsustainable development -leads to self-destruction through mismanagement, resource depletion or self-poisoning from pollution. | **(S)** Secularism, Atheism, science Intolerance, Hubris, Gluttony, Entitlement, Consumerism, Self-destruction |

111

---

[94] The Ultimate Reality becomes a phenomenal (physical, not transcendental) heaven to reincarnate into, myths become historical realities to serve the church instead of living metaphors to guide individuals to make sense of the world and discover the ultimate reality of life.

[95] The social myths become material realities to serve the objective of greed and self-satisfaction instead of serving the material needs to support the higher goals of life and spiritual self-discovery, i.e., to guide individuals to make sense of the world and discover the ultimate reality of life.

**Figure 8: How the Societal Philosophy leads to Folklore, Culture and Civilization or Barbarism**

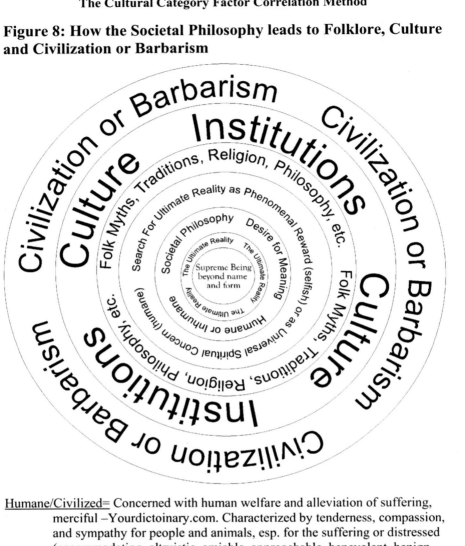

Humane/Civilized= Concerned with human welfare and alleviation of suffering, merciful –Yourdictoinary.com. Characterized by tenderness, compassion, and sympathy for people and animals, esp. for the suffering or distressed (accommodating, altruistic, amiable, approachable, benevolent, benign, benignant, broad-minded, charitable) Reference: humane. (n.d.). *Dictionary.com Unabridged (v 1.1)*. Retrieved April 11, 2007, from Dictionary.com website: http://dictionary.reference.com/browse/humane

Barbarous/Inhumane= (ignorant, primitive, rough, rude, ruthless, sadistic, truculent, uncivil, uncivilized, vicious, vulgar, wicked, wild) Reference: inhumane. (n.d.). *Roget's New Millennium™ Thesaurus, First Edition (v 1.3.1)*. Retrieved April 11, 2007, from Thesaurus.com website: http://thesaurus.reference.com/browse/inhumane

## The Standard of What Constitutes Civilization

In the book *Beyond Mythology, A Challenge to Dogmatism in Religion,* the author, Richard W. Boynton asserts that "a wide gap has opened up between the kind of thinking that is applied to the production of ever more and better material utensils and the kind that is used in dealing with the higher concerns of mankind."[96] This shift in what Boynton calls "kind of thinking", and what I would refer to more specifically as the *"societal philosophy,"* which has led to a disconnect between human existence and values based on reality, has occurred due to the technological capacity to design, create and produce more conveniences. Boynton also asserts that society (western culture), and it may be argued that this affects world modern culture since western culture dominates the world culture, is no longer "rooted"[97] in a previous traditional understanding of life. The prominent mythologist, Joseph Campbell, would say, this culture does not have a "myth to live by." We may also consider, however, that many people treat their jobs or their pleasure –seeking pursuits (such as sports, sex, family, partying) as their religion. Yet those pursuits do not yield abiding peace or balance with nature. Instead, as in a drug addiction they promote more pursuit of pleasure, more consumption, etc. without satisfaction or real contentment.

Civilization cannot be considered just as a society possessing intellectual capacity, technology, social organization, etc. These aspects are merely the basis for conducting social interactions and not necessarily required for civilization. Civilization is an expression of a mature culture which allows it to build social structures that perpetuate its existence. Promoting existence means promoting life. Promoting life means protecting life and the quality of life for all as well as the capacity to carry on life, which means also protecting nature. Since no society or culture in the world exists in a vacuum or on an island, separate from other societies or cultures, it is erroneous to believe that a civilization can advance in the absence of the general advancement of all humanity and the preservation of all nature (environmental conservation). Therefore, a society or culture's level of civilization is judged as much by its ethical social advancement, its compassion and assistance to other societies or cultures as well as it ecological conscience. Thus, a selfish or greedy society cannot be considered by these criteria as a civilization, but rather as a degraded culture {barbarism}. This means that civilization is an aspect of culture. It

---

[96] p. vii
[97] p. viii

is based on the cultural beliefs and traditions of a people and underlying this culture is a way of thinking about the world and that is based on a people's philosophy of life (Societal Philosophy), as to its meaning and purpose.

The following standard is offered as a set of cultural features needed for the determination of a society or culture's level of civilization. This list is not to be considered as final or exclusive. In order to be considered as a civilization, the society should possess and practice the following elements of civilized culture:

1. **Mystical Philosophy** – to allow the advanced members of the society to seek for the answers to the transcendental questions of life, to Know Self.

2. **Myth** – is the means by which the ethics and spiritual consciousness are transferred from generation to generation and acts as a self-definition of culture, conveying the mythic history (folklore and legends), cultural identity and common traditions of the society.

3. **Spiritual consciousness** – religion and spirituality that affirms the universal divine essence of Creation.

4. **Ethics** – philosophy of social justice to promote equality, order, peace and harmony in the absence of which a civilization cannot function efficiently.

5. **Government and Economic Organization** - The society or culture must display social organization- a group of people coming together for promoting a common goal. The form of government may be used as a factor of comparison. Two societies may have similar forms of government or even similar developments in their governmental systems due to traditional reasons, legends, or interactions. This is not necessarily a commentary on the level of development of the societies but only comparisons. The level of development may be based on a conceptual framework of socio-governmental evolution. If societies develop towards greater social support and human development we may say that ordinary governments could develop from agrarian communalism to feudalism to monarchy to republics to capitalism (as a driving force behind government, which may include physical slavery and/or economic slavery). Instead of developing towards capitalism a society could turn towards communism. Both capitalism (as practiced in the Western countries, in particular, the U.S.A. and England) and communism (as practiced in the Western

countries, in particular, the U.S.A. and England, Soviet Union and other countries) are political-economic extremes which allow power to be concentrated in the hands of the few which leads to social injustice and unrest. In the case of Ancient Egyptian society the development was from sedentism to agrarian communalism and social Pharaonic hierocracy, which lasted for thousands of years.

6. **Agriculture** - The society or culture must conduct agriculture to sustain the society and allow the members of the society to develop regular routines so as to engage in contemplative endeavors.

7. **Writing, language** or set (agreed upon) means of communication.

8. **Mathematics** – used as the foundation of distribution of resources, architecture, etc.

9. **Art** – is the means by which the ethics, spiritual consciousness and myth become visual icons for a society and through which a society views and understands the world around them. Therefore, the art of a civilization conveys its highest ethics and spiritual conscience. Art in any form may be considered as an expression of high culture if it has attained a high level of development but that high development or technical expertise should not be taken to mean that the culture is necessarily civilized; there have been many cultures throughout history that have manifested high arts but which fell to low ethics or other destructive or what we may call immature aspects of social development such as racism, fascism and imperialism. Some examples of such societies are Ancient Greece, Ancient Rome and Germany in the 20th century.


**Culture, Ethnicity, Race and Cultural Adoptions and Adaptations**

If we are to accept that the concept of race as a reality wherein human beings are viewed as separate entities due to arbitrary characteristics, external or sociopolitical factors such as their skin color, or other criteria, is bogus and therefore misleading how can the question of what is the proper way to view cultural adoptions of peoples of a particular skin color, or ethnicity, into the society and cultures of peoples of a different skin color or ethnicity be viewed? If race is not an essential cultural trait but rather one of many possible features of cultural expression what does it mean to be European, African, Asian, etc.? In other words, if race is a false classification what makes, for example, a not "white" in skin color person in European culture a part of European culture or a not "black" person in African culture a part of the African culture? Furthermore, does this mean that a person who is referred to as "white", living in European culture, for example or referred to as "brown", living in South American culture, for example or referred to as "yellow", living in Asian culture, for example can be accepted into an African society that is composed of mostly "black" people and be considered African and vise versa?

Let us begin by looking at the example of a person who would like to become a priest or priestess of Shetaut Neter (Ancient Egyptian Religion (Neterianism)). It has been demonstrated by scholars that the indigenous population that started Ancient Egyptian culture and religion as well as its philosophy, was of "black" African peoples who migrated north from the area that is today referred to as Sudan.[98] If we accept that the concept of race and its application, racism, is incorrect, then what kinds of persons are eligible to be accepted in and become practitioners of Neterian religion? If we understand that Ancient Egyptian religion contains the same fundamental religious principles and customs which are shared generally by other African peoples in other countries (societies) throughout Africa, the answer would then have to be that the Neterian priesthood is for those who follow the culture of Kemet (Ancient Egypt), which is itself part of African culture.[99]

If a person wants to be a Buddhist priest he or she would not follow Western culture and religion (Christianity, Judaism or Islam) and be Buddhist. The person must follow the culture associated with Buddhism to be a Buddhist priest. As Buddhism is primarily Indian (or by extension, Tibetan, Chinese or Japanese), they would follow that culture but since Buddhism began within Indian culture, that culture would be the primary culture associated with the tradition. There is no western independent development in Buddhist culture. Further, while Buddhism began in India (with association to Ancient Egypt)[100] one could conclude that the primary source of Buddhism should be in India and not in Japan, Tibet or China. However, while it is true that the Japanese, Tibetans and Chinese brought

---

[98] *BLACK ANCIENT EGYPTIANS* by Muata Ashby, *Egypt Revisited* (Journal of African Civilizations,) by Ivan Van Sertima, *Civilization or Barbarism: An Authentic Anthropology* by Cheikh Anta Diop, *Black Athena: The Afroasiatic Roots of Classical Civilization: The Linguistic Evidence*, Vol. 3 by Martin Bernal
[99] Fundamental Principles of African Religion. *The African Origins of Civilization, Religion, Yoga Mystical Spirituality and Ethics Philosophy*. Sema Institute of Yoga, 2002. Muata Ashby
[100] *The Ancient Egyptian Buddha* by Muata Ashby

forth positive developments in Buddhism they were following a culture that it came with (primarily Indian) to them. If we might be able to say that Zen Buddhism from Japan is a distinct form of Buddhism can we say that it is "different," that is, a different religion altogether? Further, could we say they are practicing something in contravention with the original Buddhism of India? It is all Buddhism but with its distinct cultural nuances that have developed over centuries. If Buddhism were to come to the West (as it has) can we say that a distinct western form of Buddhism has developed there? No, what is practiced are the styles brought there from the East, based on the cultures of the East. However, if the Buddhism of the west were to incorporate new traditions based on western culture then we would be forced to conclude that the western form of Buddhism is different from the original practice, and we could refer to it as an acculturated version of Buddhism which has been co-opted by the peoples of the west who adopted Buddhism but "adapted" it to their own lifestyle. Such a development could fundamentally change the meaning, purpose and goal of the practice to such a degree that it would not be considered as Buddhism at all.

The culture within which a tradition emerged is important because the philosophical tenets have references and nuances of meaning that are informed by the culture. This is why it is important to follow the culture of origin when practicing a cultural tradition; otherwise some elements of practice and or of meaning can be transformed, forgotten or even lost and the feeling, meaning and purpose of the tradition can be changed from its original form. Other examples that may be given are as follows: To be a practitioner of Islam a person would follow Arab culture, to follow Taoism a person follows Chinese culture.

Likewise, if Neterian religion were to be practiced in the West it would have to be practices along with its associated culture. There is no independent development of Neterianism in the West, it developed in Africa, and therefore the specific African culture it developed out of and within should be practiced with it. Even if over time the Kemetic religion or the Buddhist religion were to develop in the west could they ever say they are originally Western developments? No, they would always have to say they are looking to their sources, Ancient Egypt and India. The same would be true for the so called Western religions (Judaism, Christianity) since these originated in Africa and Asia Minor. However, since those religions have been so extensively altered[101] from their original forms and the adulterated and co-opted forms have been associated with Western

---

[101] see the book *The Mystical Journey From Jesus to Christ* by Muata Ashby

culture and different traditions not found in Africa and Asia Minor we cannot see the western versions as part of the original culture and must consequently classify them as different.

As Neterian religion is based in African culture, the practitioner must follow an African perspective. Since African culture and especially the Kemetic tradition, do not recognize the concept of "race" and its degraded sociopolitical application (racism), Kemetic culture does not recognize or condone segregationist or racist policies. The teachings of the Ancient Egyptian Sage Akhenaton as well as that of other Kemetic sages, enlightens us to the fact that all human beings, regardless of their skin color originate from the same spirit and the same physical creation.[102] In fact the teaching was the opposite from the modern concept of race, that all human beings have the same source and same kinship as well as the same Divine heritage. This understanding follows the modern studies of human genetics which demonstrate that all human beings alive today had the same genetic origin in Africa, and are not different or parts of "different" "racial" groups. So whether or not the person is of recent African descent ("black people") or distant African descent ("white people") the person who wants to adopt the Neterian religion should follow Kemetic-African culture.

Therefore, as long as the practitioner wants to adopt Kemetic/African culture, they can be accepted freely into the Neterian practice regardless of the ethnicity (not race) or culture they come from without fear that the tradition would be harmed or changed.

However, a person who wants to adopt a religion but also maintain the practice of a different culture would promote a process of distorted enculturation, acculturation through cooptation because that process of adopting the religion without the culture facilitates assimilation and the adulteration of the original principles and practices and the values of the original culture. Therefore, the incomplete adoption (tradition without its culture) of a culture can introduce alien cultural values that are incompatible with the tenets and values of the original culture.

---

[102] For example, from the Anicent Egyptian tradition we have: "Thou makest the color of the skin of one race to be different from that of another, but however many may be the varieties of mankind, it is thou that makes them all to live."—Ancient Egyptian Proverb from *The Hymns of Amun,* documented in the book *The African Origins of Civilization, Religion, Yoga Mystical Spirituality and Ethics Philosophy.* Fundamental Principles of African Religion. Sema Institute of Yoga, 2002.

## The Cultural Category Factor Correlation Method

One example is the Kemetic injunction, contained in the tradition of Maat, against pollution of the land and water (found in the 42 precepts of Maat[103]). The question would be how can a person in Europe, United States of America, Japan or Australia adopt Kemetic teachings but also support the right of companies and individuals to pollute the world with green house gasses and other pollutants, which is more accepted in western culture? If a non-African person in a Western country should adopt the principles and not support the pollution agenda that would mean they are rejecting the pollution principle of the Western culture and they are adopting the Kemetic/African, and can be accepted into the Kemetic culture. On the other hand, even if a "black" African person were to support a pollution agenda, they would not be considered as followers of African culture.

Another example is: In western religion/culture the central viewpoint of theism in religion is *Monotheism* i.e. there is a Single God and no other gods and/or goddesses, while African religion/culture holds that the central viewpoint of theism in religion is *Henotheism* i.e. there is a Supreme Being and lesser gods and goddesses. If a western person were to adopt that tenet of African religion they would be putting aside the monotheism of the West and adopting the African paradigm and within the parameters outlined by our scheme of culture and ethnic consistency, that the tradition should match the culture, they could be accepted into the culture without the culture suffering severe deleterious effects (acculturation, cooptation, etc.) from the newcomer.

In reference to a religious tradition, very importantly, if a person adopts a religion/culture fully they would also adopt it's concept of "Holy Land", it's sense of geographical origin and center of socio-political orientation. There is a certain concordance between the concept of the "Holy Land" and the culture and religious tradition that a person follows. It would be inconceivable to imagine a Jewish person (person who follows Judaism as their religion, not an ethnic or genetic concept)[104] looking to South Africa

---

[103] Pert m Hru – also more commonly known as the Ancient Egyptian Book of the Dead. See *The Book of the Dead* by Muata Ashby

[104] Judaism is a religion and not an ethnic designation or a racial designation. The Falashas are a native Jewish sect of Ethiopia. The name Falasha is Amharic for "exiles" or "landless ones" (the original Hebrews of the Bible Old Testament tradition were nomadic wanderers.). This is similar to the term "Hebrews" meaning "those who pass from place to place." The Falashas themselves refer to their sect as Beta Esrael ("House of Israel"). The origin of the Falashas is unknown, but one Falasha tradition claims to trace their ancestry to Menelek (Menelik), who was the son of King Solomon of Israel and the queen of Sheba (Sheba: Ancient name for a kingdom which flourished in S Yemen (Sha'abijah) at around the 1st century B.C.E. It was once renowned for gold and spices. According to the Old

as their "Holy Land"? Those who practice Christianity, Judaism, Islam, Baha'i, Sikhism, Buddhism, etc. look to either Palestine, India, etc., respectively, as their "Holy Land" and as the special place, as the source of their tradition and the place of their spiritual pilgrimage and even where they want to be buried when they die.

A person who adopts Yoruba religion, for example, but wants to continue believing in Jesus as their savior and Jerusalem as the "Holy Land" and or be buried with their family in the hills of Tennessee or the family Christian mausoleum in Scotland or Jamaica because they see that as their special final resting place, etc. is not fully following the Yoruba religious culture and its traditions; Likewise, those who want to be considered "Christians" and at the same time want to practice *Ifa* Yorba religion and who look to *Ife* as their Holy Place are in contradiction.

Thus, the understanding that the concept of race is bogus and that ethnic aspects of a culture cannot be conflated with the traditions of a culture, a culture needs to be viewed as a belief system (societal philosophy) and way of life rather than as a feature of a particular kind of people with a particular kind of "racial" makeup. Therefore, any human being can be part of a particular culture if they choose to adopt or are raised in the belief system and way of life of the culture and its traditions. Since particular traditions have developed within the matrix of its particular culture the mixing and matching of cultural elements can lead to confusion and the ineffectiveness of the belief system (societal philosophy) and way of life. For some individuals however, who are able to bridge the separations between cultures, it is possible to discover a harmony incorporating several elements from two or more cultural traditions but that is far less possible for the masses of a culture.

For the purposes of cultural studies it is important to distinguish between the similarities and apparent dissimilarities of different cultures while respecting all from an objective standpoint even while realizing the various levels of integrity or corruption they may be found in. Also, this

---

Testament, its queen visited Solomon.). Some scholars place the date of their origin before the 2nd century B.C.E. since the Falashas are unfamiliar with either the Palestinian or Babylonian Talmud (post-biblical developments of Judaism). Using Jewish culture as an example, we cannot rightly refer to Jewish culture as an example because Judaism is a religion, an aspect of cultural expression. As a religion, the traditions of Judaism developed out of the Hebrew and Ancient Egyptian cultures. Since there were no European Jews when Judaism was created but there were Asiatic and African Jews we cannot say that Judaism is a religion of "white" Europeans. It is a religion that anyone can adopt and practice if they choose to do so.

understanding can be applied to determine which elements of a culture are integral to its structure and which are grafted or alien introductions, so as to discern which elements can rightly be compared to which: indigenous social factors to the indigenous culture context, grafted social factors to the grafted culture context.

# Chapter 4: Cultural Category – Factor Correlation Method of Classifying, Studying and Comparing Categories and Factors of Cultural Expression

## How Do Cultures Interact?

How do people from different cultures interact? How do religions borrow and or adopt myths, symbols, philosophies or traditions from each other? Several examples from history will be used here to show how spirituality, as an aspect of one culture, was influenced by other cultures. The following essays relate documented historical accounts of cultural interactions of the past between two or more civilizations. They are included to illustrate how the process of cultural interaction leads to cultural exchanges, adoptions, inculturations, etc., as well as the emergence of new religions and philosophies out of teachings received from other cultures. They will also serve to provide insight into the manner in which aspects of some ancient cultures have diffused into present day cultures by introducing various basic principles of cultural interaction and how these interactions are to be recognized and studied.

## Cultural Interactions Between Christianity and Neterian Religion and Mysticism

In the case of Christianity it has been amply shown that several factors present in Ancient Egyptian Religion were adopted directly as the Christian religion developed in Egypt and the land of Canaan (now known today as Palestine). In fact the church itself admits this as the late mythologist Joseph Campbell relates in an interview with Bill Moyers.[105] (Note: Highlighted portions are by Ashby)

> M O Y E R S: If we go back into antiquity, do we find images of the Madonna as the mother of the savior child?

> CAMPBELL: The antique model for the Madonna, actually, is Isis with Horus at her breast.

---

[105] *The Power of Myth,* Bill Moyers, 1989.

MOYERS: Isis?

CAMPBELL: In Egyptian iconography, Isis represents the throne. The Pharaoh sits on the throne, which is Isis, as a child on its mother's lap.[106] And so, when you stand before the cathedral of Chartres, you will see over one of the portals of the western front an image of the Madonna as the throne upon which the child Jesus sits and blesses the world as its emperor. That is precisely the image that has come down to us from most ancient Egypt. *The early fathers and the early artists took over these images intentionally.*

MOYERS: The Christian fathers took the image of Isis?

CAMPBELL: Definitely. They say so themselves. Read the text where it is declared that *"those forms which were merely mythological forms in the past are now actual and incarnate in our Savior."* The mythologies here referred to were of the dead and resurrected god: Attis, Adonis, Gilgamesh, Osiris,[107] one after the other. The death and resurrection of the god is everywhere associated with the moon, which dies and is resurrected every month. It is for two nights, or three days dark, and we have Christ for two nights, or three days in the tomb.

No one knows what the actual date of the birth of Jesus might have been, but it has been put on what used to be the date of the winter solstice, December 25,[108] when the nights begin to be shorter and the days longer. That is the moment of the rebirth of light. That was exactly the date of the birth of the Persian God of light, Mithra, Sol, the Sun.

Along with the iconographies, symbols and rituals mentioned above, Christianity adopted many other aspects of the Neterian (Ancient Egyptian) Religion such as the Ankh-cross symbol, the anointing, the resurrection, the mutilation of the savior, the triune nature of the spirit (The Trinity), the Eucharist, as well as other symbols, motifs and

---

[106] In Ancient Egyptian mythology, the son of Isis (Aset), Heru, represents rulership and the upholding of righteousness, truth and order. Thus, the Pharaoh is Heru incarnate and when that person dies, he/she becomes Asar (Osiris ), the resurrected (Enlightened) spirit.

[107] The Asar from Ancient Egypt.

[108] December 25th is also the birthday of the Ancient Egyptian god Heru.

teachings.[109] When the Roman Emperor Justinian closed the Neo-Platonic academies in 529 A.C.E. along with other spiritual and religious institutions which were considered by him to be cult or pagan systems, such as that of the Ancient Egyptian goddess Aset (Isis), Orthodox Christianity was closing its doors on the last links to the pre-Judaic mystical philosophy of the traditions from which they had adopted so much. This led to a situation wherein the esoteric meanings of many symbols and metaphysical teachings were lost, forgotten or became dormant. Still, their subtle influences on Christianity persisted through medieval times and continued into the present because in order to be accepted, the Orthodox Church had to adopt many customs and symbols of other religions. Nevertheless, there are remnants of the Ancient Egyptian and other traditions of the past are still inherent in modern Orthodox Christianity as it is practiced today. The Christian church co-opted the customs and traditions of other religions in order to be able to convince the followers of the other religions that Christianity had those symbols and customs previous to their "pagan" religions, and therefore, they should abandon their religions in favor of the only "true" and "original" religion, Orthodox Christianity.

The evidence given by the Christian tradition and its documents suggests that many icons such as the images of the Madonna and child (Mary and Jesus) were taken during the early years of Christianity, renamed (rededicated as it were) and used in Christian worship. This practice may be described as *acculturation*[110] but this case also represents a process of deliberate *inculturation*,[111] through *co-optation*[112] of the symbols of a culture and transforming their meaning, history and heritage as if it was their own. These terms relate to the process of adopting symbols, traditions and rituals from other religions and calling them Christian, which were then officially confirmed and endorsed as official church policy. It is a practice that continues to be a means by which the church, as well as other groups, seek to expand their beliefs internationally. This process was instituted in the time of the early

---

[109] For more details see the book *The Journey from Jesus to Christ* by Muata Ashby

[110] cultural modification of an individual, group, or people by adapting to or borrowing traits from another culture

[111] Adopting cultural expressions of other cultures and making them part of one's own culture thereby subsuming the cultural factors from other cultures within the larger one and consequently dissolving the adopted culture into the larger one. Over a period of time, the original source of the tradition becomes blurred or forgotten because the original tradition is no longer presented as such. Examples: Moslem and Christian church practice of destroying indigenous temples and placing Mosques or churches, respectively, on the same sites. Christian adoption of the Ancient Egyptian cross, eucharist, resurrection, birthday of Heru, Madonna, etc.

[112] To neutralize or win over (an independent minority, for example) through assimilation into an established group or culture. (American Heritage Dictionary)

development of the Christian church. A prime example of inculturation is seen in the actions of Pope St Gregory the Great, who in a letter given to priests written in 601 A.C.E. endorsed this strategy as a means to attract followers from other spiritual traditions. He writes:

> "It is said that the men of this nation are accustomed to sacrificing oxen. It is necessary that this custom be converted into a Christian rite. On the day of the dedication of the [pagan] temples thus changed into churches, and similarly for the festivals of the saints, whose relics will be placed there, you should allow them, as in the past, to build structures of foliage around these same churches. They shall bring to the churches their animals, and kill them, no longer as offerings to the devil, but for Christian banquets in name and honor of God, to whom after satiating themselves, they will give thanks. Only thus, by preserving for men some of the worldly joys, will you lead them thus more easily to relish the joys of the spirit."

The statement above is evidence of how myth and ritual were manipulated by the early Christians to turn people towards the orthodox Christian doctrine, myth and rituals by forcing people to call their existing myths and rituals Christian. When the Roman Empire took control of Egypt, the Egyptian religion spread throughout the Roman Empire. However, later on, when Christianity took hold in Rome, the Ancient Egyptian religion and other mystical religions became an obstacle to the Christian Church which had developed divergent ideas about spirituality, and also to the Roman government which sought to consolidate the empire under Rome. Also, the plagiarized adoption of the Ancient Egyptian symbols, traditions and holidays could not be effective if there were living Ancient Egyptian Priests and Priestesses to tell and show the truth about the origins of those symbols, traditions and holidays. Further, in Ancient Egypt, religion served to refer people to Egypt as well as to mystical spiritual practice. In short, Christianity could not survive as a cult among many other more ancient religions, so it was necessary to dispose of the competition. The most politically expedient way to do this was to close all mystical religious temples.

At the end of the fourth century A.C.E. the Roman emperor, Theodosius, decreed that all religions except Christianity were to be stopped, and that all forms of Christianity besides that of the "Byzantine throne" would also cease to exist. During this time The Temple of Isis (Aset) at Philae in Upper Egypt (deep south of Egypt) temporarily escaped the enforcement of the decree. Consequently, the hieroglyphic inscriptions of this Temple, dated at 394 A.C.E., are the last known Ancient Egyptian hieroglyphs to be recorded. Also, the last demotic inscriptions there date to 452 A.C.E. It was not until the sixth century A.C.E. that Emperor Justinian entered a second decree that effectively stopped all mystical religious practices in the Roman Empire. This means that not only were the Mystery schools and temples to be closed, but also all forms of mystical Christianity which did not agree with the style of Christianity espoused in Rome were to be abolished. Therefore, the Gnostic Christians (Christians who practiced mystical Christianity), were persecuted and their churches rededicated to Roman Catholicism. Much of their writings (Gnostic Coptic) were destroyed. Thus, it is evident that the Ancient Egyptian teachings were being practiced and taught well into the Christian era.

## Theoretical Methodology for the Comparison of Cultures and their Categories of Manifestation

> A myth in its pristine state is by definition specific to a given human environment. How it fares from then on (its "life;' "afterlife'" survival, transposition, revival, rediscovery, or whatever) is a matter of historical accident. It follows that the study of any specific past body of myth has to be mainly a historical discipline employing written sources, whereas contemporary myth can be pursued by the methods of field anthropology. [113]

In the book *Comparative Mythology,* (quoted above), the author introduced certain formats for the study of comparative mythology, beginning with the premise that a myth is "specific to a given human environment." If human environment is taken to mean culture, then it follows that the study of myth needs to be carried out within the context of the culture, using the parameters of the culture. In other words, the myth needs to be studied using objective standards of universal cultural principles but from the perspective of someone living in the culture and not as an outsider. The use of objective standards refers to having a basis for cultural comparisons and is not to be understood here as objectivity. That is, a student of myth, for example, needs to practice and live the myth, to be part of the myth. Only in this way will the myth be fully understood. Otherwise, there will be a superimposition of outside cultural bias from the researcher or student on the myth being studied. This is one of the most difficult problems for any scientist to overcome, how to fully understand the object of study without projecting the researcher's biases

---

[113] *Comparative Mythology,* Jaan Puhvel

on the phenomenon being studies. The usual logic in Western scientific methodology is to strive for "objectivity."

Modern science has now accepted that research examining or studying "physical reality" cannot exist outside of the person conducting the experiments. An older theory held that the person conducting the experiment could be considered separate and apart from the phenomena being observed. Modern science now holds that nature and all phenomena occur because of an experimenter's ability to conceptualize the phenomena and to interpret it. Therefore, the observer is inevitably part of the phenomena being observed. Consequently, modern science now uses a new term for the experimenter. The new term is *Participant.* Thus, the experimenter is really a participant in the experiment because his or her consciousness conceives, determines, perceives, interprets and understands it. No experiment or observed phenomena in nature can occur without someone to conceive that something is happening, determine that something is happening, perceive that something is happening (through instruments or the senses), and finally to interpret what has happened and to understand that interpretation.

Since everything in the universe is connected at some underlying level and since human existence and human consciousness is dependent upon relationships in order to function, then it follows that objectivity is not a realistic attitude for most human beings, including scientists. The only way to achieve objectivity is to transcend "human" consciousness. That is, one must extricate one's egoistic vision of life, which is based on the limitations of the mind and senses, by discovering one's "transcendental" nature. This grants one the experience of knowing the true, unchanging and unaffected nature and essence of existence beyond the limited capacities of the mind and senses. In this capacity one can temporarily identify with the object, any object of study, and achieve a complete knowledge of the subject. This capacity has been the legacy of science and the mystical disciplines, for concentration on any subject is the key to discovering the nature of that subject. However, the mystical disciplines go a step beyond in allowing the scientists to discover their essential nature as one with the object of study. Therefore, mystical training is indispensable in the study of any subject and the acquisition of the knowledge of the essential nature of a subject or object.

This form of philosophy, described above, is antithetical to the orthodox practice of the "scientific method" but until the scientific method is adjusted to incorporate the training of the mystical disciplines, the knowledge gained from the sciences will be limited to the capacities of the logical mind and senses as well as the technological instruments that may be devised to extend the range of those limited, and therefore illusory, human abilities. So the historical and field anthropology[114] disciplines of study should be guided by the mystical experience.

When comparing two given cultures, we are not only concerned with the superficial aspects of their cultural expression, but also the underlying foundations of these. The fundamental core of any culture is its outlook or philosophy on life. This underlying philosophy is the strongest influence giving rise to the varied forms of cultural expression just as the many leaves and branches of a tree arise from a seed (common origin). The mystical philosophy of a given culture is translated by the sages and saints of that culture into an easily understandable and transmittable myth using the cultural factors available to them within that particular culture. Therefore, a sage in Ancient Egyptian culture may espouse a teaching using metaphors particular to Ancient Egyptian culture while a Christian sage may espouse the same teaching while using a different cultural metaphor which is particular to Christian culture. The myth is supported and sustained by the plots and story-lines of the folklore of the particular culture. Next, it is supported by the rituals and traditions associated with them. The rituals and traditions are supported by the combined factors of cultural expression including: architecture, iconography, artifacts and ritual objects (amulets, etc.), spiritual scriptures, language, form and function of objects produced by the culture, etc. Thus, when there is an overwhelming number and quality of synchronicities (matching category-factors of cultural expression) between the factors of expression in two cultures, a commonality in their underlying philosophies will also be discovered.

Through studies based on the factors and parameters listed above, it has been possible to show that there are at least four main world religions that have a strong basis in a common origin which transcends the cursory or superficial levels of similarity. These traditions are the Ancient Egyptian, Ancient Greek, Hindu, Buddhist and Judeo-Christian. I have already presented in-depth explorations of the Ancient Egyptian/Greek connection in my book *African Dionysus From Egypt to Greece* and the Ancient Egyptian/Judeo-Christian connection in my book *The Mystical Journey From Jesus to Christ* and the Ancient Egyptian/Hindu/Buddhist correlations in the book *Egypt and India* as well as an overall comprehensive volume *The African Origins of Civilization, Religion, Yoga and Ethics Philosophy*. Through these kinds of studies, it is possible to bring unity to seemingly disparate and conflicting points of view which lead to dissent, disagreement and misunderstanding that are based on ignorance, adherence to dogma and cultural-theological pride[115] and orthodoxy, instead of the deeper nature and purpose of culture which is to allow human beings to interact with the world and lead them to spiritual

---

[114] The scientific study of the origin, the behavior, and the physical, social, and cultural development of human beings.

[115] The belief that one's own culture is primary and superior to other cultures.

enlightenment. By such studies it is possible to lead open-minded people to understand the purpose of religion and to discover the value of all traditions which are ultimately seeking to accomplish the same task, to bring harmony, peace and order to the world and to allow human beings of all cultures to discover the supreme and essential nature of existence.

## The Standard for Determining Whether or Not a Correlation Between two Cultures is Present

Determining an objective standard for any critical study is an enormously difficult task since the human mind is ultimately what must be satisfied in a particular judgment. That is, when we are trying to determine some kind of rule or guideline to follow which will lead to an unbiased conclusion, the mind of the observer, with his/her preconceived notions, desires, leanings, etc., comes into play, and what one person may consider reasonable, another may regard as groundless. For example, a person may think a color is especially suited for a particular room while another person may say that that color is exactly the opposite of what should be used. Who is right? Well, in this question there is an arbitrary, aesthetic factor which draws upon a person's particular upbringing, particular experiences, particular education, etc. Another example seen often in modern culture is a situation where one person sees a business opportunity as clear as day, while others do not. That person will later capitalize on that opportunity. Was the opportunity there all along or was it a coincidence? In addition, we recognize factors in life that cannot be objectively proven, and yet we "know" they exist. There is a transcendental reality about them that we recognize. When that businessperson, with their training and intuition, spots an opportunity, they perceive it and register it as a reality. In this manner, scientists using training, data collection and intuition in order to "discern" the underlying truth of myths, can discover the correlating factors between cultures. Nonetheless, in the study of science, one would expect the process to be more "objective," being "either right or wrong," but even in the sciences, the ego and its prejudices can impinge on reason.

So what kind of standard can be used to discern between coincidences and synchronous correlations between cultures? Any standard to be used must be based on verifiable evidence and logical analysis, but also on reason. However, if unreasonable people review the evidence, no amount of evidence will suffice, because their minds are already prejudiced. There is often much confusion and conflict in the world due to disagreements and misunderstandings. Many have cited the lack of reason as a primary cause of human conflict. But what is reason? The following dictionary and encyclopedic definitions may provide some guidance on the meaning of "reason".

**reason: 1** to think logically about; think out systematically; analyze **2** to argue, conclude, or infer: now usually with a clause introduced by *that* as the object **3** to support, justify, etc. with reasons **4** to persuade or bring by reasoning.

**reasoning:** (-i ) *n.* **1** the drawing of inferences or conclusions from known or assumed facts; use of reason **2** the proofs or reasons resulting from this.

**in reason.** With good sense or justification; reasonably. **Within reason:** Within the bounds of good sense or practicality.

In the context of the definitions above, reason is that faculty in human consciousness wherein two minds can arrive at a conclusion that is within the bounds of practical reality based on known or assumed facts which justify or support the conclusions drawn. But how is it possible for people to apply those standards and draw rational or reasonable conclusions? Certainly, maturity in life and qualitative experience in human interactions, (i.e. based on honesty, truth, righteousness, justice and universal love) scholarship and balance in life are prerequisites for promoting soundness of the intellect and an understanding of reality within the sphere of human interactions and social intercommunications. In order to promote social order and harmony, the ancient disciplines of righteousness, known as Maat in Kamit and Dharma in India, for example, were devised. This shows that from ancient times, the necessity of promoting reason (ability to think and act by truth) as a mental faculty, in the philosophical disciplines as in government, was understood and appreciated.

**From Ancient Egyptian Hermetic Philosophy**

"Though all men suffer fated things, those led by reason (guided by the Higher Intellect), do not endure suffering with the rest; but since they've freed themselves from viciousness, not being bad, they do not suffer bad. Though having thought fornication or murder but not having committed these, the Mind-led man will suffer just as though he had committed fornication, and though he be no murderer, as though he had committed murder, because there was will to commit these things."[116]

---

[116] *Egyptian Proverbs* by Dr. Muata Ashby

## From Gita: Chapter 2: Samkhya Yogah--The Yoga of Knowledge

> "63. From anger there arises delusion, from delusion loss of memory, from loss of memory one loses the function of pure reason, and from the loss of reason one heads towards destruction."[117]

Reasoning involves objectivity and detachment. The parties must strive to pursue truth as opposed to proving a point for their own ends. The highest and best way to promote truth is to promote humility and effacement of the egoistic nature. Also, there should be deference to evidence and logic as opposed to argument and supposition or emotion. These failings are the sources of partisanship, fanaticism and disagreement. Reasoning should follow logical thinking, and logical thinking should be based on evidence. Thereby the conclusions drawn from evidences and rational thinking about those evidences will receive the correct (reasonable) weight. In this way, the misconceived notions, misjudgments, biases and desires of the deeper aspects of the personality will not impinge on the faculty of reason. Then such a person will be able to reason with other reasonable persons and arrive at reasonable conclusions or courses of action. So while defining "reason" is an abstract endeavor, certainly mature persons can rationally understand that it is a reality in principle. Life, culture and civilization cannot exist in the absence of reason, for even when there is internal disagreement with a decision or course of action, reasonable people understand they must place their personal desires aside for the collective good, or they must simply realize that other people deserve equal consideration. That is, even in arguments where two individuals may disagree, there can be an objective resolution of the disagreement. One or both parties may choose to refrain from allowing animosity to develop and to remain patient until an answer emerges from the situation or question itself, while in the mean time assisting in the development of stronger arguments which are supportable over time until the validity or invalidity of a conclusion may no longer be avoided. The calmness of a mind unfettered by emotion and desire, a hallmark of a well-adjusted self-realized human being, allows a person to disagree with a conclusion while maintaining respect for the person advancing it. This allows people to live together and organize in order to work together.

So, for the purposes of this section, as throughout this book, the opinions of scholars will not be used in place of actual evidences or if the conclusions of scholars are used they will be supported by evidences, and

---

[117] Bhagavad Gita by Swami Jyotirmayananda

"reasonable arguments" related to those evidences. In this manner, it is hoped that the discussion will be elevated to the determination of the evidences as opposed to debates over the bias of the scholars and their opinions. There are certain valid conclusions that can be drawn from the totality of evidences; these will be presented separately as summaries, conclusions or epilogues.

## Methodology for the Comparisons Between Cultures in Order to Determine the Correlations Between Cultures

The methodology for understanding mythology and its purpose, which has been presented in the previous section as well as those which will follow, present myth and metaphor as abstract principles that manifest through cultural factors in the form of recurrent themes. While these are subject to some interpretation, the possibility for bias becomes reduced as the associated factors add up to support the original conjecture about the particular factor being compared. In other words, *single event proposed correlations* (solitary or individual correlations) between cultural factors that are alleged but not yet proven or supported) between cultures can often be explained away as coincidences. However, when those correlations are supported by related factors or when those correlations are present in the framework of other correlations, then the position of bias or simple disbelief is less tenable. The basis for the objective standard will be set forth in the following logical principles which indicate congruence between the two cultural factors. In order to study and compare the Ancient Egyptian and Indian cultures, we will make use of the categories of cultural expression.

As explained earlier, in determining the common elements of different religions, there are several factors that can be used as criteria to determine whether or not cultures had common origins. If cultures are related, they will use common stories or other common factors or patterns to express the main doctrines of the religion or spiritual path, social philosophy, etc. These are listed below. Before proceeding to the items being compared, the criteria used to compare them must be understood. The following section introduces the categories of cultural expression factors and some subdivisions within them.

# The Possible Standards for Use in Determining the Correlations Between Cultures

Clifford Geertz, a prominent anthropologist, stressed that in the study of religion, as an aspect of culture, it is necessary to investigate beneath superficial meanings. The symbols (i.e., words, behavior/gestures, objects or events), are as if coverings beyond which there is a deeper meaning. Geertz called that deeper meaning their "thick description."[118] He also felt that "The thing to ask [of actions] is what their import is..."[119]

Anthropologists and sociologist attempted to follow the scientific method of the physical and natural sciences when researching in anthropology and sociology. In doing so they encountered many difficulties since humans are not machines but entities that exist in the physical world as physical forms but which also have other less discernible aspects and motivations. Even though he was influenced by Max Weber, a prominent sociologist who promoted the idea that human beings themselves create their realities, Clifford Geertz argued that there should be more humanistic hermeneutic scientific approach, a "softer"[120] science, for studies in the human sciences, such as sociology and anthropology. (Note: Highlighted {underlined} portions are by Ashby)

"Believing, with Max Weber, that man is an animal suspended in webs of significance he himself has spun. I take culture to be those webs, and the analysis of it to be therefore not an experimental science in search of law but an interpretive one in search of meaning."[121]

"The notion of what science is both varies from discipline to discipline and changes in time, and the attempt to make a simple distinction between what is legitimately rigorous and objective and what is soft and stupid is a dichotomy or dualism that could stand a little poststructural analysis. I really think we should deconstruct this dichotomy and be done with it. Much of the worst misunderstanding of my work comes from people who are trapped in that conceptual framework.... I'm speaking of the notion that, for example, literature is one thing and science is another, that they are eternally different, that they don't change, that they mean the same thing in any field. When I resist

---

[118] Geertz, Clifford. The Interpretation of Cultures. P. 3-30. Basic Books, Inc., USA. 1973
Pals, Daniel L. Eight Theories of Religion. P. 267, Oxford University Press, 2006, NY.
[119] Geertz, Clifford. The Interpretation of Cultures. P. 10. Basic Books, Inc., USA. 1973
[120] ibid
[121] Geertz, Clifford. The Interpretation of Cultures. P. 5. Basic Books, Inc., USA. 1973.

these notions, and when I resist the imposition by anthropologists (not by physicists) of hard science notions on anthropology where I think they're inapplicable, or where they don't even work, I'm often interpreted as being anti-science or unrigorous. And I think that's just wrong…But when critics divide the world into real scientists and real (or "unreal," usually) humanists and decide that this gulf is an absolute-the two-cultures notion- I think that all of what I do and a good deal of what other people in the social sciences do just drops through the cracks because it's a *third* culture, a *different* sort of thing. Many of these critics really have yet to grasp that, and when they don't grasp it then they misread. Because they see a departure from what they learned, they make distinctions between explanation and understanding that really are not sustainable.…and, therefore, misread both the intentions of my work and, indeed often enough, what is actually said on the page. [122]

## The Scientific Method for Studying Correlations Between Cultures

"Scientific Method, general logic and procedures common to all the physical and social sciences, which may be outlined as a series of steps: (1) stating a problem or question; (2) forming a hypothesis (possible solution to the problem) based on a theory or rationale; (3) experimentation (gathering empirical data bearing on the hypothesis); (4) interpretation of the data and drawing conclusions; and (5) revising the theory or deriving further hypotheses for testing. Putting the hypothesis in a form that can be empirically tested is one of the chief challenges to the scientist. In addition, all of the sciences try to express their theories and conclusions in some quantitative form and to use standardized testing procedures that other scientists could repeat."[123]

Many Western scholars adhere to the "Scientific Method" of research. This concept originated in Western Culture for the study of nature, to determine the criteria for what can be accepted as truth. The definition

---

[122] http://jac.gsu.edu/jac/11.2/Articles/geertz.htm (1991) Clifford Geertz on Ethnography and Social Construction by GARY A. OLSON
[123] Random House Encyclopedia Copyright (C) 1983,1990

above provides the step by step procedures accepted in the Western conception of a scientific method. It is further defined and contrasted from philosophy by the Encarta Encyclopedia as *(highlighted portions (italics) by Dr. Ashby)*:

> "Scientific Method, term denoting the principles that guide scientific research and experimentation, and also the philosophic bases of those principles. Whereas philosophy in general is concerned with the why as well as the how of things, science occupies itself with the latter question only. Definitions of scientific method use such concepts as objectivity of approach to and acceptability of the results of scientific study. Objectivity indicates the attempt to observe things as they are, without falsifying observations to accord with some preconceived worldview. Acceptability is judged in terms of the degree to which observations and experimentations can be reproduced. *Such agreement of a conclusion with an actual observation does not itself prove the correctness of the hypothesis from which the conclusion is derived.* It simply renders the premise that much more plausible. The ultimate test of the validity of a scientific hypothesis is its consistency with the totality of other aspects of the scientific framework. This inner consistency constitutes the basis for the concept of causality in science, according to which every effect is assumed to be linked with a cause."[124]

## Refutation of Conclusions arrived at through the Scientific Method

Conversely, if one attempts to show that a scientific conclusion is wrong, it is necessary to:

(1) show a misconception or wrongly stated a problem or question;
(2) show that the hypothesis (possible solution to the problem) based on a theory or rationale is incorrect;
(3) show that the experimentation (gathering empirical data bearing on the hypothesis) is biased or being carried out in an incorrect way;
(4) show that the process for interpreting the data and drawing conclusions has not followed a logical procedure or is biased;
(5) show that the revising process of the theory or deriving further hypotheses for testing is needed.

---

[124] "Scientific Method," Microsoft (R) Encarta. Copyright (c) 1994

(6) show that the experiment is not consistent with the totality of other aspects of the scientific framework.

(7) show evidences that contradict the conclusion.

(8) show more evidences to prove other conclusions than what have been presented to advance the other unreasonable conclusion.

## The Limitations of the Scientific Method and the study of Cultures and Religions -Part 1

### What are the soul and the mind and can western science be used to discover their mysteries?

There are several Para-psychological studies that have been done related to this the existence of and the passing of the soul when the body dies. One has detected an infinitesimal decrease in the weight of the body after death which may indicate that an aspect of the personality, the soul, has left the body. As for mind, we may consider that mind is composed of subtle elements and energies. Those elements are the subtle part of air, water, fire, ether, which compose the periodic table of elements, etc. Thus if after death we have an intact body that is not animated with less weight than the living animated body then we should conclude that the lacking part is the animating part, that is, the mind part of the personality. However, I would add that there is an aspect of mind that cannot be measured by any physical scale. Also, modern quantum physics science has demonstrated that some matter goes into and out of existence (time and space).

Since modern Western science operates as an ethnocentric scientific system, as Edgerton explains, the Western scientific method is limited and may be erroneous and unacceptable to evaluate data based in other cultures or subcultures, such as Neterian, Hindu, Buddhist and other religions not based in western culture. In his 1992 book, *Sick Societies: Challenging the Myth of Primitive Harmony* the author, Robert B. Edgerton writes: (Note: Highlighted {underlined} portions are by Ashby)

> "…not only is each culture unique unto itself, but people's thoughts, feelings and motivations are radically different from one culture to another. It follows then that any attempt to generalize about either culture or human nature must be false or trivial unless it is confined to people who live in a specific cultural system. As these relativists have said, it necessarily follows that if peoples' minds vary so much from one culture to another, Western science is only a culturally specific form of

ethnoscience, not a universally valid way of verification or falsification. In this perspective, a person from another culture remains the "Other," forever incomprehensible."[125]

The modern scientific approach is also contrary to western science in earlier times, when it was considered to be a branch of philosophy and based on or influenced by the works of Plato and his student, Aristotle,[126] the former having spent extended time in Ancient Egypt.[127]

> "Attention was directed to the final end and not to the detailed process of change from moment to moment...Greek and medieval science were primarily deductive (starting from necessary general principles and reasoning to particular exemplifications of those principles) rather than inductive (starting from particular observations and generalizing from them). This preference for deductive logic was closely related to the classical idea, particularly prominent in Plato, that knowledge is contemplation of the perfect forms of eternal truth rather than observation of their imperfect embodiment in the changing world. The goal was not primarily, as in modern science, the description, prediction, and control of a limited phenomenon but rather the understanding and contemplation of the meaning of the part in relation to the whole and to God."[128]

The Western scientific concept of a detached observer is unrealistic and also limiting. In any experiment, it is not possible for the observer (person conducting the experiment) to have complete separation or detachment; the observer is always part of the experiment and interacting with the object being studied. Therefore, the detached observer idea is illusory and therefore unworkable, as Dr. Arthur Deikman explains:

> Not only is this ideal of the objective observer theoretically impossible, and seldom achieved, but large areas of human experience require the investigator to be personally involved in the phenomena in question, since description cannot convey them.[129]

---

[125] http://newcriterion.com/archives/lead-article/10/geertz-windschuttle/

[126] Barbou, Ian G. Religion and Science. P. 5, 1997 HarperSanFrancisco, NY, NY.

[127] , Muata A. The African Origins of Civilization, Religion, Yoga Mystical Spirituality and Ethics Philosophy. p. 112. Sema Institute of Yoga, 2002.

[128] Barbou, Ian G. Religion and Science. P. 5, 1997 HarperSanFrancisco, NY, NY.

[129] Deikman, Arthur J, M.D., The Observing Self – Mysticism and Psychotherapy. P 20; 1982 Becon Press, Boston MA

Thus, the practitioner of mysticism or full religion (in its three stages) is the scientist and the object of study at the same time; yet, this arrangement need not invalidate the scientific basis and repeatability of the study:

> The mystic scientist becomes his own subject and his own consciousness in his data. Again, such an approach would seem to be quite unscientific, judging by the usual image of the scientist as a detached, objective recorder of publicly observable phenomena. That image, however, is more fantasy than reality. We know that observers are never detached in the sense of not influencing the subject of investigation. Einstein showed decisively that in measuring time and space, the observer includes himself in the measurement...[130]

The arrogance or blind acceptance of the idea that science, as it has been defined in western culture, is the only way to discover truth or reality ignores the most fundamental issue related to science itself, that there is no scientific proof that science is the only way to discover truth. This was the point made by Nobel laureate Alfred North Whitehead who said that *'This position on the part of scientist was pure bluff.' After all, if someone claims that science alone can provide valid data, then one is entitled to ask, 'what is your scientific proof of this?' The answer is 'None.'*

Societies that attain a great measure of material wealth and "scientific knowledge" like Western society, enter into a self delusion that theirs is the only true way of life and others are incorrect or primitive and therefore of lesser value. This acts as a catalyst for hubristic feelings and hegemonic tendencies in the society that exacerbate the greed, fascism and dictatorship elements within the culture that characterize their relationships with other countries and manifests through political and economic systems such as colonialism, imperialism and globalization.

Further, science is deficient because it itself and the world it purports to define are illusory in n and of themselves. In nature everything is changeable based on circumstances and based on yet unknown factors. In any case, the scientific or logical proof of any phenomena is deficient if the instruments of measuring are limited. For example, can a person smell a person a mile away? A dog can, why can't the person? The dog can because their senses are less limited, relative to yours. Likewise you cannot expect science to have all answers or for all phenomena to be explainable through science. Science can describe life processes of a cell but cannot explain why the cell lives. What is the value of science then?

---

[130] Ibid p 19

Every year scientists have to change their understanding of the body or of the universe and new text books need to be revised; if science has the definitive answers why the need for changes all the time? While science is not an absolute determiner of physical reality it can be a tool to describe and manipulate some of its aspects. For example, science cannot be used to understand history but can be used to explain dates of relative historical events to help us understand their context. Science cannot create life but can manipulate it in many cases, to extend or reduce it. So asking science to prove the existence of the soul and God is like asking a man to smell dinner from a mile away. Yet the scientific application of certain spiritual disciplines can allow a man, a sage to perceive realities that are beyond the grasp of the gross physical sciences. This is the science of the mysteries, mysticism that opens the mind to higher realities and self-discovery.

Science is an indirect means to perceive reality since it works with instruments and experiments in a universe that even quantum physicists now acknowledge is only an outer appearance of a deeper energetic reality beyond the senses, like an iceberg, with its greater vastness hidden below the unintelligible surface of the unfathomable waters. The "truth" revealed through the mysteries, the mystical philosophy, occurs through training the mind to discover and understand reality through inductive reasoning (reasoning from detailed facts to general principles)[131] and deductive reasoning (reasoning from the general to the particular (or from cause to effect).[132] Those who study mathematical principles, such as those presented in Geometry, already are practiced in this mental training. In *Logic & Mathematics* the transitive principle allows expansion of knowledge from the known to the unknown. Transitivity here means: of or relating to a relationship between three elements such that if the relationship holds between the first and second elements and between the second and third elements, it necessarily holds between the first and third elements.[133] These disciplines of reasoning, when understood and applied properly to the studies of history, nature, human psychology, religion, spirituality and mysticism then lead to direct perception of the higher reality through intuitional realization of the truth, which surpasses all indirect means. So science is the beginning of true knowledge by providing workable though conditional, facts upon which to base correct reasoning. Science is not an end in itself but a tool through which correct reasoning may be developed for correctly understanding reality.

---

[131] *WordNet® 2.1, © 2005 Princeton University*
[132] *ibid*
[133] *The American Heritage® Dictionary of the English Language, Fourth Edition Copyright © 2000*

## Part 2: The Scientific Method, Yoga Mysticism and Mystical Religion

The scientific method is an attempt to remove ambiguity from the body of human knowledge and the means by which knowledge is added to the storehouse of human learning. The problem with this method of gathering knowledge is that it necessarily receives information only from empirical evidences. However, as the great scientist Einstein and the modern day quantum physicists have proven, Creation is not absolute or absolutely empirical. Creation is composed of variables wherein some aspects operate in different ways under different circumstances. This is why the concept of cause and effect is also flawed. Ignorance of the mystical law of cause and effect known as the law of *Ari* in Ancient Egyptian philosophy and Karma in Indian philosophy, leads scientists to seek for causes or reasons for what they see in nature, somewhere within the confines of the time and space of the event in question. In reference to Yoga and mystical religion, as concerns people and their actions, mostly, what is occurring today, in a person's life could be a result of what happened in a previous lifetime (philosophy of reincarnation-already proven in parapsychology experiments).[134] As concerns nature, what occurs today is sustained by the Transcendental Essence, i.e. Supreme Being. Further, the observers, the scientists themselves, and the very perception of these experiments are factors in the experiments and are therefore, factors in the results. This is where the problem of skewing of the results and interpretations of results based on conscious or unconscious prejudices or misconceptions comes in, that is, the problem of "falsifying observations to accord with some preconceived worldview."

As the modern discipline of Quantum Physics has shown, nature itself is not what it appears. It is not solid and distinct but rather interrelated energies in varied forms of expression. Physics experiments have shown that matter is not solid as it appears but that it is rather, energy in different forms of manifestation. So the instruments used to discern reality, the logical conditioned mind, and the limited senses, are inadequate for discriminating between what is real and what is unreal. The fallacy of believing in the absolute authority of science is evident in the inability of science to discover anything that is absolute. Something absolute is unchangeable in the beginning, middle and end. Every decade medical science makes "new breakthroughs." This means that they are discovering something "new" which supersedes their previous knowledge. This necessarily means that the previous knowledge was conditional and imperfect and therefore flawed and illusory. Thus, science has its value, but it is not to be considered a reliable source for truth or as a substitute for the disciplines of self-knowledge. So, only a mind that has been trained in

---

[134] for evidences see the book *The Conscious Universe: The Scientific truth of Psychic Phenomena* By Dean Radin, Ph. D.

transcendental thinking and intuitional realization can discover "truth." Yoga and mystical religion are spiritual sciences that promote the cultivation of the higher faculties of the mind. The mystics of Yoga the world over have for thousands of years proclaimed that the mystical reality which is to be discovered through the disciplines of Yoga and Mystical religion is the same Absolute essence which has always sustained Creation and all existence, including human consciousness. It is the same essence that was discovered by Imhotep and other Sages of Kamit, the Upanishadic Sages of India, Buddha, Jesus, etc., and it is the same absolute reality that can be discovered by anyone today or in the future, who applies the teachings of Yoga and Mystical religion.

So, the idea of the objective observer or that only experimental results which can bring forth repeatable results or parameters that show "consistency with the totality of other aspects of the scientific framework" are valid is sometimes contradictory with respect to nature and logic. Nature is not a machine and even if it were to be treated as such it is not a machine for which the parts are all known and understood. There is an aspect of nature that transcends empirical observation; it must be intuited. This aspect of nature is ignored by the scientific method, by its own bindings, and therefore, the ability to use science as a tool to discover truth, is limited. Since the world is variable (relative), then it follows that any "scientific" data obtained from experiments will also be relative and variable. It is useful within the framework of science, but not beyond that framework. In other words, it cannot be used to ascertain anything about realities outside of its framework. This is why philosophy is an important tool of science. It allows the intuitive faculty of the mind to be cultivated and directed towards discovering the aspects of nature that no physical testing equipment can penetrate.

The world is not to be discerned through the intellect because the intellect is also limited. It cannot comprehend the totality of Creation. However, by intuitional (knowing that transcends the thought process) reasoning through transcendence of the relativity of nature, it is possible to discover that absolute reality which is common, and therefore uniform in its *"consistency with the totality"* of human and spiritual experience. The problem is that this aspect of existence can only be approached through a scientific application of philosophical principles and disciplines that can provide results only in the mind of an individual. The Western scientific community shuns this approach, likening it to primitive and unscientific speculations. By ignoring the "why" of things, as the definition of the scientific method above suggests, the scientific method is cutting itself off from the source of knowledge, and looking only at its effect, the "what," and then accepting this as a basis to discern reality. It is like experimenting on the sunrays, neglecting to notice the sun, but extrapolating from the limited experiments and making assertions about what the sun is. In like manner, science looks at nature and notices the relativity, but does not allow itself to explore the mystical-spiritual dimensions of cause. Rather, it seeks to ascribe factors within the realm of the flawed relative field of Creation itself, as the reason behind existence. In fact, for all the knowledge that Western Culture has amassed, in reality there is perhaps no more important knowledge than that which has been recently derived from Quantum Physics, because these clearly point to a transcendental essence of Creation.[135 / 136/137]

Western Culture's adherence to the "Scientific Method" has turned it away from the science of self-development (myth, religion and yoga mysticism) since it (spiritual evolution) cannot be proven empirically according to its current criteria as different people are at different stages of evolution and the process may require many lifetimes to complete. Here again, even the parameters set by Western Culture as the procedures of the "Scientific Method" are not being followed. The statement that there is no science beyond the existential aspect of Creation is in effect a violation of the "scientific" rule of objectivity to *"observe things as they are, without falsifying observations to accord with some preconceived world view."* The predilection to discount the transcendent as "un-provable" is a worldview which typifies Western Culture. Thus, the objectivity in the scientific method has at least two built in flaws. First, is the insistence on determining scientific fact based on evidence that can be observable to the physical senses with or without assistance from technology, and therefore can only exist in time and space. Secondly, the necessity for human standards in determining *"conclusions"* based on the data, for it has been shown that the same data can lend itself to different interpretations based on conflicting views, even within the scientific community. A true scientific method should require an objective standard which cannot be violated by the whims of the observers or scientists and is not bound or circumscribed by the requirement of having to be examined within the confines of time and space or scientifically observable reality. Its conclusions must be accepted and not refuted by opinions or desires to uphold particular worldviews. However, again, all of the best standards will be useless if the scientists are biased.

A further connotation, prevalent in Western Culture arising from adherence to the "scientific method" is that what is transcendent is imagined, superstition and unfounded illusion, and only what the "Scientific Method" deems as provable is correct and acceptable. Hence, since myth and mysticism are in the realm of the transcendent, then by this type of Western logic it follows that they are also un-provable and unreal. This is a very powerful argument that further develops into the most dangerous concept, that Western Culture is the determiner of what is truth and that the art, culture, science and religion, etc., of other cultures, past or

---

[135] *Memphite Theology*, Muata Ashby
[136] *The Tao of Physics*, Fritjof Capra
[137] *Dancing Wu Li Masters* by Gary Zukov

present, are inferior due to their primitive and "unscientific" manner of approaching nature.

## Applying the Scientific Principles and Procedures to the study Mysticism and its Practitioners

The application of scientific principles and procedures in mystical philosophy can and should be accomplished in the following manner. Firstly, a theory that the Supreme Being exists, for instance, can be developed. Now the experiment is to see how the practice of certain myths, rituals and mystical exercises (technologies) affect the personality. Then the practitioner must insightfully look within, with the assistance of expert practitioners, and see if there are any changes in the personality, and if there is anything emerging within their consciousness that transcends the personality. The scientific premise, that observable and repeatable results should be obtained, is to be understood as the result of an intuitional realization or recognition of higher (expanded) consciousness in the individual practitioners.

So, while it is possible to show many illustrations and iconographical correlations in the scientific comparison of two forms of myth, the ultimate realization of the truth behind these is to be achieved in the understanding of the observer. The mystical scriptures have long held that if this procedure is followed, any person can discover the transcendental essence of Self. This is the scientific formula for Enlightened Sagehood or Sainthood, which mystical philosophy holds to be the only goal in and purpose of life. Thus, from ancient times, the Yogic and other authentic Mystical systems have defined themselves as sciences, since the proper application of the correct philosophy, disciplines and principles of living leads to the same results of spiritual awakening in all human beings who apply them.

Due to the uniqueness of each person, when dealing with human beings, there are variables in the degree of understanding and practice. Thus, in evaluating students of the Yogic and other Mystical sciences (spiritual aspirants or initiates), the results of spiritual practices cannot be assessed in terms of an all or nothing equation or within a given time frame or situation, since evolution is occurring even when outwardly there appears to be a backward movement.

Also, spiritual evolution occurs over a long period of time encompassing many lifetimes. So these results cannot necessarily be seen in the form of ordinary data obtained in ordinary time frames, but other criteria may be used to evaluate them: a calmer personality, a human being who is expanding in consciousness, discovering the inner depths of consciousness and the universality of life, increasing contentment and fearlessness, a stronger will, and magnanimousness, wisdom and inner fulfillment. Some of these evidences cannot be put on paper, and yet they can be experienced just as the message of a painting or the love of a relative can be intuited and felt, but not explained, quantified, qualified or proven to others but yet it can be felt (experienced).

From time immemorial, the sages and saints of all world traditions have maintained the initiatic principles and technologies, the mystical philosophy and art of spiritual culture that has been handed down through time. It has been found that when human beings are properly instructed and when they engage in certain disciplines of Yoga and mystical culture, they develop expanded consciousness and spiritual awareness, as well as intuitional realization of the divine presence in a predictable manner.

The correct practice of myth and mystical philosophy in yoga requires a scientific approach, using the personality as the subject, and the mind as the instrument for proving the existence of the transcendent. It is necessary to apply philosophy scientifically, incorporating intuition and spiritual culture when engaging in any study of religion, myth, mysticism, etc.

In a scientific investigation, opinions have no place beyond the stating of the hypothesis. Also, the constraints of social propriety do not apply. For example, it is perfectly scientific to state a theory that the Ancient Egyptians were not black Africans, but rather Asiatics, or that Indian Vedic culture and not Ancient Egyptian culture gave rise to civilization. There is nothing wrong in making those statements. However, if the person stating these ideas wants to put them forth as "facts" or "reality" or consider these ideas as "proven," then a more rigorous process of supporting those ideas must be undertaken. The evidence must be accurate, available to all investigators, and it should be primary and not second-hand conjectures or based on anecdotal evidences. Therefore, the opinions of other scholars, no matter how reputable they may be, must be based on primary evidence, and that evidence cannot be substituted by the scholar's conclusions or opinions about it. Therefore, scholarly dictums[138] are worthless if the scholar cannot or does not support them with evidences. Other terms, often used synonymously in scientific discussions are "postulate" or "axiom."

---

[138] American Heritage Dictionary

An **axiom** is a self-evident or universally recognized truth; a maxim.

A **dictum** is an authoritative, often formal, pronouncement.

A **postulate** is a statement or proposition that is to be assumed to be true without proof and that forms a framework for the derivation of theorems.[139]

Many times scientists or others relying on them treat corollaries as proofs.

A **corollary** is a proposition that follows with little or no proof required from one already proven, A deduction or an inference.[140]

So corollaries, postulates, etc., are also useless in a presentation of scientific findings if unsupported by evidences. They should not even be discussed in a context of making judgments or assigning values on what is being studied because they have no merit. Sometimes merit is placed on dictums or corollaries due to the reputation of a scientist, or for political, social or economic reasons but these have no place in a scientific discussion. Thus, if a scientist is not dispassionate, an unconscious or conscious alternative agenda will be put forth. Further, if no evidence is produced to support a contention, then a scientist might be in danger of appearing biased, promoting a political or social point of view or expressing personal beliefs and sentiments about a particular issue. Over time, they themselves begin to believe in those opinions. This is the power and danger of the human mind.

---

[139] American Heritage Dictionary
[140] American Heritage Dictionary

## What is Reality? And Why is It Important For Society to be Guided by Reality when Constructing and Maintaining its Societal Philosophy?

According to the dictionary definition of "Reality" in *Philosophy* reality is:

A. something that exists independently of ideas concerning it.
B. something that exists independently of all other things and from which all other things derive.[141]

The question of *what is reality?* is important for our study because the disconnection in modern times has left society bereft of effective religious experiences in terms of ancient religious philosophy. Generally, the ancient religious philosophies recognized that the world, and in fact Creation itself, is illusory and temporal, not abiding, yet modern culture seems to tend towards the idea that the material world is The Reality to be concerned with, either for material gains to have pleasure and worldly happiness or for achieving a material heaven after death in order to experience pleasure and happiness. In this sense both are phenomenological pursuits, unlike the mystical and transcendental pursuit of ancient mystical religion. This condition has developed into a disconnection in modern culture between the concept of an Ultimate Reality that is to provide the answers and fulfillment of life and the creation of a philosophy of life that balances the material needs with the spiritual so as to allow a human being to prosper while on earth and achieve the higher essence of life after death.

In modern academia, reality would seem to be based on intellectual argument that can be supported by accumulated evidences. In ancient times reality was a factor of perceivable truths in nature. In academia reality can be created through accumulated weight of worldly evidences or other scholarly opinions. One such opinion especially in the discipline of anthropology is that religion is a worldly construct based on human needs and desires and illusions which has nothing to do with a transcendental reality or anything beyond the realm of time and space; any other ideas about religion are fiction or delusions created by its followers. We must point out here that this dictum about religion and its worth comes from atheists or secularists who only have their "faith" or "belief" in what they or others are saying about religion (opinion) as supports for their arguments. So their position is as untenable as that of the faith-based religious practitioner's. This characterization frames the argument for or

---

[141] *Dictionary.com Unabridged (v 1.1) Based on the Random House Unabridged Dictionary, © Random House, Inc. 2006.*

against religion as being related to anything beyond time and space; it relegates it to a mundane phenomenological argument about faith versus reason with religion being the unreasonable concept if not an outright delusion used by some to control the masses or a practice of self-delusion in the masses. The almost complete takeover of academia by the secular perspective on religion precludes the study of the mystical perspectives of religion.

If we are to discern reality, that reality needs to be abiding because the underlying essence of the world is abiding. Reality is not a timetable or a calendar; a calendar only circumscribes segments of a continuous stream of existence into distinct elements called "time." Time is therefore a human construct and not the natural construct found in Creation, which would be referred to by the mystics as "eternity." Arguments based on worldly experiences or opinions based on worldly logic only relates to and makes use of relative evidences and should therefore be considered limited, conditional, uncertain and therefore invalid as depictions of absolute reality. In other words, such evidences are inconclusive, provisional, contingent, and therefore subordinate. Something real is also abiding and not changeable; otherwise it is ephemeral, fleeting, impermanent, passing, short-lived, temporary, and transient.

If we were to base our knowledge on physics in order to understand the world we would not base it on the physics we find in this planet we live on, the earth, because the physical features of this world are unique. For example, the gravity of this world is not the same as on Mars since Mars is a smaller planet. Yet the universal principles of physics can be applied to calculate the specific *relative* gravity of most planets. So the universal principles of physics are the abiding reality and not the relative physics of any planet.

In the same way, the Ultimate Reality of the universe, according to a mystical philosophical perspective, is underlying universal, all-pervasive consciousness. Now, each individual religion may call that Ultimate Reality by different names, yet the abiding nature remains the same, Ultimate Reality, and the changeable names and religions are the impermanent aspect. Another way to see it is for example, when a chair is made with wood, the tree the wood came from no longer exists but the wood continues to exist in the chair; when the chair is old it can be made into something else or turned into particle board for a table. In this example, the tree, the chair and the table are the relative, impermanent and illusory aspects of reality and the wood itself is the abiding aspect.

# The Cultural Category Factor Correlation Method

Confined by the dictums of the scientific method, a scientist would look at this phenomenon and be unable to see beyond the parameters of an experimental paradigm and see the same matter in different forms but a philosopher would look at this phenomenon and reason that just as the wood is the abiding essence of the forms there is an abiding and transcendental aspect of life and Creation itself beyond forms; there is an abiding reality (Ultimate Reality) and there is also a relative reality. In terms of consciousness, when a mystic explores the inner world of the mind and spirit, he or she discovered that there is a fleeting aspect of the personality and there is also an abiding aspect; the fleeting aspect is like a drop of water and the abiding aspect is like the ocean of all water. Using this metaphor, the drop is the soul and the ocean is all-pervading spirit. So the "truth" about reality is that it needs to be based on something abiding, other wise we would be living in an illusion. This is why the practice of religion (in its full three stage practice) or mysticism and the social foundation being based upon their philosophical outlook is important. Without this discipline we would live life in accordance with illusory and or egoistic desires and delusions or misconceptions about the world. That condition would pervert our capacity to live life with a real chance of achieving abiding happiness and peace. Life would become about competition for resources and not about compassion or caring for others. The Ultimate Reality leads to a philosophy of ethical conscience and compassion or caring for others because in that philosophy there is contained an understanding that if the UR experiences prove the connection between all life and all inanimate existence, then it follows that all life is one and worthy of compassion, justice and love; nature, being part of that network of consciousness deserves caring also.

According to the dictionary definition, "Truth" means: *A.* conformity with fact or reality; verity: *the truth of a statement. B.* a verified or indisputable fact, proposition, principle, or the like: *mathematical truths. C.* agreement with a standard or original.

So "truth" is not conditional; it is based on (agreement with) abiding reality (Ultimate Reality), the "standard or original" and not conditional reality. "IF" what the sages and mystics have discovered is real, then the truth of it should be part of every aspect of society. This idea may be termed the "*societal philosophy*". Thus, any social system (religion, philosophy, government, economics, art, etc.) that is not based on the Ultimate Reality is bogus, illusory and ultimately detrimental to the successful functioning of the society in terms of its sustainability and in reference to the possibility for the success of its individuals in attaining meaningful experiences that will lead to personal fulfillment, happiness and contentment while on earth and or after death. A societal philosophy can be based on the Ultimate Reality, derived from sagely investigations and experiences or on concepts based on egoistic illusions and desires (philosophy of greed, philosophy of pleasure-seeking, philosophy of political power, philosophy of superiority, philosophy of racism, philosophy of sexism, etc.). Religion as well as the secular must both adhere to the mystical axiom that culture should be based on the understanding of the Ultimate Reality and its implications. This means that faith-based religions cannot be considered as reality based systems of spiritual practice if they solely base their religious practice on having faith in God or believing in God. The mystic philosophy leads to a culture of mysticism and humanitarianism and the egoistic illusions lead to cultures of greed, warfare and barbarism.

## How the philosophy of a culture impels, shapes culture and expresses through the cultural factors of that culture:

Culture

7. Form and function of objects and institutions produced by the culture

6. Ritual and Tradition

5. Plots and story-lines of the myth

4. Language (linguistics-phonetics) -Spiritual scriptures

3. Myth

2. Societal outlook based on societal philosophy (Civilized or Barbarous, Humane or Inhumane)

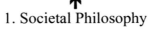

1. Societal Philosophy

150

# Comparative Mythology Approaches, The Factors That Make Cultures Distinct and the Methodology for Comparing Them

In the book *Comparative Mythology,* the author, Jaan Puhvel, introduces two formats or models for the study of comparative mythology, based on the concepts of abstraction and generalization.

> Comparative mythology of separately localized and attested traditions can be practiced on different levels of abstraction and generalization.

> "Universal mythology" is essentially reduced to explaining accordances (and, if relevant, differences or contrasts) by appeal to human universals or at least common denominators based on similarities of psychological patterning, environment, or levels of culture. Needless to say, it has to pursue the typical and usual at the expense of the specific and unique.

> "Diffusionary mythology" studies how traditions travel, charting the spread and transmission of myth. The trouble is precisely that myth does not "travel" very well and, when it does travel, frequently moves from its specific historical and geographical fulcrum into the international realm of legend, folktale, fairy tale, and other debased forms of originally mythical narrative.[142]

While the above author speaks primarily of mythological studies, the ideas are relevant to our study since mythology is an integral if not central aspect of culture. In our study, we will strive to raise the methodology for the comparative cultural study to a high standard that goes beyond the universalistic aspects of culture, that is, those factors that are innate to all human beings from a general perspective to a format based on specific delineated and categorized factors of cultural expression.

The author quoted above also works with the premise that mythology becomes "debased" or degrades due to the changes and additions it experiences over time. While this model occurs and may even be considered as the norm, it is also possible to see a sustained practice of myth and other aspects of culture from one group to the next. However, the deterioration of a myth in the area of plot, that is, the story may lose some aspects from the original, does not necessarily mean that the theme

---

[142] *Comparative Mythology,* Jaan Puhvel

and its import are lost or debased. The determination of any degradation may be made through the comparison of the function and metaphorical significance changes over time in the cultural factors of the cultures being studied. That is, if the function and metaphorical significance of the cultural factors is lost over time, the model above is correct. However, if the function and metaphorical significance of the cultural factors are sustained over time, even if some plot elements are lost, this would tend to indicate a closer correlation between the two cultures due to closer and stronger connection that led to the adoption of the cultural factor.

The closer bond can be expected in the indigenous relationship of a culture with its own legacy. That is, a modern culture can be expected to exhibit a lesser degree of deterioration of indigenous fundamental cultural factors as opposed to those that have been imported (considering the imported ones and the indigenous ones at the same point in time). For example, a culture being exposed to another culture would tend to have a closer bond to its own cultural legacy as opposed to the new culture it is being exposed to. Over time, if the older culture is suppressed or overwhelmed the bond with the indigenous culture can become weaker and the culture may adopt the new cultural traits or co-opt the old ones into the new.

The model presented in ordinary comparative mythology studies is that myth may retained its form but degrade in content. If a sustained (un-degraded) correlation can be demonstrated between two cultures over time (one emerging after the other), then it is possible to maintain that the cultures are not separate and disparate but actually elements of a continuous manifestation of cultural expression. An example of this can be Western culture emerging out of the ruins of the Roman Empire. Western culture retained certain cultural factors including Latin and Christianity. The cultural "form" (Roman architecture, customs, traditions, etc.) were lost but certain essential elements of the content of what was retained continued on. In other words, the two cultures were actually part of one evolving culture.

Another factor to be considered is the concept of a study that works within the framework of different levels of abstraction and generalization. The principles under which this current study of culture will be conducted is based on the contention that when several cultural factors can be correlated or matched, then the study becomes more concrete and specific as opposed to abstract and general. This of course raises the validity of the conclusions drawn from the comparative studies since the statistical probability of the indications is quantifiably more empirical.

> "The twentieth-century search for universally applicable "patterns" that so clearly marks the ritualist and psychoanalytic approaches to myth is also characteristic of

the trends that remain to be mentioned, the sociological and the structuralist. Whereas ritualism had its roots in England and psychoanalysis in the German cultural orbit, the French contribution is important here, starting with the sociological school of Emile Durkheim and Marcel Mauss. Durkheim's "collective representations," Mauss's seminal studies on gift giving and sacrifice, and Bronislaw Malinowski's views on myths as social "charters" all recognized the paramount role of myths as catalysts in cementing structured human coexistence. The structural study of myth, with Claude Levi-Strauss as its most flamboyant paladin, also stresses the role of myth as a mechanism of conflict resolution and mediation between opposites in the fabric of human culture and society, not least in the great dichotomy of nature versus culture itself. But Levi-Strauss's analytic method is one of binary oppositions influenced by structural linguistics (especially the work of Roman Jakobson) and folklore (starting with Vladimir Propp's *Morphology of the Folktale* [1928]), which themselves are but manifestations of the vast structuralist movement in science and scholarship."[143]

The view that myth is a manifestation of ritual or of a psychological state is a barrier between scholarship and myth; this is because the very premise for the study is flawed. Created by sages, saints, seers, etc., mystical mythology is an "explanation" of something that is transcendental, something that exists in a form that cannot be communicated by rational thinking or linear logical conceptualizations. When mystical mythology is reduced by scholars to a support for rituals, manifestations of the psyche or a tool to "glue" or bind members of a culture to a common concept, such as social cohesion, the original intent of myth is displaced and the resulting conclusions about myths, their import and pervasiveness, will be elusive. These models may be grouped together and referred to as logical models since they neglect to take into account the transcendental aspects of myth and indeed, also the human experience. The models that take into account the mystical nature and purpose of myth along with the disciplines of anthropology, archeology, philology and historical linguistics, phonetics and phonology, may be referred to as mystic or intuitional models. In another section, the author continues to outline the previous approaches taken by other mythologists in an attempt to determine the benefits or pitfalls of their concepts and methodologies.

"While Levi-Strauss himself, after starting with the Oedipus myth, has for the most part resolutely ranged from Alaska to the Amazon, structuralist ideas have begun

---

[143] Ibid

to seep into the study of classical myth and "historical" mythology in general. The obvious danger is that the approach is by nature generalist, universalizing, and ahistorical, thus the very opposite of text oriented, philological, and time conscious. Overlaying known data with binaristic gimmickry in the name of greater "understanding" is no substitute for a deeper probing of the records themselves as documents of a specific synchronic culture on the one hand and as outcomes of diachronic evolutionary processes on the other. In mythology, as in any other scholarly or scientific activity, it is important to recall that the datum itself is more important than any theory that may be applied to it. Hence historical and comparative mythology, as practiced in this book, is in the last resort not beholden to any one theory on the "nature" of myth or even its ultimate "function" or "purpose." But it is fully cognizant that myth operates in men's minds and societies alike, that it is involved in both self-image and worldview on an individual and a collective level (being thus tied to religion and its manifestations such as ritual and prayer, and to societal ideology as well), and that it creates potent tensions of language and history (speaking of timeless happening, narrating eternal events in the grammatical frame of tense forms for [usually]) past or [rarely] future occurrences [as in the case of prophecy], never in the generalizing present)."[144]

While there have been a wide range of scholars and writers who have taken note of and even asserted the similarities of the myths of widely varying cultures by citing simple similarities, there have been relatively few serious, rigorous, scholarly researches and documentations. Mostly, there have been many anecdotal and or unsubstantiated claims that do not reconcile history with the events that are being artificially connected. Further, there is little accounting for the discrepancies and inconsistencies that arise. While it is true that all humanity emerged from the same source, it is not necessarily correct to say that all cultures are related since people, having moved away from their original ancestral home (Africa) when humanity first appeared on earth, may have developed varying ways of life and cultural expression based on local cultural factors. So making the standard too tight or too loose leaves us with either biased conclusions or unsubstantiated conjecture respectively. The author ends his introduction to comparative mythology with a caveat for entering into those studies.

---

[144] Ibid

"Thus the twentieth-century lessons of ritualism, psychoanalysis, sociology, and structural anthropology alike deserve to be heeded by the historical and comparative student of myth and religion, but only to the extent that they offer viable insights into a study that is by definition historical, and more specifically philological, rooted in the minute and sensitive probing and comparison of primary written records."[145]

If the categories of cultural expression are found to match in several areas, the mythic principles will have survived the passage of time even as cultures interact with others and adopt new factors into their culture. In our model the factors of cultural expression are recognized as elements that will remain embedded in the culture as layers upon which new traditions, names and parochial idiosyncrasies[146] have been developed or acquired. This layering of symbol, myth and metaphor is starkly evident in several examples that will be presented in this section. This pattern of diffusion was noticed early on in the study of the correlations between the myths of varied cultures. The writings of Count Goblet D' Alviella present a typical example, referring to the Sacred Tree symbolism.

"Each race, each religion has its independent type, which it preserves and develops in accordance with the spirit of its own traditions, approximating it, however, by the addition of extraneous details and accessories, to the equivalent image adopted in the plastic art of its neighbors. Thus the current which makes the Lotus of Egypt blossom on the Paradisaic Tree of India has its counter-current which causes the *Asclepias acida* of the Hindu Kush to climb upon the Sacred Tree of Assyria. Art and mythology comply, in this respect, with the usual processes of civilization, which is not the fruit of a single tree, but has always been developed by grafts and cuttings between the most favoured branches of the human race."[147]

---

[145] Ibid

[146] A structural or behavioral characteristic peculiar to an individual or a group.

[147] *The Migration of Symbols,* Count Goblet D' Alviella, 1894

# Chapter 5: Application of The Cultural Category-Factor Correlation Method

## Correlations based on Universal Forms of Human Expression due to the Innate Common Human Expressive Capacity or due to Cultural interactions.

In order to proceed with our study we must differentiate between ordinary human inspired correlations and correlations based on cultural interactions between two cultures. Using the example presented by D' Alviella above, of the Lotus of Ancient Egypt and the Tree of India we may illustrate the difference between a correlation of two artifacts belonging to two cultures either due to an innate human form of expression or due to cultural interaction.

1.  (A) If the creation of a symbol is based on the innate human need to express the concept of spiritual awakening {Universal Forms of Human Expression based on the Innate Common Human Expressive Capacity} then these two cultural factors (Lotus, Tree) may be seen as correlatable as innate human factors of cultural expression but we can not say that they developed based on cultural contact since we only have a single unsupported correlation (mythic significance).

| (A) | | Mythic significance Spiritual enlightenment | | |
|---|---|---|---|---|
| Artifact in culture A EGYPT | Lotus | ☑ | | |
| Artifact in culture B INDIA | Paradisaic Tree | ☑ | | |

This kind of occurrence, when we have two items which seem to have one area of correlation we may refer to as *single event proposed correlation*. If this *single event proposed correlation* does not have any other aspects or factors in common we may refer to it as an *unsupported single event proposed correlation*.

2.  (B) If the correlation of the artifact in the two cultures involves two, three or more additional "correlatable", factors that are found to be equivalent, then we could begin to assert with greater

confidence that the artifacts (cultural factors) were developed in a way influenced by cultural contact. For example:

| (B) | | Mythic significance Spiritual enlightenment | Form/ Makeup vegetation | Function meditation |
|---|---|---|---|---|
| Artifact in culture A EGYPT | Lotus | ☑ | ☑ | ☑ |
| Artifact in culture B INDIA | Paradisaic Tree | ☑ | ☑ | ☑ |

In example #2 we were able to match three factors related to the artifact. This finding could give us greater confidence to say that there is a relationship, a correlation between the factors related to the artifact and the cultures to which it belongs. This kind of occurrence, when we have two items which seem to have more than one area of correlation we may refer to as *multiple event proposed correlation*. Since this *multiple event proposed correlation* does have other aspects or factors in common we may also consider it as a *supported proposed correlation*.

In other cases we may find that there are many correlatable factors of cultural expression, for the same artifact, but there are also, at the same time, some factors that are not correlatable. In such a case that artifact may be partially correlatable which could suggest that there was some contact but that the contact yielded only partial adoption of the complete artifact; some aspects of the cultural essence were lost, forgotten or are dormant in one of the cultures.

Universal Forms of Human Expression based on the Innate Human impetus to express a feeling, desire or will using Common Human Expressive Capacities based on the similar environments.

In other words, it is possible that two artifacts may be similar in one or more ways because two separate human beings are trying to express the same universal idea, based on an "innate human impetus" due to "common urges" experienced by all human beings, using the same capacity that all humans have. For example: two separate individuals belonging to two separate cultures may wish to express the idea of rising from the earth to the heavens so they each draw a picture of a tree and attach that meaning to it because it rises from the earth to the sky.

- In this example, the hypothesis (proposed explanation of the phenomena (apparent correlation) is that there is a correlation between the two artifacts which could be explained as innate human impetus or as cultural interactions.
- the innate human impetus is the desire to express "rising from the earth to the heavens".
- The artifact in this case, the tree, is the universal Form of the Human Expression.
- The common human expressive capacity is drawing. Generally, all humans have the concept of a body with limbs and generally those conceptualized bodies have the same capacities (walking, lifting, pointing, working, etc.).
- The similar environment is the earth.

Now, taking this example a few steps further, if more factors of those same trees of the two cultures were treated in similar ways it would mean that there is more than one coincidental apparent factor of commonality. So if the trees were found to have more common factors of cultural expression we would be able to move beyond the hypothesis to say with more clarity that the similarity is due to the innate human impetus and common capacity or it is due to cultural interaction. The following factors of cultural expression could be applied to the artifacts in order to go beyond an anecdotal or unsupported correlation and if found to present matches or no matches could allow us to make a determination about the correlation and the cultures or further revise the theory or derive further hypotheses for testing.

- Decorated in the same way,
- Named in the same way,
- Mythologized in the same way,
- Ascribed to the same origins,
- Trimmed in the same way,
- Etc.

## Simple Probability and Statistical analysis in the Cultural Category-Factor Correlation Method

We may assess the mathematical probability of a correlation between the factors of two given cultures in the following way. Using the example above, what is the probability that the cultural factor (artifact) of Egypt, the Lotus, and the cultural factor (artifact) of India, the Tree that were correlated based on a single factor of cultural expression was due to cultural interaction? Also, what can we learn about the artifacts from this study? We may construct the equation by first assessing the major cultures around in the time when Ancient Egypt was in existence and then we may assess the ones we know had contact with Ancient Egypt and then determining which ones adopted the artifact from Egypt. We could also begin to develop a basis of knowledge to determine if there is a tendency to find Egyptian artifacts in countries that had contact with Ancient Egypt. If we were to find that the artifacts are correlatable in more respects that one, we could develop greater insights into the nature of their meaning and usage by combining the knowledge about the artifacts.

### Table 7: Cultures in contact with Ancient Egypt

|   | Culture | Artifact | Contact with Egypt | Similar meaning to Egyptian Lotus |
|---|---------|----------|--------------------|-----------------------------------|
| 0 | Ancient Egypt | Lotus | | |
| 1 | India | Tree | ☑ | ? |
| 2 | Mesopotamia | | ☑ | ? |
| 3 | Greece (classical) | Lotus from Egypt used in Mysteries of Isis | ☑ | ? |
| 4 | Nubia | Lotus from Egypt | ☑ | ? |
| 5 | Libya | unknown | ☑ | ? |
| 6 | Minos | unknown | ☑ | ? |
| 7 | Assyria | unknown | ☑ | ? |
| 8 | Persia | unknown | ☑ | ? |
| 9 | Rome | | ☑ | ? |
| 10 | Byblos (Lebanon) | unknown | ☑ | ? |
| 11 | Canaan/Jewish Hebrews | See ref. | ☑ | ? |

| 12 | **Phoenicia** | See ref. | ☑ | ? |
| 13 | **Christians** | See ref. | ☑ | ? |

**Probability calculations:**[148] In the situation above an event $E$ can happen $h$ ways out of a total of $n$ possible equally likely ways. The possibility of getting a match (*success*) between the Ancient Egyptian lotus and an artifact in one of the other cultures is:

$P = Pr\ \{E\} = h/n$

The probability of an event is a number between 0 and 1. if the event cannot occur (its possibility of happening is *impossible*), then its probability is "0". If the event has to occur (its possibility of happening is *certain*) no matter what then its probability is "1".

Therefore:

$P = Pr\ \{E\} = h/n = 1/13 = $ or 1 out of $13 = 0.08$

The chance of the occurrence (match) not occurring (*failure*) may be calculated as follows:

$q = Pr\ \{not\ E\} = (n - h) / n = 1 - (n - h) = 1 - p = 1 - Pr\ \{E\}$

Therefore:

$q = Pr\ \{not\ E\} = (n - h) / n = (13 - 1)/13 = 12/13 = .92$

If $p$ is the probability that an event will occur, the *odds* in favor of that occurrence actually happening are $p : q$ in other words "$p$ to $q$". So the odds *against* the occurrence of an event are $q : p$ or "$q$ to $p$". Therefore, in our case (the event discussed above) the *odds against* a match between the ancient Egyptian Lotus and a similar artifact in another ancient culture is:

$q : p = 12/13 : 1/13 = $ "12 to 1"

---

[148] Schaum's Easy Outlines Statistics by Murray R. Spiegel

# The Cultural Category Factor Correlation Method

Now what matches do we actually get between the Ancient Egyptian Lotus and other similar artifacts in cultures that were in contact with Ancient Egypt in ancient times?

## Table 8: Matching the Egyptian Lotus with similar artifacts in other cultures

| | Culture | Artifact | Contact with Egypt | Similar meaning to Egyptian Lotus |
|---|---|---|---|---|
| 0 | **Ancient Egypt** | Lotus | | |
| 1 | **India** | Tree | ☑ | ☑ |
| 2 | **Mesopotamia** | | ☑ | ☑ |
| 3 | **Greece (classical)** | Lotus from Egypt used in Mysteries of Isis | ☑ | ☑ |
| 4 | **Nubia** | Lotus from Egypt | ☑ | ☑ |
| 5 | **Libya** | unknown | ☑ | — |
| 6 | **Minos** | unknown | ☑ | — |
| 7 | **Assyria** | unknown | ☑ | — |
| 8 | **Persia** | unknown | ☑ | — |
| 9 | **Rome** | | ☑ | ☑ |
| 10 | **Byblos (Lebanon)** | unknown | ☑ | — |
| 11 | **Canaan/Jewish Hebrews** | See ref. | ☑ | ☑ |
| 12 | **Phoenicia** | See ref. | ☑ | ☑ |
| 13 | **Christians** | See ref. | ☑ | — |

In the Table above we find 7 matches. That means that 7 out of 13 cultures have an apparently similar artifact to the Ancient Egyptian Lotus. That outcome was higher than the previously predicted probability calculation. Now what if we add more factors to be matched in order to find out more definitively if the matches mean that the artifact has some relation to the ancient Egyptian (was due to cultural interaction or adoption from Ancient Egyptian culture). In the table below we will add three more factors of cultural expression to the matching criteria for the artifact and see if there are any artifacts in the other cultures that are closer matches to the Ancient Egyptian Lotus.

# The Cultural Category Factor Correlation Method

## Table 9: Correlating 5 Factors of Cultural Expression to the Egyptian Lotus

| | Culture | Artifact | Contact with Egypt | Mythic significance | Form/ composition | Function | Usage | # of Matches 4 |
|---|---|---|---|---|---|---|---|---|
| | | | | Spiritual enlightenment | vegetation | meditation | smelling | |
| 0 | **Ancient Egypt** | Lotus | ☑ | ☑ | ☑ | ☑ | ☑ | ↓ |
| 1 | **India** | Tree | ☑ | ☑ | ☑ | ☑ | — | |
| 2 | **Mesopotamia**[149] | | ☑ | ☑ | ☑ | ☑ | ☑ | ↓ |
| 3 | **Greece (classical)** | Lotus from Egypt used in Mysteries of Isis | ☑ | ☑ | ☑ | ☑ | ☑ | ↓ |
| 4 | **Nubia** | Lotus from Egypt | ☑ | ☑ | ☑ | ☑ | ☑ | ↓ |
| 5 | **Libya** | unknown | ☑ | — | — | — | — | — |

[149] North Syrian Ritual of the Lotus and Winged Sundisk 1100 B.C.E. See the book *The African Origins of Civilization* by Muata Ashby, Plate 21

## The Cultural Category Factor Correlation Method

| # | Culture | | | | | | |
|---|---|---|---|---|---|---|---|
| 6 | Minoans | unknown | ☑ | — | — | — | — |
| 7 | Assyria | unknown | ☑ | — | — | — | — |
| 8 | Persia | unknown | ☑ | — | — | — | — |
| 9 | Rome[150] | — | ☑ | ☑ | ☑ | ☑ | — |
| 10 | Byblos (Lebanon) | unknown | ☑ | — | — | — | — |
| 11 | Canaan/Jewish Hebrews[151] | See ref. | ☑ | ☑ | ☑ | — | — |
| 12 | Phoenicia[152] | See ref. | ☑ | ☑ | ☑ | — | — |
| 13 | Christians[153] | See ref. | ☑ | — | ☑ | — | — |

---

[150] Alder tree – symbol of resurrection. Also, the Palm, in association with the mysteries of Osiris from Egypt. *Women's Dictionary of Symbols and Sacred Objects* by Barbara G. Walker

[151] Palm tree of cult of the god Baal-Peor with similar meaning as in Ancient Egypt- worshipped at Jesish Tabernacle until practice was stopped. *Women's Dictionary of Symbols and Sacred Objects* by Barbara G. Walker

[152] Palm tree in cult of the god Baal-Peor with similar meaning as in Ancient Egypt. *Women's Dictionary of Symbols and Sacred Objects* by Barbara G. Walker Baal was ichnographically and philosophically related to the Ancient Egyptian god Asar (Osiris) *The African Origins of Civilization* by Muata Ashby

[153] Tree of life upon which Jesus was crucified. Represents resurrection, not Enlightenment. *Women's Dictionary of Symbols and Sacred Objects* by Barbara G. Walker

# Comparative Mythology, Cultural and Social Studies

## Table 10: Possible outcomes in our study (from data collected in the previous Table).

|   | Spiritual enlightenment | vegetation | meditation | smelling |
|---|---|---|---|---|
| 0 | ☒ zero | ☒ zero | ☒ zero | ☒ zero |
| 1 | ☑ |  |  |  |
| 2 | ☑ | ☑ |  |  |
| 3 | ☑ | ☑ | ☑ |  |
| 4 | ☑ | ☑ | ☑ | ☑ |

For each culture there are 5 possible outcomes (E= event):

0 matching ☒
1 matching ☑
2 matching ☑☑
3 matching ☑☑☑
4 matching ☑☑☑☑

- So for each attempted culture match up there is 1 chance out of 5 of getting an exact match.
- Therefore, there is 1 chance out of 65 (13 cultures X 5 chances) of getting 1 set of all 4 matching criteria between two cultures.

**Probability calculations:** In the situation above an event $E$ can happen $h$ ways out of a total of $n$ possible equally likely ways. The possibility of getting a match (*success*) between the Ancient Egyptian lotus and an artifact in one of the other cultures is:

$P = \Pr \{E\} = h/n$

Therefore:

$P = \Pr \{E\} = h/n = 1/65 =$ or 1 out of $65 = 0.02$

The chance of the occurrence (match) not occurring (*failure*) may be calculated as follows:

$q = \Pr \{not\ E\} = (n - h) / n = 1 - (n - h) = 1 - p = 1 - \Pr \{E\}$

Therefore:

$q = \Pr \{not\ E\} = (n - h) / n = (65 - 1)/65 = 64/65 = .98$

If $p$ is the probability that an event will occur, the *odds* in favor of that occurrence actually happening are $p : q$ in other words "$p$ to $q$". So the odds *against* the event occurring are $q : p$ or "$q$ to $p$". Therefore, in our case the *odds against* a match between the ancient Egyptian Lotus and a similar artifact in another ancient culture is:

*Odds against finding a match* $= q : p = 64/65 : 1/65 =$ "64 to 1"

## Conclusions:

What is the probability of getting a perfect match (all 4 Factors of Cultural expression) between the Ancient Egyptian Lotus and another artifact in another culture? What is the probability that the matches we found are truly related to Ancient Egyptian culture? From the example above we obtained four matches and we found that the closest matches tended to be in cultures that had direct adoption of the Ancient Egyptian religion of Asar and Aset (Isis and Osiris). We also found that when we applied the Category Factor Correlation Method by comparing more Factors of Cultural expression related to the particular artifact being compared the matches were quickly reduced from 7 to 4 and that the

Indian Paradisaic Tree no longer matched to the Ancient Egyptian Lotus in more exact parameters or criteria of comparison.

If we are to consider that random chance would inform us that the probability of an even occurring are 50% or 1/2 or 1 to 2 or one out of two, equal chance for or against the event occurring, we may conclude that the matches that may be found overcame the high odds against them, indicating a high probability that the match is possibly highly related to Ancient Egyptian culture. Indeed, when we look at documented studies related to the cultures where matches were positive (successful) we find that the cultures had direct or close contact with Ancient Egypt and/or adopted the Ancient Egyptian religion that included the practice of the use of the artifact in question, in this case, the Lotus. We may also note here that while the comparison of the Ancient Egyptian Lotus with the Indian Paradisaic Tree was not highly correlated, there is an Indian Lotus artifact that would be highly correlatable.[154]

As stated earlier, the probability of an event is a number between 0 and 1. If the event cannot occur (its possibility of happening is *impossible*), then its probability is "0". If the event has to occur (its possibility of happening is *certain*) no matter what then its probability is "1". The probability related to this experiment is closer to "0" than to "1".

We could also extend our inquiry to discern which cultures had heavy, moderate or minimal contacts. Since the matches occurred in cultures that had close contact with Ancient Egypt we might conclude that the heavier the contact the higher the probability is of having a match in a factor of cultural expression. How would our table look if we included cultures that had not contact with the ancient Egyptians?

---

[154] Item for Comparison **Error! Main Document Only.**: The Lotus Symbol of Ancient Egypt and Indian Hinduism, in book *The African Origins of Civilization* by Muata Ashby

## Table 11: Comparing the artifact in Cultures with and without contact with Ancient Egypt

| | Culture | Artifact | Contact with Egypt | Similar meaning to Egyptian Lotus[155] |
|---|---|---|---|---|
| 0 | Ancient Egypt | Lotus | | |
| 1 | India | Tree | ☑ | ☑ |
| 2 | Mesopotamia | | ☑ | ☑ |
| 3 | Greece (classical) | Lotus from Egypt used in Mysteries of Isis | ☑ | ☑ |
| 4 | Nubia | Lotus from Egypt | ☑ | ☑ |
| 5 | Libya | unknown | ☑ | — |
| 6 | Minoans | unknown | ☑ | — |
| 7 | Assyria | unknown | ☑ | — |
| 8 | Persia | unknown | ☑ | — |
| 9 | Rome | | ☑ | ☑ |
| 10 | Byblos (Lebanon) | unknown | ☑ | — |
| 11 | Canaan/Jewish Hebrews | See ref. | ☑ | ☑ |
| 12 | Phoenicia | See ref. | ☑ | ☑ |
| 13 | Christians | See ref. | ☑ | — |
| 14 | Aborigines of Australia | Unknown | — | — |
| 15 | Inca | Unknown | — | — |
| 16 | Eskimos | Unknown | — | — |
| 17 | Norse | Unknown | — | — |
| 18 | Vikings | Unknown | — | — |
| 19 | Anasazi | Unknown | — | — |
| 20 | Cheyenne | Unknown | — | — |
| 21 | Arawac | Unknown | — | — |
| 22 | Biloxi | Unknown | — | — |
| 23 | Apache | Unknown | — | — |

---

[155] Spiritual Enlightenment

In the example above we found:

1.  the successful correlation of the Ancient Egyptian Lotus tended to occur in cultures that had some contact with Ancient Egypt.
2.  that there were only correlations of the Ancient Egyptian Lotus artifact in cultures that had contact with Ancient Egypt.

Therefore we may conclude that in order to obtain a successful correlation, the finding of the Lotus with the same meaning as in the Ancient Egyptian culture, there needs to be contact between the Ancient Egyptian culture and the other culture.

# Principles for using the Cultural Category Factor Correlation Method to Compare Cultures

The cultural and or mythological comparative models presented in this book adopt the mystic understanding of myths and cultures in the determination of their compatibility. While this study makes use of such disciplines as anthropology, archeology, philology and historical linguistics, phonetics and phonology, it lays heavy emphasis not so much on the historicity of the factors of cultural expression, although this forms an important aspect of the evidences related to prior contact, but rather on the substance or symbolic, philosophical and metaphoric significance of the items in question with increasing specificity in order to decrease the random or chance matches or matches occurring do to innate common human cultural expressions. Written records do constitute an essential aspect of the study but this definition needs to be broadened to include iconography, as symbol, metaphor, and iconography are also forms of language. The following principles will be used in this comparative cultural system or method.

## Step 1: Theoretical Correlation

Firstly we collect artifacts (can be an amulet, symbol, myth, parable, architecture, etc.) that seem to possess one or more similar characteristics. This stage is like the formulation of a theory which will then be tested using the *Cultural Category Factor Correlation Method*. Having read the artifacts and determined their provenance, usage, form, intent, or any number of relevant factors that may apply to them we may determined which artifacts we will compare. Thus, we may proceed in the following way to determine if the artifacts selected (Factors of Cultural Expression) have a basis in commonality and are "correlatable."

Next we will proceed to collect data about the artifact and tabulate that data in a manner that will facilitate our determination about the possible correlations between the artifacts in the cultures being compared. The following principles are to be applied in the process of comparing the artifacts.

# Principle 1: Correlation of Categories and Factors of Cultural Expression

## Single Event Proposed Correlation (one occurrence) Match in one cultural category factor is Un-supported by Matches in Other Factors

Example: If one artifact looks the same (correlation of form) in two separate cultures, *this single event proposed correlation* might be explained as a coincidence perhaps based on the "Universal Forms of Human Expression based on the Innate Human Impetus to express a feeling, desire or will using Common Human Expressive Capacities which may also be based on the similar environments." But if the primary factor upon which the conjecture is based, for example, *form,* is supported by correlations in other factors such as usage, philosophy, myth, etc., then the argument that it is only a coincidence becomes less tenable. That is, just because the *ontology*[156] of two cultures is expressed through mythology does not suggest a correlation between the two cultures. In order to be considered as a *proposed correlation* for the purpose of determining the congruence of the two cultures, the simple correlation must be supported by at least one or more matching elements of cultural expression. So if there is no other match beyond the initial apparent match this proposed correlation will be considered as being "unsupported."

### A- Example of an *Unsupported single event proposed correlation:*

The Primary Category proposed as a correlation between two cultures is *Myth.* A mythic factor (plot, theme, character, etc.) seems to be the same in the two cultures. So the mythic factor becomes the primary category of this proposed correlation.

Typically, the common forms of evidence used to support the theory of cultural connections is a Single Event (one occurrence) Unsupported Match in One Cultural Category which may or may not occur in the presence of other unrelated single event matches in the same or in related but separate cultural categories.

---

[156] Ontology, in philosophy, the branch of metaphysics that studies the basic nature of things, the essence of "being" itself.

| Single Event Unsupported Match | Culture A | Culture B |
|---|---|---|
| The primary matching Category | *Mythic Character 1* | *Mythic Character 1* |

If the *single event proposed correlation* is devoid of additional supports (ex. correlation is of form only). The correlations here are basic and superficial, usually of appearance, and yet they are suggestive of a deeper connection. However, if it is found along with other *single event proposed unsupported correlations* (see Table 12) in the same category or other cultural expression categories, then the conclusion that the correlating factors are simple coincidences is less supportable because the frequency of correlations rises beyond the threshold of chance as would be determined by statistical analysis of the normal probability of the existence of such correlations.[157]

If the mythic factor is supported by another factor, for example, iconography (of the character) then the iconography factor becomes the secondary category and first (primary) support of the primary category for this proposed correlation.

| Single Event Supported Match | Culture A | Culture B |
|---|---|---|
| The primary matching Categories | *Mythic Character 1* | *Mythic Character 1* |
| The primary supporting factor ➜ | *Iconography* | *Iconography* |

---

[157] *Statistics-probability-* A number expressing the likelihood that a specific event will occur, expressed as the ratio of the number of actual occurrences to the number of possible occurrences. (American Heritage Dictionary)

The Cultural Category Factor Correlation Method

## Table 12: Example of a Single Category Multiple Factor Event Supported occurrence with Matches in One Cultural Category

| Single Event Unsupported Match | Culture A | Culture B | Culture A | Culture B | Culture A | Culture B | |
|---|---|---|---|---|---|---|---|
| The primary matching Categories | *Mythic Character 1* | *Mythic Character 1* | *Mythic ritual* | *Mythic ritual* | *Mythic gender* | *Mythic gender* | ← *Same category (myth)* |
| | | | | | | | *Different Factors* |
| The primary supporting factor → | *Iconography* | *Iconography* | *Iconography* | *Iconography* | *Iconography* | *Iconography* | ← Matches |

This example has matches in the same category (Myth) but with different factors of mythic expression (character, ritual, gender). The mythic category matches are supported by the iconography factor. So the appearance of the character, the ritual and the gender is the same in each comparison. Each factor is part of the same myth but not part of the same artifact within the myth.

## Additional criteria for Principle 1:

*Single event proposed correlations* that are unsupported by other factors and unrelated to other categories require a more rigorous standard of discernment in order to be included as evidence of congruence. A *single event proposed correlation* that is unsupported by other factors and unrelated to other categories will be accepted as strong evidence of congruence if it occurs in the presence of at least two or more other unrelated single event matches in the same or other cultural factor categories. In this way we may work towards establishing a medium for assigning the relative strengths of proposed correlations.

## Table 13: Categorizing the relative strength of correlation for single event findings

| Ranking | |
|---------|---|
| Strong | 1 category match plus 2 or more supporting matches |
| Moderate | 1 category match with 1 supporting match |
| Weak | 1 category match with no (0) supporting matches |

The Cultural Category Factor Correlation Method

**Table 14: Example of a Multiple Event (more than one Category of cultural expression) Supported Match Occurring in the Presence of Other Unrelated[158] Single Event Matches in the same culture but in separate Cultural Categories**

| Multiple Event Single[159] Supported Match | Culture A | Culture B | Culture A | Culture B | Culture A | Culture B | |
|---|---|---|---|---|---|---|---|
| The primary matching Categories | *Mythic Character 1* | *Mythic Character 1* | *Architecture* | *Architecture* | *Ritual* | *Ritual* | ← *Different* Category - factors |
| The primary supporting factors → | *Iconography* | *Iconography* | *Style* | *Style* | *Tradition* | *Tradition* | **Apparent** ← **Matches** |

The primary categories above support each other in a horizontal or breadth-wise format so the idea that culture A and culture B are related is suggested by the finding of several category matches between the two cultures.

---

[158] related by being part of the same cultures but unrelated in that the factors are from different categories.
[159] Only has one primary supporting cultural factor match

## APPLICATION:

For the application of this Cultural Comparison System we will use cultural factors related to the two cultures known as Ancient Egypt and India. Various factors were compared in the book African Origins OF CIVILIZATION, RELIGION, YOGA MYSTICAL SPIRITUALITY, ETHICS PHILOSOPHY BY MUATA ASHBY.

The following example compares two goddesses, one of Ancient Egypt (Aset) and of India (Saraswati), as well as two artifacts, one of Ancient Egypt (hetep) and India (lingam yoni). So it contains more than one Category matches supported by a single supporting category or factor match. The two categories relate to the same culture but not to each other. The mythic character belongs to the same culture and the ritual artifact belongs to the same culture also but to a different aspect of the culture. In other words, the goddesses do not use the ritual object but both of the artifacts being compared here, goddesses and libation instruments, belong to the same respective religion (Shetaut Neter, Hindu) and culture (Ancient Egyptian, Indian), which correlate.

The Category Factor Cultural Comparison Method

**Table 15: Multiple Category Event Single Supported Match**

| Single Event Unsupported Match | Culture A ANCIENT EGYPT | Culture B ANCIENT INDIA | Culture A ANCIENT EGYPT | Culture B ANCIENT INDIA | Supported Matches |
|---|---|---|---|---|---|
| The primary matching Categories | *Mythic Character 1* | *Mythic Character 1* | *Ritual* | *Ritual* | ← Matches |
| The primary supporting factors → | *Iconography* | *Iconography* | *Tradition* | *Tradition* | ← Matches |
| name | *Goddess Aset (Isis)* | *Goddess Saraswati* | *Hetep* | *Lingam-Yoni* | |
| References | | | *see* the book African Origins Of Civilization, Religion, Yoga Mystical Spirituality, Ethics Philosophy by Muata Ashby, page 516, Item for Comparison 1: The Goddess of Wisdom- Aset (Isis) of Kamit and the Avian Saraswati of India and the Principle | *see* the book African Origins Of Civilization, Religion, Yoga Mystical Spirituality, Ethics Philosophy by Muata Ashby, page 517, Item for Comparison 2: The Ancient Egyptian Hetep (Offering) Slab and the Hindu Lingam Yoni | |

# Principle 2: Depth (deepness-vertical) pattern of correlations

The depth pattern of correlation finds factors about a single category artifact that correlate so the correlation pattern is not of several categories necessarily but several factors in a few categories that also match between the two cultures. If two or more (B), (C), (D), (E), (F), etc. independent factor matches occur within one category (A), and they are supported by 2 or more other factor matches they will be considered as a part of a pattern strengthening the proposed correlation between the two artifacts and strongly suggesting correlation between the two cultures. These correlations will be considered as equivalencies within a particular category of expressions such as, art, architecture, myth, etc. This pattern is referred to as a *depth pattern of correlations* and the category will be accepted as evidence in the determination of congruence between two cultures. The depth pattern is vertical.

**<u>Example of a *Depth Pattern Supported Single event proposed correlation:*</u>**

Primary Category proposed as a correlation between two cultures➔➔➔ (A) *Myth*  ⬅ Supported by
                                                                                                              (B)*Iconography*

                                                                           ⬆⬆⬆
Cultural elements (Factors) that may support the primary factor    ➔➔➔ (C) Plot,
                                                                           (D) gender,
                                                                           (E) theme,
                                                                           (F) action,
                                                                                etc.

In this example, the myth category of the two cultures match wholly or partially, first in iconography, and then in plot, gender, theme, action, etc. Therefore, the initial correlation hypothesis (iconography) is supported by more than three factor matches. (see table below).

**Table 16: Depth Pattern–Multiple Correlations Occur Within the Same Cultural Category**

| Supported Matching Cultural Factors | Culture A<br>ANCIENT EGYPT | Culture B<br>ANCIENT INDIA | Supported Matches |
|---|---|---|---|
| The primary matching category → | Iconography | Iconography | ← Matches |
| | ↑↑ Supporting Factors | ↑↑ Supporting Factors | |
| The primary supporting factor →<br>Secondary supporting factor →<br>Tertiary supporting factor →<br>Quaternary supporting factor → | Plot,<br>gender,<br>theme,<br>action, etc. | Plot,<br>gender,<br>theme,<br>action, etc. | ← Matches<br>← Matches<br>← Matches<br>← Matches |

The Category Factor Cultural Comparison Method

**APPLICATION** of the Depth Pattern - Multiple Factor Correlations Occur Within the Same Cultural Category (Iconography) using Ancient Egyptian and Indian artifacts (Goddesses) (Part 1)

| Supported Matching Cultural Factors | Culture A Goddess Aset (Isis) ANCIENT EGYPT | Culture B Goddess Saraswati ANCIENT INDIA | Supported Matches |
|---|---|---|---|
| The primary matching category ↑ | Iconography Avian quality | Iconography Avian quality | ← Matches |
| The primary supporting factor ↑ Plot, | (R-1) Ignorant but virtuous aspirant needs enlightening | (R-2) Ignorant but virtuous aspirant needs enlightening | ← Matches |
| Secondary supporting factor ↑ gender, | (R-3) female | (R-4) female | ← Matches |
| Tertiary supporting factor ↑ theme, | (R-5) Wisdom-philosophy | (R-6) Wisdom-philosophy | ← Matches |
| Quaternary supporting factor ↑ Role of the character in the myth | (R-7) Teacher-preceptor | (R-8) Teacher-preceptor | ← Matches |

# References: (R)

R-1- The Divine child Heru is born in ignorance and needs to be enlightened. *see* the book African Origins Of Civilization, Religion, Yoga Mystical Spirituality, Ethics Philosophy by Muata Ashby, page 576, Item for Comparison 3: The Divine Mother and Child of Ancient Egypt and India and the Metaphor of Blackness. See also the book *African Religion Vol 4. Asarian Theology* by Muata Ashby

R-2- *see* the book African Origins Of Civilization, Religion, Yoga Mystical Spirituality, Ethics Philosophy by Muata Ashby, page 557, *The Story of Lila* –Lila is instructed by goddess Saraswati in the ways of the mysteries so she may attain enlightenment.

R-3- *see* the book African Origins Of Civilization, Religion, Yoga Mystical Spirituality, Ethics Philosophy by Muata Ashby, page 516, Item for Comparison 4: The Goddess of Wisdom- Aset (Isis) of Kamit and Saraswati of India and the Avian Principle

R-4- ibid

R-5-Goddess Aset represents wisdom philosophy in Kemetic myth and legend. *see* the book African Origins Of Civilization, Religion, Yoga Mystical Spirituality, Ethics Philosophy by Muata Ashby, page 516, Item for Comparison 5: The Goddess of Wisdom- Aset (Isis) of Kamit and Saraswati of India and the Avian Principle

R-6- Goddess Saraswati represents wisdom philosophy in Indian-Hindu myth and legend. *see* the book African Origins Of Civilization, Religion, Yoga Mystical Spirituality, Ethics Philosophy by Muata Ashby, page 516, Item for Comparison 6: The Goddess of Wisdom- Aset (Isis) of Kamit and Saraswati of India and the Avian Principle. *see also-* page 557, *The Story of Lila*

R-7-Aset acts as spiritual preceptor to the Divine child Heru who is born in ignorance and needs to be enlightened. *see* the book African Origins Of Civilization, Religion, Yoga Mystical Spirituality, Ethics Philosophy by Muata Ashby, page 576, Item for Comparison 7: The Divine Mother and Child of Ancient Egypt and India and the Metaphor of Blackness. See also the book *African Religion Vol 4. Asarian Theology* by Muata Ashby

R-8- Saraswati acts as spiritual preceptor to the Lila who is born in ignorance and needs to be enlightened. *see* page 557, *The Story of Lila*

## APPLICATION of Depth Pattern-Multiple Correlations Occur Within the Different Cultural Categories using Ancient Egyptian and Indian artifacts Part 2

For the application of this Cultural Comparison System we will use cultural factors related to the two cultures known as Ancient Egypt and India. Various factors for these two cultures were compared in the book AFRICAN ORIGINS OF CIVILIZATION, RELIGION, YOGA MYSTICAL SPIRITUALITY, ETHICS PHILOSOPHY BY MUATA ASHBY.

**Figure 9: Below left – The Ancient Egyptian Goddess Aset (Isis) in her avian aspect (all-encompassing flight of wisdom, i.e. intuitional vision)**

In Ancient Egyptian (Egyptian) myth, the Goddess of Truth, Justice and Righteousness is MAAT. Her symbol is the feather. Maat is an aspect of goddess Aset. Aset assumes the winged from as a swallow or a hawk. The name "Aset" means "wisdom." She also is known as "Urt-Hekau," the "lady of words of power." In the Asarian Resurrection myth, goddess Aset outwits Set, who symbolizes egoism and vice. She gets him to admit his wrongdoing without him realizing it. This philosophical teaching embedded in the myth relates the power of wisdom to work in the unconscious mind to make a person speak truth in spite of themselves.

**Figure 10: Above right: Hindu Goddess of wisdom, truth and learning, Saraswati, in her avian aspect.**

The image of goddess Saraswati is often shown on a white swan indicating purity of consciousness. In several epics and parables of Hindu myth, Saraswati is the goddess of wisdom and order, righteous speech. In the myths her power to "twist" the tongues of the unrighteous is legendary, as in the story of the demon Kumbakarna in the Indian *Ramayana* myth. He practiced austerity and earned a boon from the god Brahma. Kumbakarna planned to ask Brahma to make him stay awake for 6 months of the year and then sleep for only one night, so he would be able to indulge in his pastime of eating people. The gods, realizing he was going to ask for this went to the goddess Saraswati, the goddess of speech and intellect, and asked for her assistance so that he would not be able to make this request which would surely destroy the world. So, when Kumbakarna was about to speak, the goddess twisted his intellect so that he requested the opposite, to be asleep for 6 months of the year, and only awake for 1 day. Here we have a correlation of gender, form, function and mythological plot. The avian motif is present in both mythic characters (Aset and Saraswati).

## Table 17: Comparing some Factors of Cultural Expression of the Ancient Egyptian Goddess Aset (Isis) and the Indian Goddess Saraswati

| Multiple Event (several categories) Supported Match | Culture A<br><br>ANCIENT EGYPT | Culture B<br><br>ANCIENT INDIA | |
|---|---|---|---|
| The primary matching Categories | *Mythic Character 1*<br>*Goddess*<br>*Aset (Isis)* | *Mythic Character 1*<br>*Goddess*<br>*Saraswati* | |
| The primary supporting category/factor ➔ *Iconography* | *Solar disk* | *Solar disk* | ⬅<br>**Match** |
| The secondary supporting factor ➔Gender | *Gender* | *Gender* | ⬅<br>**Match** |
| The tertiary supporting factor ➔avian (zoomorphic) | *The goddess displays avian quality.* | *The goddess displays avian quality.* | ⬅<br>**Match** |
| The quaternary supporting factor ➔Philosophy/ Symbolism / meaning | *Wisdom Goddess And goddess of righteous speech* | *Wisdom Goddess And goddess of righteous speech* | ⬅<br>**Match** |
| | | | |
| Reference | see the book African Origins Of Civilization, Religion, Yoga Mystical Spirituality, Ethics Philosophy by Muata Ashby, page 516, Item for Comparison 8: The Goddess of Wisdom- Aset (Isis) of Kamit and Saraswati of India and the Avian Principle | | |

The Category Factor Cultural Comparison Method

## Principle 3: Breadth (wideness-horizontal) pattern of correlations

The pattern may appear as a consistent number of single event correlations discovered in different cultural categories. For example, several correlations in a study of comparative culture may be found in any of the cultural categories discussed earlier. If two or more instances of matching categories and two or more instances of matching factors are discerned then this pattern is referred to as a breadth (wideness-horizontal) pattern of correlations and the category will be accepted as evidence of congruence.

**Table 18: Example-Supported Matching Cultural Factors within the wide range of Cultural Factor/Categories**

| *Breadth pattern of correlations* Factors | Culture A | Culture B | Culture A | Culture B | Culture A | Culture B |
|---|---|---|---|---|---|---|
| The primary matching Categories | *Mythic Character 1* | *Mythic Character 1* | *Architecture* | *Architecture* | *Ritual* | *Ritual* |
| The supporting factors ↑ ↗ ↗ | ↑↑↑ Supporting Factors / *Iconography* Plot, gender, theme, action, etc. | ↑↑↑ Supporting Factors / *Iconography* Plot, gender, theme, action, etc. | ↑↑↑ Supporting Factors / *Iconography* Plot, gender, theme, action, etc. | ↑↑↑ Supporting Factors / *Iconography* Plot, gender, theme, action, etc. | ↑↑↑ Supporting Factors / *Iconography* Plot, gender, theme, action, etc. | ↑↑↑ Supporting Factors / *Iconography* Plot, gender, theme, action, etc. |

# The Category Factor Cultural Comparison Method

## Principal 4: Breadth (wideness-horizontal) and Depth (vertical) pattern of correlations

The Breadth patter can occur in a format with many *Moderate Correlations, that is, correlations with only one category* match and with one supporting correlation for each match. This could indicate moderate evidence of correlation and or the possibility of cultural interactions between the two cultures which led to the apparent correlation of the categories and factors.

**Table 19: Example-*Strong* Breadth and Depth Supported Matching Cultural Factors within the Cultural Factor/Category: Myth**

| Depth pattern of correlations | Culture A | Culture B | Culture A | Culture B | Culture A | Culture B | Supported Matches |
|---|---|---|---|---|---|---|---|
| The primary matching categories | *Myth* | *Myth* | *Mythic Character 1* | *Mythic Character 1* | *Mythic Theme* | *Mythic Theme* | |
| The supporting factors ↑ ↗ ↗ ↗ | ↑↑↑ Supporting Factors | ↑↑↑ Supporting Factors | ↑↑↑ Supporting Factors | ↑↑↑ Supporting Factors | ↑↑↑ Supporting Factors | ↑↑↑ Supporting Factors | |
| | Iconography Plot, gender, theme, action, etc. | Iconography Plot, gender, theme, action, etc. | Iconography Plot, gender, theme, action, etc. | Iconography Plot, gender, theme, action, etc. | Iconography Plot, gender, theme, action, etc. | Iconography Plot, gender, theme, action, etc. | ← Matches ← Matches ← Matches |

## Principle 5: Cross-Cultural Correlations

Principle #1 represents the most common form of evidence that can be presented as proof of congruence between two cultures. Therefore, this is the principle within which most simple correlations between cultures are to be found. However, the nature and exactness of the correlations of the factors between the two cultures may be deserving of greater weight. An example of this is the correlation between the relationship of the numbers used in Indian, Icelandic and Chaldean myth, presented earlier in this text.[160] Cross-cultural correlations (correlations between three or more cultures) may be observed in the unsupported or supported state. They may most likely be found in the weak or moderate breadth pattern of distribution. This pattern of correlation suggests a *diffusion* of the expressions of the cultural factors from one original source and / or a relationship between the cultures being studied.

**Table 20: Single Event Supported Cross Cultural Correlations (*Weak*)**

| Cross-Cultural Correlations | Culture A | Culture B | Culture C | Culture D | Culture E | Culture F |
|---|---|---|---|---|---|---|
| The primary matching category | *Mythic Character 1* | *Mythic Character 1* | *Mythic Character 1* | *Mythic Character 1* | *Mythic Character 1* | *Mythic Character 1* |
| The primary supporting factor ➜ | *Iconography* | *Iconography* | *Iconography* | *Iconography* | *Iconography* | *Iconography* |

---

[160] *see Chapter 2: Principles of Cultural Expression*

# Examples of Cross-Cultural Congruence: HORUS, JESUS AND KRISHNA

Heru (Horus)          Krishna          Jesus

**Figure 11:** Top center: Horus the child in control of the forces of nature in the form of animals. At left: Krishna in the same aspect. At right: Jesus in the same aspect.

Lord Krishna is a God form or symbol within the Indian Hindu mythic system. He represents an incarnation of the Supreme Being or Brahman. Literally translated, the name "Krishna" means "Black" or "The Black One." The God Asar (Osiris) of Ancient Egypt myth, like Lord Krishna, was also known as "The Black One." Krishna of India, Horus of Egypt and Jesus of Egypt/Cannaan have equivalent symbolisms in that they show, through their myths, what is correct action that leads the way to salvation.

Jesus, the savior of Christianity, was persecuted at birth by the reigning King, because Jesus was prophesied to be the next king who would bring salvation and freedom. In the same way that Horus, of Neterian (Ancient Egyptian) Religion was persecuted after his birth by the King of Egypt, his uncle, Set, who had murdered Horus' father (Osiris), Jesus was persecuted after his birth because the ruling king feared that Jesus would take the throne which was rightfully his. Like Horus, who was persecuted by his uncle at birth, Krishna, of Indian Hindu religion, was also viciously persecuted from the time of his birth by his uncle, the king, because he, like Heru, was also prophesied to be the righteous king who would end the injustices of the existing king. The evil King Kamsa, Krishna's uncle, foresaw that Krishna would assume the kingship and defeat him, so Kamsa ordered that all male children

189

born around the same time as Krishna be killed (this part also parallels the story of Jesus).

Like the eyes of Horus, the eyes of Krishna represent the Sun and the Moon, duality unified into one whole. Krishna was born of a virgin mother as were Horus and Jesus, to fight the forces of evil on earth. As with Horus, he contained the entire Universe in his essence, as do all humans.

Horus, Jesus Christ and Krishna are symbols of the Soul in each individual which is the innermost Self that is constantly engaged in a battle of opposites (duality) within our minds and physical bodies over good-evil, virtue-vice, light-dark, yin-yang, positive-negative, prosperity-adversity, etc.

The correspondence in the birth stories of Horus, Krishna and Jesus is only one correlation out of many which point to a common origin of these traditions. If these myths are understood literally, then it would be odd to discover exact stories which match in almost every detail in different lands. The chance of this occurring is low at best. However, if they are seen as mythological stories with deeper messages, then we are able to see that there is a common origin and that these stories refer not to an event which occurred long ago, but to a mythic ongoing process which is occurring in the life of every human being even now.

From a mythic standpoint, the story surrounding the birth of a savior was never intended to be understood in a factual or literal sense or as referring to a single character or personality in history. There is something more important, beyond the actual facts themselves, which the ancient sages sought to convey. Principally, we are to understand that a savior is a metaphor for that principle within each of us which seeks to be saved from the clutches of egoism and to discover true peace and happiness.

Thus, myths surrounding these three saviors point to a special connection between ancient Egyptian Religion which worshipped Horus as the incarnation of Osiris, Indian Vaishnavism -Vasudeva cult which worshipped the God Krishna as the incarnation of Vishnu and Christianity which worships Jesus Christ as an embodiment or incarnation of God (the word of God) on earth.

**The Category Factor Cultural Comparison Method**

**Table 21: Supported Cross Cultural Correlations (*Strong*)**

| Cross-Cultural Correlations | Culture A | Culture B | Culture C | Culture D | Culture E | Culture F | Supported Matches |
|---|---|---|---|---|---|---|---|
| The primary matching category | *Mythic Character 1* | *Mythic Character 1* | *Mythic Character 1* | *Mythic Character 1* | *Mythic Character 1* | *Mythic Character 1* | Matches ← |
| The primary supporting factor → | *Iconography* | *Iconography* | *Iconography* | *Iconography* | *Iconography* | *Iconography* | Matches ← |
| Other possible additional supporting factors → ↗↗↗↗ | Function Actions Gender Age Metaphoric significance | Function Actions Gender Age Metaphoric significance | Function Actions Gender Age Metaphoric significance | Function Actions Gender Age Metaphoric significance | Function Actions Gender Age Metaphoric significance | Function Actions Gender Age Metaphoric significance | ↓↓↓↓↓ |

191

**Comparative Mythology, Cultural and Social Studies**

## Table 22: EXAMPLE: Data Collection Seeking Supported Cross-Cultural Correlations using savior gods (Basic)

| Cross-Cultural Correlations | Culture A Ancient Egypt Heru | Culture B India Krishna | Culture C Aryan Mitra | Culture D Persian Mithra/Meher | Culture E Zoroastrianism Mithra | Culture F Christianity Jesus |
|---|---|---|---|---|---|---|
| The primary matching category | *Mythic Character 1* | *Mythic Character 1* | *Mythic Character 1* | *Mythic Character 1* | *Mythic Character 1* | *Mythic Character 1* |
| | Gender *Male* | Gender *Male* | Gender *Male* | Gender *Male* | Gender *Male* | Gender *Male* |
| The primary supporting factor ➜ | Symbolic meaning *Savior* | Symbolic meaning *Savior* | Symbolic meaning *Savior* | Symbolic meaning *Savior* | Symbolic meaning *Savior* | Symbolic meaning *Savior* |
| The secondary supporting factor ➜ | Enemy of darkness, evil, unrighteousness | Enemy of darkness, evil, unrighteousness | Enemy of darkness, evil, unrighteousness | Enemy of darkness, evil, unrighteousness | Enemy of darkness, evil, unrighteousness | Enemy of darkness, evil, unrighteousness |
| | *God of Ethics, righteousness* | *God of Ethics, righteousness* | *God of Ethics, righteousness* | *God of Ethics, righteousness* | *God of Ethics, righteousness* | *God of Ethics, righteousness* |
| The tertiary supporting factor ➜ | Iconography *God of Light/sun* | Iconography *God of Light/sun* | Iconography *God of Light/sun* | Iconography *God of Light/sun* | Iconography *God of Light/sun* | Iconography *God of Light/sun* |

In this table we discovered that there are some divinities that appear in several cultures that seem to have several characteristics (Factors of Cultural manifestation) in common. If we explore further using fundamental cultural factors we may discover some differences between them that may suggest that the correlations are not due to cross cultural interaction in all of them.

The Category Factor Cultural Comparison Method

## Table 23: EXAMPLE: Data Collection Seeking Supported Cross-Cultural Correlations using savior gods (Detailed study)

| Cross-Cultural Correlations | Culture A Ancient Egypt *Heru* | Culture B India *Krishna* | Culture C Aryan *Mitra* | Culture D Persian *Mithra/Meher* | Culture E Zoroastrianism *Mithra* | Culture F Christianity *Jesus* |
|---|---|---|---|---|---|---|
| The primary matching category | *Mythic Character 1* | *Mythic Character 1* | *Mythic Character 1* | *Mythic Character 1* | *Mythic Character 1* | *Mythic Character 1* |
| | Gender *Male* | Gender *Male* | Gender *Male* | Gender *Male* | Gender *Male* | Gender *Male* |
| *Matching?* | ☑ | ☑ | ☑ | ☑ | ☑ | ☑ |
| The primary supporting factor → | Symbolic meaning *Savior* | Symbolic meaning *Savior* | Symbolic meaning *Savior* | Symbolic meaning *Savior* | Symbolic meaning *Savior* | Symbolic meaning *Savior* |
| *Matching?* | ☑ | ☑ | ☑ | ☑ | ☑ | ☑ |
| The secondary supporting | Enemy of darkness, evil, unrighteousness | Enemy of darkness, evil, unrighteousness | Enemy of darkness, evil, unrighteousness | Enemy of darkness, evil, unrighteousness | Enemy of darkness, evil, unrighteousness | Enemy of darkness, evil, unrighteousness |
| factor → | *God of Ethics, righteousness* | *God of Ethics, righteousness* | *God of Ethics, righteousness* | *God of Ethics, righteousness* | *God of Ethics, righteousness* | *God of Ethics, righteousness* |
| *Matching?* | ☑ | ☑ | ☑ | ☑ | ☑ | ☑ |
| | | | | | | |

193

Comparative Mythology, Cultural and Social Studies

| | | | | | | |
|---|---|---|---|---|---|---|
| The tertiary supporting factor → | Iconography *God of Light/sun* | Iconography *God of Light/sun* | Iconography *God of Light/sun* | Iconography *God of Light/sun* | Iconography *God of Light/sun* | Iconography *God of Light/sun* |
| *Matching?* | ☑ | ☑ | ☑ | ☑ | ☑ | ☑ |
| The quaternary supporting factor → | Iconography *Hawk* Anthropomorphic and zoomorphic | Iconography *human* Anthropomorphic | Iconography *human* Anthropomorphic | Iconography *human* Anthropomorphic | Iconography *human* Anthropomorphic | Iconography *human* Anthropomorphic |
| *Matching?* | *Partial match* | ☑ | ☑ | ☑ | ☑ | ☑ |
| The fifth supporting Factor → | **Mythic plot Dies, resurrected, becomes king** | Mythic plot Dies, resurrected, becomes king | Mythic plot Dies, resurrected | Mythic plot Dies, resurrected | Mythic plot Dies, resurrected | Mythic plot Dies, resurrected, becomes king |
| *Matching?* | ☑ | ☑ | *Partial match* | *Partial match* | *Partial match* | ☑ |
| The sixth supporting factor → | Mythic plot *Persecuted at birth* | Mythic plot *Persecuted at birth* | | | | Mythic plot *Persecuted at birth* |
| *Matching?* | ☒ | ☒ | ☒ | ☒ | ☒ | ☑ |
| The sixth supporting factor → | "great bull" "eye of the Sun" | Solar God | "great bull of the Sun" | "great bull of the Sun" | "great bull of the Sun" | Solar God |
| *Matching?* | ☑ | *Partial match* | ☑ | ☑ | ☑ | *Partial match* |
| | | | | | | |

194

## The Category Factor Cultural Comparison Method

| The sixth supporting factor → | *great traveling teacher and master.* | *great traveling teacher and master.* | *great traveling teacher and master.* | *great traveling teacher and master.* | *great traveling teacher and master.* | *great traveling teacher and master.* |
|---|---|---|---|---|---|---|
| *Matching?* | ☑ | ☑ | ☑ | ☑ | ☑ | ☑ |

In this table above we discovered more common factors between the artifacts of the different cultures but as we get more specific we see partial or no matches in some factors. Here the *Fundamental Cultural Factors* (see next chapter) become more important in determining possible cultural relationships and real cultural borrowings or adoptions from each other. If the mismatches are in areas of folk manifestation but the fundamental category-factors match, the differences may be explained by local folk differences which do not discount the substantive fundamental matches.

## Table 24: Categorizing the relative strength of correlation findings for Depth and Breadth findings

| Pattern of Correlations | Ranking |
|---|---|
| Depth correlations of one category match plus 2 or more supporting Factor matches. | Strong indication of correlation between the two artifacts. |
| Breadth correlations of 2 or more separate Categories of Cultural Expression with 1 category match plus 2 or more supporting Factor matches for each category. | Strong indication of correlation between the two cultures and artifacts if they belong to the same Category of cultural expression. |
| Depths & Breadth correlations together. | Strongest indication of correlation between the two cultures and artifacts or between the two cultures even if the artifacts do not belong to the same Category of cultural expression. |
| Depths & Breadth correlations together covering 3 or more cultures. | Strongly suggests cross cultural interaction, influence and or adoption of Factors of Cultural Expression between the cultures. |

# Determining Cultural Relationships and Influences with the Cultural Category- Factor Correlation Method

In order to present strong indication of cultural interaction in the presentation of artifacts of two different cultures it should be possible to demonstrate correlation evidences that rise above random chance matches. It is thought that the following criteria will constitute such evidence.

A. **CULTURAL INTERACTION-** In order to establish evidence to suggest the influence of one culture on another it must be possible to show exact Depth and Breadth concordances in at least 3 categories, including Evidence of Contact, and /or shared Ethnicity.

    a.   Each category of cultural expression match must be supported by at least three additional factor correlations

B. **CULTURAL PRIMACY-** In order to demonstrate that one culture has come first in history and that the later (secondary) culture has drawn cultural factors from the primary culture, it is necessary to first establish

    a.   Evidence of Contact, and /or shared Ethnicity.
    b.   Relative historical dating of the two cultures (when they existed relative to each other) and demonstrate a chronology in which the primary culture is shown to have developed previous to the secondary culture.
    c.   Show Matching Depth and Breadth Category-Factors of Cultural Manifestation as described in (A) above.
    d.   Relative historical dating of the artifacts of the two cultures (when the artifacts existed or were used relative to each other) and demonstrate a chronology in which the primary culture is shown to have used the artifact previous to the secondary culture.

C. **COMMON CULTURAL ORIGINS-** In order to establish evidence to suggest common origins of two given cultures it must be possible to show Evidence of Contact and or common Ethnicity.

# Chapter 6: The Fundamental Cultural Factors

What is it that distinguishes one culture from another? What parameters determine whether or not a cultural factor is borrowed by one group from another, and what criteria determines that a culture is not simply influenced, but is actually part of another culture? In order to proceed with our study we will need to outline what the fundamental aspects of cultural expression are and how to judge cultural interactions. In the book *The New Comparative Mythology, An Anthropological Assessment of the Theories of Georges Dumézil,* the author, C. Scott Littleton, discusses aspects of the theoretical models of *Georges Dumézil* and Claude Levi-Strauss. Dumézil and Lévi-Strauss drew heavily upon linguistic models and linguistics for their comparative studies which were confined to cultures using the same language family. Nevertheless, some of their efforts are useful for our wider study of myths and intercultural relations.

> To be sure, Lévi-Strauss had come to a similar conclusion about the relationship between the phenomena in question (Leach 1970, P. 50), but he extrapolated from it a *single* set of structural principles (the dialectic relationship between oppositions) far beyond any single historical tradition.
>
> In short, while both scholars took an important step beyond Durkheim, Dumézil has remained convinced that the underlying ideological principles (for Lévi-Strauss read "structural principles") that one may discover in a given tradition, principles that are replicated throughout the several social and supernatural paradigms characteristic of that tradition, are in fact an integral part of the tradition itself and not to be considered part of any larger, more abstract conception of the human thought process.[161]

The concept of "ideological principles" (Dumézil) or "structural principles" (Lévi-Strauss)has been advanced to deal with underlying aspects that might be treated as recurring characteristics in the process of the study of "social and supernatural paradigms" in a given tradition. However, the "ideological principles" or "structural principles" here are treated as characteristic only in that given tradition, that is, as a conception related to that particular tradition and not related to a wider common

---

[161] *The New Comparative Mythology, An Anthropological Assessment of the Theories of Georges Dumézil,* by C. Scott Littleton, p. 270

human paradigm. Here we will introduce *Core Fundamental Category-Factors of Cultural Expression* (or simply "Fundamental Factors") that should not be thought of as paradigms or themes but rather as avenues of cultural expression. For example, two individual drivers may take a trip from Madrid to Moscow. In this analogy, the desire to drive to Moscow is the *innate human impetus;* Moscow is the *Ultimate Reality,* the goal; the paths taken are the *"Category-Factors of Cultural Expression".* If they choose different routes, each route becomes the *cultural expression* (or tradition) of each driver. If they were to choose most or all of the same route then we could see correlations and be able to see if they may have traveled together, or perhaps they discussed the route and agreed on it, maybe one went first and then told the other the best route and the other agreed or perhaps they both received the same instruction and thought it best to use the same route. The actual roads themselves, the way of choosing them, the way of naming them and the way of naming their starting point and the destination as well as themselves as travelers, constitutes the mythic nature of their journey, composed of categories and factors of cultural expression.

The journey could be from Egypt to Ethiopia or Shanghai to Beijing; the locations are all the same from an archetypal point of view and the names of the roads might or might not be the same but their usage could be a unique way of correlating them with other forms of usage; the manner in working out the journey can be different but "correlatable". Joseph Campbell referred to a similar idea in his concept of a "Hero's Journey". He wrote: *"A hero ventures forth from the world of common day into a region of supernatural wonder: fabulous forces are there encountered and a decisive victory is won: the hero comes back from this mysterious adventure with the power to bestow boons on his fellow man."* Campbell explained that major myths of the world that survived for millenia, all tend to share a fundamental structure, that he called the *monomyth.* This fundamental structure, of a monomyth, according to Campbell, contains a number of stages, which include:[162]

(1) a *call to adventure,* which the hero has to accept or decline,
(2) a *road of trials,* regarding which the hero succeeds or fails,
(3) *achieving the goal or "boon,"* which often results in important self-knowledge,
(4) a *return to the ordinary world,* again as to which the hero can succeed or fail, and finally,
(5) *application of the boon* in which what the hero has gained can be used to improve the world.

---

[162] *The Hero with a Thousand Faces* by Joseph Campbell (1949)

Campbell's exposition is simplified, for general consumption especially for Western readers and also may appear to have a phenomenological outlook; the terms adventure, trials, and boon may appear to most people to relate to worldly adventures, like a road trip or winning a lottery or a trip to Africa. Yet, they refer to deeper psycho-spiritual aspects of human existence. Though, item #5 of Campbell's scheme can be equated with service to humanity that the hero performs upon returning to ordinary life, after the life changing journey. That boon or, in our terms, the discovery of the "Ultimate Reality", does not serve to improve the world directly but rather indirectly if those who have made the journey are allowed to instruct others, especially the leadership of society, in the ways of wisdom.

Our concept of *psychomyth,* organizes the scheme of the human journey as follows:

1. The innate desire to discover the "Ultimate Reality" of life compels and impels a person to seek for it in search of the true nature of Self, abiding peace, happiness and contentment.
2. the person's *innate human impetus,* causes them to embark on a journey of discovery by,
3. learning the societal philosophy of life contained in the culture and myth of the society,
4. then by living the myth, as its protagonist, including practicing the rituals of the myth, that have been set up in their culture, for that purpose and is based on the *societal philosophy* in order to make the myth effective and not just as an object of faith or belief,
5. then the practitioner struggles to perfect the ethical conscience enjoined by the myth and its philosophy through the trials, struggles and tribulations of life,
6. finally, the now wise, contented and transformed personality can live the rest of their life in fulfillment and as an example, a model for others who may listen and adopt the path.

As explained earlier, the innate human desire to engage in a mystical movement in life to discover the "Ultimate Reality" is the catalyst for the spiritual journey, the *psychomythic* movement. The final success of the journey can take lifetimes. In terms of comparison, the journeys of two myths do not have to be the same in terms of their folklore, even though they are the same in terms of psychomythic archetype. If we were to find the same archetypal journey and the same or many of the same folkloric factors of cultural expression we could consider that the differences would constitute the "Folk" component of the culture, the variable feature of cultural manifestations.

There are fundamental variables, aspects of cultural expression that would be less variable and denote unmistakable correlations between cultures. The journey is the archetype so that is not correlated since everyone has the journey. However, if the manner (factors of cultural expression) of the journey turns out to be the same in its fundamentals and variables the two cultures could be highly correlated. So the archetypes are basic human endeavors and can be correlated in and of themselves as common human paradigms since they apply to all human beings. As archetypes they are not considered either as cultural expression categories or factors but only structures of cultural expression or its scaffolding; they are not used for cultural comparison purposes. Instead, the manner (way of expressing) of working out the journey, that was chosen by a culture, can be compared. If commonalities or non-commonalities exist in those *Category-Factors of Cultural of Expression* of each culture they can be catalogued and quantified and their degree of similarity or dissimilarity can be calculated.

As stated earlier the concept, under which this current study of culture is based, is the contention that when several Category-Factors of Cultural Expression can be correlated or matched, and when these matches can be supported by varied aspects within the two cultures, then the study becomes more concrete and specific as opposed to abstract and general. The higher level of specificity raises the validity of the arguments and the conclusions drawn from them. But where is the threshold wherein it becomes obvious that a group of peoples is related to another? The following cultural principles are offered as criterion for such a determination. *Societal Philosophy, Myth, Rituals and Traditions* (related to the myth), *Evidence of Contact* and *Ethnicity*) may be considered as the basic qualities which define a culture and which it carries forth over time. These cultural factors may be thought of as the core fundamental elements of cultural expression which constitute a unique form of expression from the standpoint of the determination of its kinship to another culture. Contact is considered here because proven contact bolsters the overall findings of correlation.

1) **Philosophical synchronism**
   a) Same meaning in concepts presented
   b) Same meaning in wisdom instruction (same teaching)
2) **Myth synchronism**
   a) Same Plot elements (same situations with same interactions)
   b) Same Theme
3) **Rituals traditions synchronism**
   a) Same ritual procedure (particular way of usage of an artifact)
4) **Contact – evidence of prior contact (relationships)**
   a) Evidence of contact may substitute for direct ethnic relationship
5) **Ethnicity – both groups matching in their ethnic background**

a)   Ethnic correlation may substitute for Evidence of contact.

So under this model, even if people born in Ancient Egypt were to be found in India, if their lives and activities did not match in the other pertinent cultural factors, they would not be considered as members of the same culture for the purposes of this study. Accordingly, it must be understood here that though some have defined ethnicity as "people of the same race or nationality who share a distinctive culture," the term "ethnicity" does not specifically or exclusively relate to race bur rather to nationality (using the nomenclature presented in this definition (nationality is a relatively new concept in human history)). The word "ethnic" may have originated from the Biblical term "ethnos" meaning *"of or pertaining to a group of people recognized as a class on the basis of certain distinctive characteristics, such as religion, language, ancestry, culture, or national origin."* So, using this latter definition, the term ethnicity has much in common with the term culture in the sense that ethnicity is the group that follows a particular culture. Since the concept of "race" is erroneous anyway, it does not apply to this program of study. It would apply in studies of those groups and individuals who believe in and adhere to the socio-political, economic and psychological concepts and institutions founded upon the concept of racism.

## Figure 12: Fundamental and Secondary Cultural Category-Factors of Cultural Expression

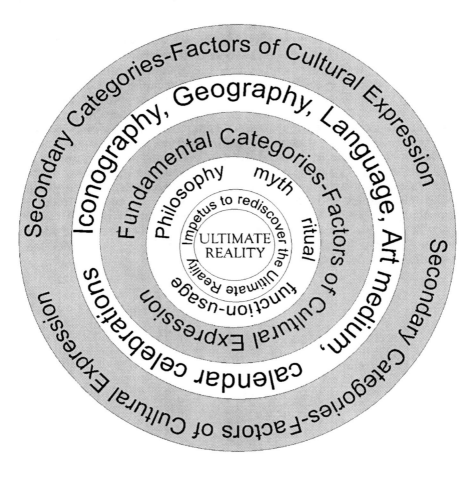

## Table 25: : Fundamental and Secondary Cultural Category-Factors of Cultural Expression

| | **Cultural Expressions** | |
|---|---|---|
| | ⬆ | |
| Secondary Categories- Factors of Cultural Expression | Other folk expressions Iconography, ‡ Geography, Language, Art medium, calendar celebrations, | ‡secondary unless used as an expression of the philosophy |
| | ⬆ | |
| Fundamental Categories- Factors of Cultural Expression | Evidence of Contact** function-usage ritual, Myth, Philosophy | **fundamental when study used to determine cultural interactions, borrowings, adoptions, influences etc. |
| | ⬆ | |
| | Impetus to rediscover the Ultimate Reality | |
| | ⬆ | |
| Most power motivating*** factor in pre-modern culture to create culture | ULTIMATE REALITY*** | ***A culture can have three motivating movements:<br>• Rediscover ultimate reality<br>• Pursue worldly pleasures, power and wealth<br>• Mixed |

# The Importance of Evidence of Contact as a method to establish cultural relations and the problem of Bias in Looking at Possible Evidences that may establish Evidence of Contact between two cultures

## General forms of contact between cultures:

a. Concurrent – cultures develop at the same time - equal exchanges relationship
b. Dependent – one culture depends on the other for technology, instruction - Donor – recipient relationship
c. Common Origins- Cultures originate from the same point with the same primary categories and then branch off and develop factors of cultural expression independently.
d. Eye witness accounts
e. Self descriptions – Their own writings acknowledge the contact.
f. Pacts – treaties, etc.

Evidence of contact is a special feature of cultural comparative studies because without it our assertions of cultural correlations would only go as far as being considered possible statistical probabilities. The finding of evidence of contact between two cultures solidly allows not only the possibility of past cultural exchange but also provides a solid foundation for findings of correlation in the categories between two cultures. The nature of the contact may differ and may be influenced by which culture is primary or which culture is strongest in its cultural expressions (the primary culture may not be the stronger as far as cultural expressions). Therefore, a secondary[163] culture could in theory more strongly influence the primary culture it comes into contact with. If the primary is the stronger then it is more likely that the influence would be from the primary to the secondary culture. If the primary culture was in existed prior to the secondary culture then it is more likely that the influence would be from the primary to the secondary culture.

---

[163] emerged after the primary

# Forms of Contact between cultures and Kinds of Evidence already documented by researchers.

As explained earlier, the ages of human existence (Stone Age, Metal Age, Copper Age, Iron Age and the Bronze Age, etc.) were experienced at different times in different geographical areas of the world in accordance with the particular culture's capacity for technological ingenuity or contact with other technologically advanced groups.

Many people have tried to assert the veracity of the Judeo-Christian Bible through evidence of contact. However, that evidence has been scarce. The work of Darwin (theory of evolution) and other scientists caused major controversies in Western society. A case in point is the attempt to correlate the events of the Biblical story of Exodus with those of the Ancient Egyptian Pharaoh, Ramses II. The argument for the interaction between the Jews and the Egyptians is predicated upon Evidence of Contact and then extrapolating to the assumption of contact between Moses and Ramses. Firstly, while there is evidence of a group of Hebrews who may have been the group later referred to, in modern times, as the Jews of the Bible,[164] there are no accounts of any conflict between the Jews and the Egyptians in any Ancient Egyptian records yet discovered, beyond an inscription at the Karnak temple in Egypt stating that the Jews were one of the tribes under Egyptian rule in Palestine. Secondly, there are no corroborating records of the events chronicled in the Bible in any of the contemporary writings of its time, from countries that had contact with the Ancient Egyptians and should have been able to know of or have had contact with the Jews as well. Thirdly, there were at least eleven kings who went by the title Remises (Remises I, II, III, IV, etc.), spanning a period dated by traditional Egyptologists from 1,307 B.C.E. to 1,070 B.C.E. The name Remises was so powerful that the term Pharaoh came to be synonymous with the term Remises; so we would need more specific data to correlate a specific Pharaoh with the supposed Jews which we also do not have sufficient data to substantiate the existence of. Further, some localities were also referred to as Remises.

The aforesaid brings up an important issue that affects the reliability of evidence of contact findings, that of corroboration. This assertion of the historicity of the Bible is referred to as *Literalism.* Practitioners in orthodox religions have adopted the stance of literalism and prefer to

---

[164] The Merenptah Stele –also known as Israel Stele, see the book *The Limits of Faith* by Muata Ashby

distance themselves from myth especially since the term myth has been likened in Western culture to a falsehood or an untruth. Also, since myth has been found to be such an integral part of non-Western religions, the Western religions would distance themselves further so as not to be compared or amalgamated with those religions. Many people have come to believe that the Bible contains historical and infallible information that does not require outside verification. Consequently those people believe anything the Bible says even though most personalities and events in it, especially those items related to historical events that supposedly occurred and personalities that supposedly existed, have no independent corroboration. It is important to realize that the mythic value of the Biblical stories such as that of Moses, Jesus, etc. is not at issue here. What is at issue is the claim of the historicity of the Biblical stories. When we look at myth we do not assert their historicity even though we may generally determine when they were / are observed, rather, we look for archetypal truths that may be universal or related to specific cultures, which inform us about the nature of human existence, cultural expressions and or cultural interactions.

When we compare two cultures or aspects of two cultures we are to compare two actual similar or compatible artifacts and not the claim of artifacts; that is to say, we are to compare for example, a ritual in one culture to a ritual in another. If we compare personalities those are to be compared independent of history unless that history can be verified independently. So, for example, we may compare a tenet of Judaism in the Bible to an Ancient Egyptian tenet but we cannot compare a personality such as Moses to a personality in Ancient Egypt such as Imhotep since there is no independent verification that Moses existed in ancient times, except in the Bible but there is evidence that Imhotep existed as a living personality. We may compare Moses as a mythic personality to a mythic personality in Ancient Egyptian culture but we cannot compare Moses to a historical personality in Ancient Egyptian or any other culture.

## EXAMPLE: Contacts between Ancient Egypt and Ancient Sumer

A brief study of the knowledge about Sumerian religion reveals many similarities to Ancient Egyptian religion in its basic respects. Sumer was known as the southern region of ancient Mesopotamia. This area was later known as the southern part of Babylonia and today it is known as south central Iraq. Like Ancient Egypt, it was an agricultural civilization. While Egyptian civilization emerged within Africa, the Sumerian culture emerged in Asia Minor.  It is widely accepted that Sumerian culture emerged during the 3rd millennia B.C.E. The geological evidences related to the Great Sphinx and other evidences demonstrate that Ancient Egyptian civilization is much older. It must be noted that the revised history, which is based on new archeological and geological evidences, shows that Ancient Egyptian civilization, including the invention of writing, arose prior to Sumerian Civilization and the Indus Valley Civilization. The evidence of contact and the correlations in the myths and other artifacts (factors of cultural expression) between Ancient Egyptian, Sumerian and the Indus Valley Civilizations again point to an influence of the Ancient Egyptian culture and its philosophy on the emerging civilizations.

The land of the Sumerians was called Sumer and was referred to as Shinar in the Bible. The Sumerians, up until recently, have been credited with forming the earliest of the ancient civilizations. However, their origins are obscured in the past. They are not believed to have been Semites like most of the peoples of the region. They apparently spoke a language which was unrelated to other known tongues. It is believed that they may have come to southern Mesopotamia, the area of Ur, from Persia, or northeastern Mesopotamia before 4,000 B.C.E. However, this is speculation by archeologists. It has also been widely circulated that the Sumerians were the first to create writing and that they influenced Ancient Egyptian culture. The syllabic signs of Ancient Egyptian Hieroglyphic language did not indicate differences in vowel sounds, as did the Sumerian script. While the Sumerian language has been thought by some scholars to be related to the Ancient Egyptian, the similarities are only due to general correspondences which all pictographic languages have in their original forms. Thus, Ancient Egyptian, Sumerian and Mayan (Native American) scripts show several similarities, but these cannot, in and of themselves in the absence of other supporting evidences, be used to say that one necessarily originates from the other. Also, the Sumerian language is believed to be agglutinative and unrelated to any other known language. The Ancient Egyptian language is related to the Hamitic (African) family of languages. [165] Nevertheless, a comparison of some of the mythic features of the two cultures yields several matches which may be used for comparative studies, apart from the linguistic aspects. The following table lists some correlatable cultural factors.

---

[165] Copton's Encyclopedia

## Table 26: Ancient Egyptian Mythology and Extrapolated Sumerian Mythology

| SUMERIAN RELIGION[166] / [167] | ANCIENT EGYPTIAN RELIGION |
|---|---|
| A- The Sumerians believed that the universe was ruled by a pantheon of divinities comprising a group of living beings, human in form, but immortal and possessing superhuman powers. They believed these beings to be invisible to mortal eyes, and that they controlled and guided the cosmos in accordance with well-laid plans and duly prescribed laws. | A- The Ancient Egyptian Religion was headed by a pantheon. It was comprised of Ra or Pa-Neter, the Supreme Being, and from him emanated the neteru or gods and goddesses. They were depicted with human forms, but were symbolic of unseen cosmic principles. |
| B- The Sumerians recognized four leading deities. They were known as gods of creation. These gods were An, the god of heaven, Ki, the goddess of earth, Enlil, the god of air, and Enki, the god of water. Thus, heaven, earth, air, and water were considered as the four major constituents of the universe. | B- The main gods and goddesses of the Ancient Egyptian pantheon of the city of Anu were: |
| Enlil – Air<br>Enki – Water<br>Ki – Earth<br>An – Heaven, Sky | Shu- Air<br>Tefnut- Moisture (water)<br>Geb- Earth<br>Nut- Sky, Heaven |
| C- It was held that the act of creation was accomplished through the utterance of the divine word. The deity doing the creating had only to make plans mentally and then pronounce the name of the thing to be created. | C- Creation was accomplished by God in the form of Neberdjer, by uttering his own name. God could create by merely thinking it into existence. The same creative word teaching was later adopted by the Greeks (logos) and the Christians (John 1:1 - *In* |

---

[166] "Funk and Wagnals New Encyclopedia"
[167] Random House Encyclopedia.

| | |
|---|---|
| | *the beginning was the Word, and the Word was with God, and the Word was God.).* |
| D- To maintain the universe in harmonious and continuous operation and to avoid conflict and confusion, the gods brought the "me" into being. It was a set of unchangeable and universal rules and laws that all beings were required to obey. | D- In order to maintain the universe, God instituted Maat. Maat is the principle and philosophy of cosmic order, justice, righteousness and harmony which all nature follows. All human beings were required to practice Maat in order to live in harmony with nature and each other, and to reach the eternal abode to live with God after death. |
| E- Each of the important deities was the patron of one or more Sumerian cities. Large temples were erected in the name of the deity, who was worshiped as the divine ruler and protector of the city. Temple rites were conducted by many priests, priestesses, singers, musicians, sacred prostitutes, and eunuchs. Sacrifices were offered daily. | E- The cities of Ancient Egypt were known as Nomes. Each had a patron deity. Many temples survive to this day. Daily rituals were performed by Priests and Priestesses. |
| F- The Sumerians believed that human beings were fashioned of clay. | F- The Ancient Egyptians believed that God, in the form of Khnum, fashioned human beings on a potter's wheel. |
| G- When human beings die, it was believed that their spirits descend to the netherworld. | G- When human beings die, they go to the Duat (netherworld) where they are judged in accordance with their deeds while on earth. |

The Gilgamesh Epic is an important Middle Eastern work of literature. It was written on twelve clay tablets in cuneiform about 2000 B.C.E. The Gilgamesh Epic relates the story of its hero, Gilgamesh, and includes the city of Uruk which is known in the Bible as Erech (now Warka, Iraq). The Sumerians created an advanced culture which included the development of cuneiform writing but their country soon fell to outside invasions. There was a brief Sumerian renaissance centered on Ur, which continued until c.1950 B.C.E. when Semitic Amorites overran much of Sumeria. This was the beginning of a long period of instability in Mesopotamia until the first Babylonian Dynasty was founded in 1830 B.C.E., which reached its height with Hammurabi. This date is believed to mark the end of the Sumerian state. Thereafter the Sumerian culture was then adopted almost completely by Babylonia. The dates for Abraham's departure from Ur are possibly mythically related to this period since there were undoubtedly many migrations out of the area during that time. It is clear to see that Abraham was influenced by Sumerian culture and there is evidence that there was trade between the Sumerians and the Ancient Egyptians.

The Image of the Sphinx, the Quintessential Ancient Egyptian Symbol of Spiritual Enlightenment appears in Mesopotamian and Greek iconography

**Figure 13: Ancient Egyptian Winged Sphinx**

**Figure 14: Left- Assyrian Winged Sphinx. Above: Right: Greek Winged Sphinx**

**Figure 15: Left- Ancient Egyptian Sefer (Griffin). Above: Right: Griffin of Asian and Western myth**

The Griffin is a mythical creature, originally thought to have originated in Asia Minor and Persia, the supposed guardian of hidden treasure, with the body, tail, and hind legs of a lion, and the head, forelegs, and wings of an eagle.[168] One of the most important Ancient Egyptian stories about the Sefer is the Myth of Hetheru and Djehuti.[169] The Sefer has the head of the Hawk (Falcon) because it is related to the Supreme Divinity *Heru*, whose main symbol is the Hawk.

In Egyptology, prior to the 1970's the orthodox view of the creators of the civilization today known as Ancient Egypt were asserted to be from Mesopotamia (Asia Minor) and not Africans from Africa. This view was unchallenged even though it was based on theories assuming that Mesopotamian culture (Sumeria) arose before or was contemporary with Ancient Egypt. Dr. Cheikh Anta Diop presented eleven categories of evidence, at the 1974 Unesco conference of Egyptologists, to support his argument for a native black African KMT[170]. One of those evidences involved an analysis of four issues involving possible evidence of contact or evidences of the expected effects of such contact if it had occurred. This analysis was not refuted by the Egyptologists who had claimed the Mesopotamian origin theory.

> Item #3: There were no data presented to show that Ancient Egyptian temperament and thought were related to Mesopotamia.

---

[168] Copyright © 1995 Helicon Publishing Ltd
[169] See the book *The Glorious Light* by Muata Ashby
[170] Kamit (Ancient Egypt)

Item # 5: There was no evidence of large-scale migration between Kamit (Ancient Egypt) and Mesopotamia. There were no Mesopotamian loan words in Ancient Egyptian: (therefore the two cultures could have no genetic linguistic relationship or be populated by the same people.) For comparison purposes, mention was made of the fact that when documented contact with Kamit was made by Asian Hyksos around 1700 B.C.E., loan words were left in ancient Kamit.

Item #7: Muslim Arabs conquered Kamit during the 7th century of the Common Era. Therefore, Arabic culture is not a part of Kamit during any part of the 3,000 years of dynastic Kamit.

Item #8: Genetic linguistic relationships exist between the African languages of Ancient Egyptian, Cushitic (Ethiopian), Puanite (Punt or Somaliland), Berber, Chadic and Arabic. Arabic only covered territory off the continent of Africa, mainly in adjacent Saudi Arabia, an area in ancient times that was as much African as Asian.

## EXAMPLE: Contacts between Ancient Egypt and other African nations

Edward Wilmot Blyden (1832 - 1912) was one of the first African American theologian/scholars to recognize a connection between Ancient Egypt and the West African nations. He began to notice that the trade routs across the Sahara desert, which can be seen even today, transported goods and people, creating an inexorable connection between Northeast and West Africa. This contact existed since ancient times. The evidence of its existence can be found on the walls of the tombs of the nobles in Egypt – below (picture by Ashby (2000)). These are the same trade routs that were used by the Arabs, who conquered north Africa later in history, to communicate, extend trade and spread the Islamic faith to West Africa, and they did so from their base in Egypt.

214

**Figure 16: Ancient Traders: Painting from the "Tombs of the Nobles" in Ancient Egypt**

_**Ancient Traders:**_ Painting from the "Tombs of the Nobles" in Ancient Egypt (New Kingdom) showing desert traders coming from other parts of Africa to Egypt. Note the hat of the first man from the right. This is the same type of hat used by traders in the present day region of West Sahara (Western Sudan) and it is also used by present day Dogons.

Cheikh Anta Diop presented compelling evidences to show that the Wolof language (Senegal) is derived from the Ancient Egyptian.[171] Yoruba is a term that refers to a people (Oyo, Ife, Ilesha, Egbe, and Ijebu), a culture and a language originally based in Africa, as well as a religion. There are many parallels between Ancient Egyptian religion and the Yoruba religion. Both incorporate a system of divinities which represent cosmic forces, and many direct correlations can be observed between them. The Yoruba people reside in Western Africa (Nigeria). While many scholars of Yoruba openly state that there is little or no connection between these systems of spirituality, others have attempted to show that there are linguistic correlations and there was contact in ancient times. As in the Dogon culture, some practitioners of Yoruba religion openly acknowledge their lineage to Ancient Egypt. The Asarian (Ancient Egyptian religion of the god Osiris) artifacts that have been discovered

---

[171] _The African Origin of Civilization_, _Civilization or Barbarism,_ Cheikh Anta Diop

elsewhere in Africa[172] show that there was contact between Ancient Egypt and other countries in the interior of Africa. The Ancient Egyptian clergy carried with them certain aspects of spiritual knowledge which became incorporated in other cultures, through the influence of the clergy. In the late period of Ancient Egyptian history the Ancient Nubians fully adopted the Ancient Egyptian religion and culture. Therefore, by looking at the mythology of Yoruba and Shetaut Neter (Ancient Egyptian Religion), direct correlations in the fundamental theological principles of the religions are found which establish a relationship between the two.

## EXAMPLE: Contacts between Ancient Egypt and Ancient Greeks

In the area of the relationship between the early Greek Philosophers and the ancient Egyptian philosophers the Greek philosophers, Thales, Pythagoras, Plato and others acknowledged their debt to the Ancient Egyptian sages for their instruction in art, music, philosophy, etc.

The Greek philosopher, Plato, wrote about a mythic land he was told about by the Ancient Egyptian priests called "Atlantis". Many writers and scholars have speculated throughout history about the location of Atlantis. In most every way the known history and remains of the Minoan civilization on the island of Crete best fit the description of Atlantis. Artifacts confirming trade and contact with the Ancient Egyptians, such as art and architecture that seem to copy the Ancient Egyptian, have been discovered on Crete up to the reign of Pharaoh Amenhotep III, which also confirms the date of 1400 B.C.E. (explosion at Santorini). In the Ancient Egyptian records, the Cretans are referred to as the *Keftiu*.

---

[172] *The African Origin of Civilization*, Cheikh Anta Diop – *Civilization or Barbarism*, Cheikh Anta Diop

## Figure 17: Minoans offering tribute to the Egyptian king Djehutimes III

Above: Minoans offering tribute to the Egyptian king Djehutimes III (Thutmose 18th Dynasty). The Cretans are distinguishable by their clothing. (Norman de Garis Davies; Tomb of Rekh-mi-Ra at Thebes, vol. II, plates 19 and 18)

This civilization of the Minoans flourished between 2000 B.C.E. and 1400 B.C.E. when it was apparently disrupted by a cataclysm that caused the civilization to cease. The art and culture of the Minoan civilization shows influences in artistic forms and customs that are unmistakably Ancient Egyptian in character, and there is ample physical evidence as proof of contact between the two cultures. As Ancient Egypt was the older civilization (beginning around 10,000 B.C.E. or before), it is no surprise that the Ancient Egyptians retained knowledge of the Minoans after the cataclysm destroyed the Minoan civilization, especially as there was a close relationship between them. The fact that the Ancient Egyptians did have knowledge and the Greeks of the Classical Period had little or no knowledge about the Minoans points to the degradation of culture which the Greeks had sustained, and the level of disconnection with their own past history, even in ancient times.

The bull figures prominently in Minoan art and spirituality. One of the Minoan myths relates that there was a great Bull who lived in the underground labyrinths beneath the great palace; king Minos defeated it. The bull was called Minator. Another myth relates that it was to be given *seven virgins.* In Ancient Egyptian mythology, the bull is the symbol of Asar, one of the most important divinities. He is given seven cows, who in turn give rise to Creation. Some examples of the similarities between the Ancient Egyptian and Minoan cultures using the cultural factors, *art* and *iconography,* are below.

## Figure 18: Depictions of the Bovine Iconography in Ancient Egypt

**Above left: The god Asar-Hapi, also known in later times as Serapis by the Greeks and Romans,**
**depicted as part bull and part human (mixed zoomorphic and anthropomorphic, respectively).**
**Above center: the Asar-Hapi bull in full zoomorphic form.**
**Above right: Asar-Hapi (bottom tier) and the seven Hetheru cows.**

## Figure 19: the Minoan bull.

Above left: the Minoan bull. Above right: a late period Minoan statue of a person wearing the bull horns with upraised arms.

## Figure 20: The Griffin of Ancient Egypt and the Ancient Minoans

Above left: Ancient Egyptian *Sefer* (Griffin). Above right: Minoan Griffin (palace relief)

The Category Factor Cultural Comparison Method

## Figure 21: Processions in Ancient Egyptian and Minoan Iconography

Above: Procession of red colored men and white colored women bringing offerings to the mummy of Any (Papyrus of Any 18th Dynasty-Ancient Egypt)

Above: Minoan sarcophagus with red colored men and white colored women bringing offerings to the dead personality.

## EXAMPLE: Contacts between Ancient Egypt and Ancient Pre-Judaic Mesopotamian cultures

The goddess Lilith is an important deity that shows the connection between Ancient Egyptian Religion and Pre-Judaic Mesopotamian religion and Judaism. According to Hebrew legends, Lilith was regarded as the first wife of Adam, the first man in the Jewish Bible. However, her story was later omitted from the Bible cannon when its books were compiled. She was repudiated because of her independence and sexual freedom. Nevertheless, the images of the goddess are clearly Ancient Egyptian in origin (see below). Given the known evidence of contact between Sumerian culture and the Ancient Egyptian, it is clear that she was adopted into Mesopotamian culture at a date prior to the formation of Judaism (2,000 B.C.E.-1,000 B.C.E.) According to a Hebrew legend, Adam married Lilith because he was tired of having sex relations with animals. This practice was prohibited in the Bible (Deuteronomy 27:21). At the time when the Old Testament was being compiled, Lilith was seen as a demoness because, according to a legend, she refused to have sexual relations while in the missionary position (male on top, female on bottom).[173] This practice of keeping women on the bottom was a product of a male oriented and patriarchal culture and it is one of the fundamental differences between the Western religions (Judaism, Christianity, and Islam) which developed out of the cultures of Asia Minor during the Counter Reversion era. In African and East Asian Religions mythologically the female is almost always found to be on top and the male on the bottom. In African and East Asian Religions the woman is considered as the heavens and the man is earth because she does the work of Creation (movement like the clouds) and he is Spirit which is the regarded as the "unmoved mover" (in nature the earth is sedentary and heaven is dynamic). The Muslims repudiated this kind of sexual position and so did the Christians. Muslims have expressed the opinion: "Accursed be the man who maketh woman heaven and himself earth."[174] Christians stated that any sexual position that did not maintain male dominance was sinful.[175] The contact between the early Hebrews and the Ancient Egyptian culture, which has been documented, facilitated the adoption of the Lilith iconography from the Ancient Egyptian Goddess. So Lilith was adopted by the Hebrews in pre-Judaic times[176] but was later discarded when the religion of Judaism turned away from a balance between male and female and placed more importance on the male aspect of divinity.

---

[173] *Woman's Encyclopedia of Myths and Secrets* by Barbara Walker
[174] *The Jewel in the Lotus,* Edwardes, Allen, Lancer Books, 1965, p 157
[175] *Hebrew Myths*, Robert Graves and Raphael Patai, 1964, p 67
[176] Before the formation of the Jewish religion.

# Cultural Interactions Throughout History Demonstrating Evidence of Contact

## Cultural Interactions Between Judaism and Ancient Egypt

The next prominent example of adoption of religious culture comes from the relationship between Judaism and Ancient Egypt. Many times in the emergence of new mythologies throughout history, the founders or followers of the new system of religion will create stories to show how the new system surpasses the old. The story of Exodus is such an example. Moses went to Mount Sinai to talk to God and brought back Ten Commandments. As we saw earlier, at the time that Moses was supposed to have lived (1,200?-1,000? B.C.E.), Ancient Egypt was the most powerful culture in the ancient world. However, at the time when the bible was written (900 B.C.E.-100 B.C.E.), Egypt was on a social and cultural decline from its previous height as the foremost culture in religious practice, art, science, social order, etc. So it apparently became necessary for the Jews, a small group of Ancient Egyptians (according to the Bible, the early Jews were ethnic Ancient Egyptians),[177] to legitimize the inception of their new theology by claiming to have triumphed over the mighty Egyptian gods with the help of their new "true god" who defeated the "weak" gods of Egypt. This triumphant story would surely bring people to convert to the new faith, since up to that time, the Ancient Egyptian gods and goddesses had been seen not only as the most powerful divinities, but also, according to the Greeks, as the source of other deities in other religions. So in effect, by saying that the Jewish God "defeated" the Ancient Egyptian God by freeing the Jews, it is the same as saying that a new, more powerful religion is to be followed. This form of commencement for a spiritual tradition is not uncommon. As an example of inculturation, the similarity between the story of Moses of the Jews and Sargon I from Assyria (reigned about 2,335-2,279 B.C.E.) is instructive. Like the later Moses of the Jewish Bible, Sargon also was placed in a basket and floated down a river to be picked up by the royal household. So part of the story of Moses is borrowed from Assyrian history.

In almost the exact same expression as one of the Ancient Egyptian creation myths, the original Jewish Bible and related texts also describe the Creation in terms of an act of sexual union. *Elohim* (Ancient Hebrew for gods/goddesses) impregnates the primeval waters with *ruach,* a Hebrew word which means *spirit, wind* or the verb *to hover.* The same word means *to brood* in Syriac. Elohim, also called El, was a name used for God in

---

[177] From more details see the book *Christian Yoga: The Journey from Jesus to Christ* by Muata Ashby

some Hebrew scriptures. It was also used in the Old Testament for heathen gods. Thus, as the Book of Genesis explains, Creation began as the spirit of God "moved over the waters" and agitated those waters into a state of movement. In Ancient Egyptian myth the god Ra stirred the waters with his movements in the form of *Nun* or as the giant serpent of the world or with his divine *"boat of millions of years."* The same concept appears in Ancient Egyptian Memphite Theology and in the theology of the goddesses of Ancient Egypt as well, being one of Ancient Egyptian religion's most prominent teachings.

In Western traditions the active role of Divinity has been assigned to the male gender, while the passive (receiving) role has been assigned to the female gender. This is in contrast to the Southern and Eastern philosophical views where the passive role is assigned to the male gender, and the active role to the female.

## Cultural Interactions Between Judaism and Babylonia

In this area of study, an important figure from Mesopotamia is Hammurabi. Hammurabi is believed to have lived around 1,792-1,750 B.C.E. He was king of Babylonia in the first dynasty. He expanded his rule over Mesopotamia and organized the empire by building wheat granaries, canals and classified the law into the famous "Code of Hammurabi." The divine origin ascribed to the Code is of particular interest to our study. Hammurabi can be seen receiving the Code in a bas-relief in which he is depicted as receiving the Code from the sun-god, Shamash, in much the same way that Moses would later receive the Ten Commandments from God, who had appeared as the burning bush (fire is a solar motif). In Ancient Egypt the Precepts of Maat were given through the divinities Maat and Djehuti. This mode of introducing a teaching or new order, by claiming it to be divinely ordained, may be seen as in reality an attempt to impress on the masses of people the authenticity, importance and force with which the new teaching was received and must therefore be followed. Like Moses, Hammurabi created the laws himself, or in conjunction with others, wishing to institute a new order for society. Whether or not they were divinely inspired relates to the degree of communion they were able to achieve with the Divine Self, God. This they could only ascertain for themselves. Some observers feel that the motivation behind the introduction of the legal codes in this way is that it is possible that spiritually immature people tend to follow a teaching when they believe that it was inspired by God, even if they cannot know for certain intellectually. They feel they somehow "know" in their hearts as they are urged by passionate preachers to have faith. However, if people are fanatical instead of introspective and sober in their religious practice, they may follow the teachings of those who are not authentic spiritual leaders and be led blindly, even to their death.

## Cultural Interactions Between Ancient Egypt and Ancient Greece

Greek Myth is a conglomeration of stories related to certain divine personalities and their interactions with each other and with human beings. The main stories about the Greek divinities (gods and goddesses) are contained in the epics, *The Iliad* and *The Odyssey,* written by Homer (900 B.C.E.). The main functions of the gods and goddesses and their mingling with human beings was outlined in these early Greek myths. The early Greeks also spoke of the origins of their gods and goddesses. It must be clearly understood that at the time when the early Greeks organized themselves sufficiently enough in order to take up the task of learning art, culture and civilization, they had very little in the way of culture, and what they did have was primitive by Ancient Egyptian standards thousands years earlier. The force of the Ancient Egyptian culture created perhaps the strongest impression, but it was not the only impression, since the Greeks traveled to other lands and attempted to assimilate the teachings of others as well. This, coupled with their own ideas, caused a situation wherein they created a synthesis of religious philosophies. The expression of Greek culture and philosophy in later periods is reflective of this synthesis. In short, what is regarded as Greek myth was in reality a patchwork of differing ideas that had their basis in Ancient Egyptian philosophy, but which did not follow its precepts entirely as the following statement from Herodotus suggests. *(Bold portions are by Ashby)*

> 35. "Almost all the names of the gods came into Greece from Egypt. **My inquiries prove that they were all derived from a foreign source, and my opinion is that Egypt furnished the greater number.** For with the exception of Neptune and the Dioscuri, whom I mentioned above, and Juno, Vesta, Themis, the Graces, and the Nereids, the other gods have been known from time immemorial in Egypt. This I assert on the authority of the Egyptians themselves."
>
> - Herodotus

> **"Solon, Thales, Plato, Eudoxus** and **Pythagoras** went to Egypt and consorted with the priests. **Eudoxus** they say, received instruction from Chonuphis of Memphis,* **Solon** from Sonchis of Sais,* and **Pythagoras** from Oeniphis of Heliopolis."*
> –Plutarch (Greek historian c. 46-120 A.C.E.)
> *(Greek names for cities in Ancient Egypt)

Greek Philosophy has been equated with the origin of Western civilization. Ancient Greek philosophers such as Thales (c. 634-546 B.C.E.) and Pythagoras (582?-500? B.C.E.) are thought to have originated and innovated the sciences of mathematics, medicine, astronomy, philosophy of metaphysics, etc. These disciplines of the early Greek philosophers had a major impact on the development of Christianity since the version of Christianity which was practiced in the Western (Roman) and Eastern (Byzantine) empires was developed in Greece, alongside Greek culture and the Greek language[178] which was steeped in Ancient Egyptian culture and its legacy. However, upon closer review, the ancient writings of contemporary historians of those times (early Christianity) also point to sources other than Greek Philosophy, and hence we are led to discover similarities in philosophy by tracing their origins to a common source.

There is evidence that shows how Ancient Egypt supported not only the education of the early Greek philosophers who came to study in Ancient Egypt itself, but Egypt also supported the Ancient Egyptian Mystery Temples that were established in Greece. Some Egyptian pharaohs sponsored and financed temples abroad which taught mystical philosophy as well as other disciplines. One such effort was put forth by the Ancient Egyptian king, Amasis, who financed the reconstruction of the famous Temple of Delphi in Greece, which was burnt down in 548 B.C.E.[179] This is the Temple which made the saying "Know Thyself" famous.[180] The Ancient Egyptian philosophy of self-knowledge was well known throughout the ancient world. The oracle of Zeus at Dodona was the oldest; and the one at Delphi, the most famous. Herodotus records a Greek tradition which held that Dodona was founded by the Priesthood in Egyptian Thebes. Further, he asserts that the oracle at Delos was founded by an Egyptian who became the king of Athens in 1558 B.C.E. This would be one of the earliest suggested dates for the existence of civilization in Greece, and it is being attributed to an Ancient Egyptian origin by the Greeks themselves, in their own myth and folklore. The connection to and dependence on Ancient Egypt for the creation of Greek culture is unmistakable and far-reaching. Along with this is the association between the Greek city of Athens and the Ancient Egyptian city of Sais. These two were known as "sister cities" in ancient times. The Greeks and Egyptians regarded the goddesses of those cities as being one and the same, i.e. Athena of Greece and Net (Neith) of Egypt. Also, the original rulers of Athens were Egyptians.

---

[178] see the book *The Journey from Jesus to Christ* by Muata Ashby
[179] Stolen Legacy, George G.M. James
[180] Inscription at the Delphic Oracle. From Plutarch, Morals, *Familiar Quotations,* John Bartlett

Thales was the first Greek philosopher of whom there is any knowledge, and therefore he is sometimes called the "Father of Greek Philosophy." After studying in Egypt with the Sages of the Ancient Egyptian temples, he founded the Ionian school of natural philosophy which held that a single elementary matter, water, is the basis of all the transformations of nature. The similarity between this teaching, the Ancient Egyptian Primeval Waters and the creation story in Genesis may be noted here. The ancient writings of the Greeks state that Thales visited Egypt and was initiated by the Egyptian priests into the Egyptian Mystery System, and that he learned astronomy, surveying, engineering, and Egyptian Theology during his time in Egypt. This would have certainly included the theologies related to Asar, Amun and Ptah. Pythagoras was a native of Samos who traveled often to Egypt on the advice of Thales and received education there. He was introduced to each of the Egyptian priests of the major theologies which comprised the whole of the Egyptian religious system based on the Trinity principle (*Amen-Ra-Ptah*). Each of these legs of the Trinity were based in three Egyptian cities. These were Heliopolis (Priesthood of Ra), Memphis (Priesthood of Ptah) and in Thebes (Priesthood of Amen {Amun}) in Egypt.

In reference to the Ionian school that Thales founded after his studies in Egypt, a student from that school, Socrates, became one of the most famous sage-philosophers. Socrates (470? -399? B.C.E.) was regarded as one of the most important philosophers of ancient Greece. He ended up spending most of his life in Athens, however, he was known to have studied under the Ionian philosophers. This establishes a direct link between Socrates and his teaching with Ancient Egypt. Socrates had a tremendous influence on many disciples. One of the most popular of these was Plato. Plato in turn taught others, including Aristotle (384-322 B.C.E.) who was Plato's disciple for 19 years. After Plato's death, Aristotle opened a school of philosophy in Asia Minor. Aristotle educated Philip of Macedon's son, Alexander (Alexander the Great), between the years 343 and 334 B.C.E. Aristotle then returned to Athens and opened a school in the Lyceum, near Athens; here Aristotle lectured to his students. He urged Alexander onto his conquests since in the process, he, Aristotle, was able to gain in knowledge from the ancient writings of the conquered countries. After Alexander's conquest of Egypt, Aristotle became the author of over 1,000 books on philosophy. Building on Plato's *Theory of the Forms*, Aristotle developed the theory of *The Unmoved Mover*, which is a direct teaching from Memphite Theology in Ancient Egypt. Among his works are *De Anima, Nicomachean Ethics and Metaphysics.*[181]

---

[181] For more details on the interaction between Ancient Egypt and Greece see the book *From Egypt to Greece* by Muata Ashby.

Another interesting area of cultural interaction is in the area of the alphabet. Up to the late 20th century, it had been thought that the alphabet that is used in western countries was derived from the Phoenicians, through a man called Cadmus. However, scholarship has determined that the Phoenician alphabet that was later used in Asia Minor and even later, taken over and altered by the Greeks, was derived from a "**Proto-Canaanite**" – also known as "**Proto-Sinaiatic**" form which was itself developed mostly by taking characters from the ancient Egyptian Hieroglyphic script (signs). In recent years further evidence has been discovered that supports the earlier finding that the alphabet originated in Ancient Egypt.

## Carvings set off debate about early alphabet
*By Salah Nasrawi, Associated Press writers*

CAIRO, Egypt -- A new scholarly debate reveals it's not as easy as A-B-C to determine when civilization moved toward its first                                                      alphabet.
Yale researcher John Coleman Darnell announced in November he had found alphabetic tracings in an Egyptian valley dating to between 1900 and 1800 B.C. Soon after, word came that Greek archaeologist Panikos Chrysostomou was claiming to have found even older traces -- dating to 5300 B.C. -- of a possible writing system in northern Greece (Nasrawi (1999)).

In the documentation of the actual research findings Dr. Darnell wrote:

The internal evidence- the specific paleographic models used for certain signs, the mixture of both hieratic and hieroglyphic models, and vertical orientation of otherwise predominantly horizontally oriented signs-indicates the early Middle Kingdom as the probable period of alphabetic origins-or at least this is the probable time when the Egyptian hieratic peculiarities became fossilized in many of the signs in these inscriptions (early to mid-12th Dynasty, ca. 1900 B.C.E.). (Darnell, Dobbs-Allsopp, Lundberg, McCarter, Zuckerman & with the assistance of Manassa, (2005) p. 90)

This scholarship supports the claims of the Ancient Egyptians. According to ancient Greek legends Cadmus was a Phoenician prince who founded Thebes in

Boeotia,[182] and among several other things *invented the alphabet*. In spite of the popularity of this tradition (supported by Herodotus, 450 B.C.), this was doubted even in ancient times. For instance, Tacitus[183] says:

> The Egyptians also claim to have invented the alphabet, which the Phoenicians..
> appropriated the glory, giving out that they had discovered what they had really been taught. (*Annals* 11.14)

## Diodorus (1st Cent. B.C.) states that Cadmus was an Egyptian citizen and also expressed caution in the acceptance of this Phoenician "invention":

> "Cadmus, who was a citizen of Egyptian Thebes..." (*Lib. Hist.*, Book 1. 23. 1-5)

> "Men tell us . . . that the Phoenicians were not the first to make the discovery of letters; but that they did no more than change the form of the letters; whereupon the majority of mankind made use of the way of writing them as the Phoenicians devised." (*Lib. Hist.*, Book V).

So the alphabet characters we have today appear to have been derived from the ancient Egyptian signs, but also the derived characters were also of Egyptian origin. They were taken by Asians and developed in to a Proto-Syniatic system which in turn developed into Canaanite, Cuneiform, Aramaic, Phoenician, Hebrew, Arabic, Greek, Roman and from Roman into the Romance languages, English, Spanish, French, etc.

## Figure 22: The Ancient Egyptian God Djehuti and the Greek God Hermes

**Below: The Ancient Egyptian god Djehuti (A) holds the caduceus (from the Temple of Seti I-Abdu, Egypt). The caduceus is the symbol of the life force power wielded by the god, which sustains life and leads to spiritual enlightenment. The Greeks adopted the teaching of Djehuti (Thoth) and called him Hermes. (B)**

---

182 An ancient region of Greece north of Attica and the Gulf of Corinth. The cities of the region formed the Boeotian League in the seventh century B.C. but were usually under the dominance of Thebes.

183 Roman public official and historian whose two greatest works, Histories and Annals, concern the period from the death of Augustus (A.D. 14) to the death of Domitian (96).

(A)

(B)

The images above of the Ancient Egyptian god Djehuti, who was known by the Greeks as Hermes (image below) at first look may not appear to be similar. Upon closer inspection however, the main elements of their iconographies can be correlated. Firstly, we know from the Greek writings that the god Hermes is a Greek rendition of the Ancient Egyptian god. Hermes appears with the head of a man (anthropomorphic) while Djehuti appears with the head of an Ibis (zoomorphic). However, they are both male, both represent wisdom and the transmission of the Supreme Being's will to the world. The caduceuses they use appear slightly different but yet they are composed of the same elements, a staff with serpents and both caduceuses which represent the same meaning. In the

Ancient Egyptian texts the Ancient Egyptian god is referred to as Thrice Greatest One. In the same way Hermes is referred to as Thrice Greatest in the Greek texts.

"Djehuti aah-u" is an ancient Egyptian title of the god Djehuti. It means "three times great." This same title in the Ancient Egyptian language makes use of the glyph "aah" which means "great." In Ancient Egyptian grammar the use of three glyphs is taken to mean three or plural. The same term appears in the Hermetic period of Greek culture in association with Ancient Egypt in the term "Hermes Thrice Greatest". Hermes is the Greek name for the Ancient Egyptian god Djehuti. Therefore, the ancient tradition in the form of the title was transferred into Greek philosophy during the late period of Ancient Egyptian history and the post-classical period of Greek history. From the Greek "Corpus Hermeticum" we read the following passage, which has clear reference to Hermes as the "Thrice greatest one", and as an Egyptian sage with intimate knowledge about Egypt,

Thou dost not mean their statues, dost thou, 0 Thrice greatest one?

*Tris.* [I mean their] statues, 0 Asclepius-dost thou not see how much *thou* even, doubtest?-statues, ensouled with sense, and filled with spirit, which work such mighty and such [strange] results statues which can foresee what is to come, and which perchance can prophesy, foretelling things by dreams and many other ways[statues] that take their strength away from men, or cure their sorrow if they do so deserve.

Dost thou not know, Asclepius, that Egypt is the image of the Heavens or, what is truer still, the transference, or the descent, of all that are in governance or exercise in Heaven? And if more truly [still] it must be said-this land of ours is Shrine of all the World.[184]

---

[184] **Thrice Greatest Hermes: Studies in Hellenistic Theosophy and Gnosis Being a Translation of the Extant Sermons and Fragments of the Trismegistic Lite** by G. R. S. Mead

## Cultural Interactions Between Greece, Rome, Egypt and Ethiopia, and the Indian, Egyptian and Ethiopian relationship.

As Rome emerged as a powerful military force in the period just prior to the birth of Christ (200 B.C.E.-30 B.C.E.), they adopted Greek customs, religion and art, seeing these as their legacy. Just as the Greeks adopted *The Illiad* and *The Odyssey*, the Romans enthusiastically embraced *The Aeneid* as their national epic. Vergil or Virgil (70-19 B.C.E.) was a Roman poet who wrote *The Aeneid* in the Latin language.[185] *The Aeneid* is actually a story that was written in the same form as *The Odyssey* and *The Illiad* of the Greek writer Homer. It was widely distributed and read throughout the Roman Empire. Thus, *The Aeneid* is considered to be a classical Latin masterpiece of ancient world literature, which had enormous influence on later European writers.[186] Some portions of these texts have important implications to understand the relationship between the Egyptians, the Ethiopians and the Indians in ancient times. *(italicized portions are by Ashby)*

> Mixed in the bloody battle on the plain;
> *And swarthy Memnon in his arms he knew,*
> *His pompous ensigns, and his Indian crew.*
>      - *The Aeneid*, Book I, Vergil or Virgil (70-19 BC)[187]

In Greek myth, Memnon was a king from Ethiopia, and was openly referred to as being "burnt of skin", i.e. "black."[188] He was the son of Tithonus, a Troyan (Trojan) prince, and Eos, a Greek goddess of the dawn. Tithonus and Eos represent the sky and romantic love, respectively. During the Troyan war, Memnon assisted Troy[189] with his army. Even though he fought valiantly, he was killed by Achilles. In order to comfort Memnon's mother, Zeus, the king of the Greek gods and goddesses, made Memnon immortal.[190] The Greeks revered a colossal statue of the Ancient Egyptian king Amenhotep III as an image of Memnon. During the times of Greek (332 B.C.E.-30 B.C.E.) and Roman (30 B.C.E.-450 A.C.E.) conquest of Egypt, it became fashionable for Greek and Roman royalty, nobles and those of means from all over the ancient world, especially Greece, to take sightseeing trips to Egypt. The "Colossi of Memnon" were

---

[185] Random House Encyclopedia Copyright (C) 1983,1990
[186] "Vergil," Microsoft (R) Encarta. Copyright (c) 1994
[187] *The Aeneid By Virgil*, Translated by John Dryden
[188] Recall that the term Ethiopians means "land of the burnt (black) faces."
[189] Troy (Asia Minor), also Ilium (ancient Ilion), famous city of Greek legend, on the
        northwestern corner of Asia Minor, in present-day Turkey. "Troy (Asia Minor),"
        Microsoft (R) Encarta. Copyright (c) 1994
[190] "Memnon," Microsoft (R) Encarta. Copyright (c) 1994

big attractions. The Colossi of Memnon are two massive statues that were built under Amenhotep III, 1,417-1,379 B.C.E.[191] The statues fronted a large temple[192] which is now in ruin, mostly depleted of its stonework by nearby Arab inhabitants who used them to build houses.

This passage is very important because it establishes a connection between Ethiopia, Egypt and India. Further, it establishes that the Indians made up the army of Memnon, that is to say, Ethiopia. Thus, in the time of Virgil, the cultural relationship between north-east Africa and India was so well known that it was mythically carried back in time to the reign of Pharaoh Amenhotep III, the father of the famous king Akhnaton. Pharaoh Amenhotep III was one of the most successful kings of Ancient Egypt. He ruled the area from northern Sudan (Nubia) to the Euphrates river. The Euphrates river is formed by the confluence of the Murat Nehri and the Kara Su Rivers. It flows from East Turkey across Syria into central modern day Iraq where it joins the Tigris River. The land referred to as Mesopotamia, along the lower Euphrates, was the birthplace of the ancient civilizations of Babylonia and Assyria, and the site of the ancient cities of Sippar, Babylon, Erech, Larsa, and Ur. The length of the river is 2,235mi (3.598km).[193] So again we have support for the writings of Herodotus and Diodorus who related the makeup of the ethnic groups in Mesopotamia as belonging to the Ancient Egyptian-Nubian culture.

At first inspection, this relationship appears to be perhaps an allusion to Virgil's times when it is well known and accepted that there was trade and cultural exchange, not only between India and Egypt, as we and other scholars have shown, but also between India and Greece.

Also, in contrast to present day society, there is no racist concept detected or being implied in the Greek writings. Also, there is no apparent aversion to having a personage of African descent (someone from a different ethnic group) in the Greek religion as a member of the family of Greek Gods and Goddesses. There is a remarkable feeling in reading the Greek texts that they had no compunction about admitting their association with Africa and Africans. The Greeks received much in terms of civilization and culture from Africa, in particular, Ethiopia and Ancient Egypt. This may be likened to modern college graduates who are proud to boast of their successful attendance at prestigious schools. There seems to be an eagerness to admit traveling to Egypt, as if it were a stamp of approval for their entry into society as professionals in their fields. There

---

[191] Random House Encyclopedia Copyright (C) 1983,1990
[192] *The Complete Temples of Ancient Egypt*, Richard Wilkinson, (C) 2000
[193] Random House Encyclopedia Copyright (C) 1983,1990

are other passages of interest in *The Aeneid,* which support the cultural connection similar to the previous verse.

**Figure 23: The Pharaoh Amenhotep III**

**Figure 24: The Colossi of Memnon- built under Amenhotep III, 1,417 B.C.E. -1,379 B.C.E. 59 feet tall**

> Ceasar himself, exalted in his line;
> Augustus, promised oft, and long foretold,
> Sent to the realm that Saturn ruled of old;
> Born to restore a better age of gold.
> *Africa and India shall his power obey;*[194]
> - The Aeneid, Book VI, Vergil or Virgil (70-19 BC)[195]

---

[194] *italicized portions are by Ashby*
[195] *The Aeneid By Virgil*, Translated by John Dryden

This seen, Apollo, from his Actian height,
Pours down his arrows; at whose winged flight
*The trembling Indians and Egyptians yield,*[196]
- The Aeneid, Book VIII, Vergil or Virgil (70-19 BC)[197]

In the first passage above, Africa and India are being linked as two countries that will be controlled by the Roman emperors (Ceasar, Augustus). Also, this statement implies that Egypt is an African country and not an Asiatic country. The time when this text was written is the period just prior to the Roman conquest of Ancient Egypt (30 B.C.E.). Therefore, it follows that the intent of the Romans, based on this passage, was to expand their empire to encompass north-east Africa and India. This repeated reference to India in conjunction with Africa and Egypt seems to imply a connection between the two countries, relating to a vast empire with two major geographic locales (Ancient Egypt and India).

## Cultural Interactions Between Hinduism and Vedic Culture In India

In India, the emergence of Hinduism saw a similar situation as with the one that occurred between the Jewish and Ancient Egyptian Religion. In a later period (c. 800 B.C.E.-600 B.C.E.), the earlier Vedic-Aryan religious teachings related to the God Indra (c. 1,000 B.C.E.) were supplanted by the teachings related to the Upanishadic and Vaishnava tradition. The Vaishnava tradition includes the worship of the god Vishnu, as well as his avatars (divine incarnations), in the form of Rama and Krishna. The Vaishnava tradition was developed by the indigenous Indian peoples to counter, surpass and evolve beyond the Vedic religious teachings. In the epic stories known as the Ramayana and the Mahabharata[198], Vishnu incarnates as Rama and Krishna, respectively, and throughout these and other stories it is related how Vishnu's incarnations are more powerful than Indra's, who is portrayed as being feeble and weak. Some of the writings of the Upanishadic Tradition,[199] the writings which succeed the Vedic

---

[196] *italicized portions are by Ashby*

[197] *The Aeneid By Virgil*, Translated by John Dryden

[198] *Mahabharata* (Sanskrit, *Great Story*), longer of the two great epic poems of ancient India; the other is the *Ramayana*. The *Mahabharata* was composed beginning about 300B.C.E. and received numerous additions until about 300 A.C.E.. "Mahabharata," *Microsoft® Encarta® Encyclopedia 2000.* © 1993-1999 Microsoft Corporation. All rights reserved.

[199] Any of a group of philosophical treatises contributing to the theology of ancient Hinduism-Vedanta Philosophy, elaborating on and superseding the earlier Vedas.

234

tradition, contain specific verses which seem to profess that the wisdom of the Vedas is lesser than that of the Upanishads, and that they therefore supersede the Vedas. One such statement can be found in the *Mundaka Upanishad*. The following segment details the view of the two sets of scriptures in relation to each other and the two forms of knowledge. (italicized portions are by Ashby)

> Those who know Brahman (God)... say that there are two kinds of knowledge, the higher and the lower. *The lower is knowledge of the Vedas* (the Rik, the Sama, the Yajur, and the Atharva), and also of phonetics, grammar, etymology, meter, and astronomy. *The higher is the knowledge of that by which one knows the changeless reality.*

## Cultural Interactions Between Hinduism and Buddhism

A similar situation that transpired with Ancient Egyptian religion with respect to Judaism, and with Hinduism with respect to Vedic religion, as discussed above, occurred between Hinduism and Buddhism with the advent of Buddhism. The story of Buddha's struggle to attain enlightenment, the inceptive and most influential work of Buddhist myth, relates how he strove to practice the austere paths of Hinduism (Upanishadic wisdom, Vedanta, Brahmanism, austerity, yoga, etc.). He practiced renunciation of the world and all sorts of penances and asceticism, even to the point of almost starving himself to death. Then he "discovered" a "new" path, "The Middle Path," and for a long time it was held to be superior to Hinduism by many. It found a great following in China and Tibet, as well as other countries of Indo-China.[200] Currently in the west, Buddhism is rarely related to its roots in Hinduism and Yoga philosophy. Upon close examination, the roots of the teaching of the middle path, along with the other major tenets of Buddhism such as the philosophy of *Karma* (action), *Maya* (cosmic illusion) and *Samsara* (philosophy of worldly suffering) can be traced to the Upanishadic Tradition,[201] especially in the Isha Upanishad. Thus, the early Buddhist teachers found it necessary to disparage the other practices in order to highlight the Buddhist faith, and yet what developed is a reworking of the same teaching that was there previously, not only in Indian mystical philosophy, but also in the mystical and yogic teachings of Ancient Egypt.

---

[200] The Indochinese peninsula includes a small part of Bangladesh, most of Myanmar (Burma), Thailand, Cambodia, and parts of Malaysia, Laos, and Vietnam.

[201] Spiritual tradition in India based on the scriptures known as the Upanishads. It is also referred to as Vedanta Philosophy, the culmination or summary of the Vedic Tradition whish is itself based on the scriptures known as the Vedas.

Buddha emphasized attaining salvation rather than asking so many questions. He likened people who asked too many intellectual questions to a person whose house (lifetime) is burning down while they ask, "How did the fire get started?" instead of first worrying about getting out of the house. Further, Buddha saw that renouncing attachment to worldly objects was not primarily a physical discipline, but more importantly, it was a psychological one. Therefore, he constructed a philosophical discipline, based on already existing philosophical tenets, from Hinduism, that explained the psychology behind human suffering and how to end that suffering. The Middle Path emphasized balance rather than extremes. He recognized that extremes cause mental upsets because one extreme leads to another, and the mind loses the capacity for rational thought and intuitional awareness which transcends thought itself. Therefore, Buddha reasoned that mental balance is the way to achieve mental peace and serenity, which will allow the transcendental vision of the Self to emerge in the mind. The following segment from the *Isha Upanishad* shows that having a balanced approach and proceeding according to the *"middle path"* with respect to the practice of spiritual disciplines was already addressed as being desirable for spiritual growth prior to the emergence of Buddhism. Buddhism later represented an accent or emphasis on this feature of the doctrine so it is clear that Buddhism "adopted" many pre-existing philosophical principles from Hinduism.

"To darkness are they doomed who devote themselves only to life in the world, and to a greater darkness they who devote themselves only to meditation.
Life in the world alone leads to one result, meditation alone leads to another. So we have heard from the wise. They who devote themselves both to life in the world and to meditation, by life in the world overcome death, and by meditation achieve immortality. To darkness are they doomed who worship only the body, and to greater darkness they who worship only the spirit."

This Buddhist Yogic psychological discipline became known as the Noble Eight-fold Path, the disciplines of Buddhist Yoga which lead to spiritual enlightenment. The "Middle Path," is also the central feature of Maat Philosophy from Ancient Egypt. It was referred to as "Keeping the Balance."[202]

In India, five to six hundred years before Christianity, Buddhism had caused a renaissance of sorts. The Brahmanic system (based on the Vedic

---

[202] *"The Wisdom of Maati,"* Dr. Muata Ashby. *"The Egyptian Book of the Dead,"* Dr. Muata Ashby.

Tradition) of ritual, asceticism and elaborate myth began to lose favor with many aspirants who were seeking a more psychologically based approach to the pursuit of spiritual enlightenment that did not include the use of deities for supreme worship or elaborate symbolism. The ideas inherent in Buddhism such as Karma, (the law of cause and effect and reincarnation), *Maya*, (Cosmic Illusion) and *Buddhi* (Intellect) existed in the Vedantic and Yogic scriptures of India prior to the formulation of the Buddhist religion. However, the spiritual system developed in the sixth century B.C.E. by Gautama, the Buddha, represented in a way a reform as well as a refinement of the older teachings which were already widely accepted. Especially emphasized was the idea that God, the ultimate reality, alone exists and that everyone is equally able to achieve oneness with that reality. However, the concept of God in Buddhism is that God is not to be considered as a deity, but as an abstract state of consciousness which is achieved when the mind is free of desires and consequently free of the fruits of action impelled by the desires. Buddhism also placed important emphasis on non-violence which certainly became a central part of the Christian doctrine as well, in philosophy if not in practice. In the same sense that Buddhism proclaims everyone can have *Buddha Consciousness* (or *Buddha Nature*) and thus become a Buddha, Gnostic Christianity affirms that everyone can achieve *Christ Consciousness* and thus become a *Christ*.

As explained earlier, the Buddha or *"The Enlightened One"* developed a philosophy based on ideas that existed previously in the Upanishads and other sources. In much the same way as the term Christ refers to anyone who has attained "Christhood," the term Buddha refers to any one who has attained the "Buddha Consciousness," the state of Enlightenment. In this context there have been many male and female Christs and Buddhas throughout history, since the earliest practice of mystical spirituality in Ancient Egypt.

Prior to Buddha, other teachings such as those of the "Brahmins," (followers of the teachings related to Brahman of the Upanishads) the *Samnyasa* or renunciates, and the Jains promoted the idea that one was supposed to renounce the apparent reality of the world as an illusion by detachment, privation and austerity. The Buddhists as well as the Jains[203] deny the divine origin and authority of the Vedas. The Buddhists revere Buddha and the Jains revere certain saints who espoused the Jain philosophy in ancient times. Buddha recognized that many people took the teachings to extreme and saw this as the cause of failure in attaining progress in spirituality. Teachings such as reducing one's Karma by

---

[203] Religion founded by Mahavira, a contemporary of Buddha. "Jainism," Microsoft (R) Encarta. Copyright (c) 1994

reducing one's worldly involvements were misunderstood by many to mean escaping the world by running away to some remote forest or mountain area.  Also, the teachings of non-violence which stressed not harming any creatures were taken to the extreme by some in the Jain religion, to the point that they would not physically move so as not to step on insects, or not breathe without covering the mouth and nostrils, so as not to kill microorganisms. Others felt that they should not talk to anyone or interact with others in any way. These teachings were taken to such extremes that some aspirants would remain silent so long as to lose their capacity to speak at all. Others starved themselves while others practiced severe austerities such as meditating in the cold rivers or not sleeping and thereby causing harm to themselves. Others became deeply involved with the intellectual aspects of philosophy, endlessly questioning, "Where did I come from? Who put me here? How long will I need to do spiritual practice? Where did Brahman (God) come from?" etc. These questions were entertained ad-infinitum, without leading to answers that promote the attainment of enlightenment. Buddha saw the error of the way in which the teaching was understood and practiced. He therefore set out to reform religion.

## The Rediscovery and or Reconstruction of Mythic Culture and Religion Through Reconstruction of the Essence of Religion: Mysticism

Many scholars and world renowned spiritual masters have recognized the strong connections between India and Ancient Africa, namely Joseph Campbell, R.A. Schwaller de Lubicz, Omraam Mikhael Aivanhov, and Swami Sivananda Radha. However, what they stated amounted to a few pieces of a larger puzzle, which until now had not been pursued in an extensive manner.

All of this comes down to the following. Mystical spiritual culture is not the exclusive property of any culture. Further, mystical philosophy operates through culture and is not culture itself. Culture relates to the mannerisms, customs, icons, language and traditions that are specific to a particular group of people. These may be related, adopted or influenced by other peoples. However, mysticism transcends cultural conventions; it is universal. Therefore, if one understands mystical philosophy, one can understand the expression of mystical philosophy through any culture. This means that if a mystic of India were to examine the mysteries of China, that mystic would understand those mysteries. Likewise, by understanding one form of mysticism, another may be recognized. Thus, by collecting the pieces of Ancient Egyptian mysticism which have survived in various cultures, the mysticism of Egypt may be fully understood and rediscovered.

Mysticism is a special cultural factor within the category of religion. It provides us with a good example of a universal or fundamental human cultural pursuit that reflects similar human expression beyond the outer or folkloric aspects of its manifestations.

Since Judaism, Christianity, Hinduism, Buddhism, Islam, Dogon and Yoruba spirituality have been demonstrated to be related to Ancient Egyptian Religion and philosophy, by this author, the authors mentioned above and others, the basic principles of Ancient Egyptian Mysticism can be traced through those religions back to Ancient Egypt. Besides these there are other less known and less numerous groups of people who follow the Ancient Egyptian tradition and who claim to be descendants of the Ancient Egyptians living in present day Asia Minor and in Africa itself. Their traditions also correlate with the evidences gathered from the other systems. However, in the case of Ancient Egypt and Ancient India, there is sufficient evidence to show that there was a cultural and social connection between the two cultures so close that it is possible to say that Indian spirituality is a development of Ancient Egyptian religion and mystical philosophy.[204] There is also sufficient evidence to demonstrate the same relationship between Ancient Egyptian religion and Christianity.[205]

Thus, by tracing the historical connection between the two countries and tracing the evolution of culture, it is possible to see the living manifestations which match in their major mystical principles. So even though the modern Indians may not uphold the exact disciplines or even acknowledge the Ancient Egyptian origins of their systems of spirituality, nevertheless the living Ancient Egyptian tradition can be discerned in the Indian traditions, customs and symbols.[206]

It is possible to recreate Ancient Egyptian religion and mysticism through studies based on comparison of ancient Egyptian scriptures, myths, and other cultural factors to the present day forms of religion and mysticism as practiced especially in the religions that had contact with Ancient Egyptian culture (Christianity and Hinduism). It may be said that the Ancient Egyptian tradition never ceased but its elements, its cultural factors, became dormant or embedded in other traditions. So this perspective as related to the study and reconstruction of a culture such as the Ancient Egyptian, through comparative cultural studies, is more along the lines of outlining the essential elements of Ancient Egyptian religion and culture as they survive in present day cultures, demonstrating their compatibility or identical natures, rather than recreating or deducing based on modern unrelated systems of spirituality. The key to the rediscovery of Ancient Egyptian spirituality as presented in the book *Egyptian Yoga*[207] was due to the understanding that is a yogic mystical system is present in the Ancient Egyptian religion whose goal is to promote spiritual enlightenment, called *Nehast,* which is not unlike the Hindu concept of Moksha or liberation or the Buddhist Nirvana. This is why past attempts at reconstructing Ancient Egyptian religion were frustrated.

Thus it has been possible to understand the mysteries of Ancient Egypt as an original source for many of the most fundamental teachings surviving not just in Hinduism but also Ancient Greek Philosophy, Judaism and Christianity. So, the research that led to the Neterian book series and the revival of Ancient Egyptian culture was like tracing back to the source, like discovering the seed from which a plant has grown. Also, in knowing the seed it is possible to know the plant (spirituality) and its

---

[204] See the book *The African Origins of Civilization* by Muata Ashby
[205] See the books *The African Origins of Civilization* and *The Mystical Journey from Jesus to Christ* by Muata Ashby
[206] See the books *Egypt and India* by Muata Ashby
[207] author Muata Ashby

240

branches (the religions) better and vise versa, thereby illuminating them in modern times with the depth of their own deeper history which leads back to the place where all life and civilization was born. So to summarize, five important methods have been used to reconstitute the Ancient Egyptian Mysteries.

## The Methods to Rediscover and Reconstruct a Culture and its Civilization

The fundamental aspects of a culture (its categories of cultural expression) can be rediscovered through the following methods of cultural anthropology[208] and the Cultural Category Factor Correlation Method (CCFCM). The following investigatory procedure is to be applied first to the *Fundamental Category-Factors of Cultural Expression* and then to the *Secondary Category-Factors of Cultural Expression*.

1. Studying the writings or evidences of the *societal philosophy* left by the culture itself. This is the first and foremost method. A tradition is to be defined by its own cultural philosophy of life first.

2. Studying the myth(s) and ritual traditions of descendants (if any) who are trying to carry on the original ancient tradition.

3. Studying the cultural factors of the other cultures (if any) that had contact with the culture being reconstructed and which have described interactions with the "ancient" culture; For example: In reference to Ancient Egypt, Greek philosophy and religion, Mesopotamian culture and religion, varied cultures of Asia Minor, Judaism, Christianity, Hinduism, Buddhism, Islam, Dogon and Yoruba qualify.

4. Studying the cultural factors of related or non-related cultures with traditions, which may outwardly appear to be similar to the main culture being reconstructed and may contain diluted, dormant, adopted or co-opted knowledge, rituals or traditions, that is carried on by the descendants (if any). Example: Mystery Traditions, Judaism, Christianity, Hinduism, Buddhism, Islam, Dogon and Yoruba qualify as religions related to Ancient Egypt some of which are practiced by descendants of the Ancient Egyptians.

---

[208] The scientific study of the origin, the behavior, and the physical, social, and cultural development of human beings.

# More on the Recovery of Myth and Culture

Linguists and others who study "dead" languages are always on the look out for a "Rosetta Stone" that will allow them to decipher the language they are studying. The Rosetta Stone is a slab upon which an edict was written on behalf of the King of Egypt. The special thing about it is that it was written in three different languages, Hieroglyphic, Demotic and Greek. Since the closing of the Ancient Egyptian temples at about 450 A.C.E. had forced the hieroglyphic text into disuse, it has become forgotten by the world. Even if the letters of a word are understood a language may not be understood because there is no context to understand the meaning of each word and then to relate them to each other in order to formulate rational sentences in order to derive ideas and thoughts. Such an example is the Meroitic language. Its letters have been deciphered but the language remains a mystery. As far as the Rosetta Stone however, since Greek was still understood and since the texts are a translation of the same message. It was possible to discover the "context" of the images (words) upon the slab. This led to the decipherment of the Ancient Egyptian Hieroglyphic language.

In like fashion, mythologists search for "Factors of Cultural Expression" the methods in which the "Categories of Cultural Expression" such as symbols, artifacts, myths, architecture, traditions, customs, etc., are used. The Categories are the expressive aspects of all cultures but these may have different forms of manifestation and thus may not relate to each other. If the factors match then this provides a context in which to understand the Categories of the no longer "dead" culture. Taking this a step further, when the previously "Dead" culture has left a language it is possible to verify the findings of the Cultural Anthropology studies. That is, the context that has been established can be verified by the ideas and thoughts contained in the language of the "previously dead culture." Ancient Egypt is such a case. These studies have yielded a framework through which to understand and bring back to life the culture of Ancient Africa. Having decoded the language of myth, a mythologist can understand when the fundamental principles of myth are being espoused and {she/he} can also determine the nature of those expositions in order to see if the methods used coincide with others and thereby establish relationships between myths of different peoples. Joseph Campbell and others accomplished this work successfully in their areas of study. The same success can be achieved in other Categories of Cultural Expression besides Myth. When the Factors of varied Categories are studied a quite complete picture can emerge of what the previously dead culture was all about, and this of course can lead to a revival of that culture.

So the objective of this kind of study is to discover which factors of Cultural Expression correlate (match) between the "extinct" culture and the "living" culture. Those matching Factors of Cultural Expression (aspects of culture that are proven as borrowings from one culture to another) constitute practices in common between the ancient culture and the modern culture. A partial match such as adoption of a symbol but not the meaning of a symbol denotes a possible initial adoption of the symbol and a loss of the interpretation over time due to cultural changes. Thus, an "extinct" culture whose customs, traditions, teachings and symbols have been transferred to writings, descendants, other cultures religions or philosophies cannot be said to be "dead" or "extinct" since these aspects of culture "live" on albeit in a dormant state in the present day "living" culture.

The methods of cultural anthropology outlined above are very difficult to apply in the study of most ancient cultures. This is because their impact was not felt to the degree of leaving those traces of traditions, symbols etc. with descendants of other cultures. Sometimes they have no writings about themselves for researchers to go on. The writings of a people are the primary source material for discovering a people. Archeology is an inexact profession and cannot be relied upon completely for such determinations. There need to be language studies, cultural anthropology studies and if possible hard science evidences such as geological evidences in order to confirm the findings of archeology. Fortunately, in the case of Ancient Egypt, unlike the case of the Sumerians, we are in the position to engage in all of the methods of study outlined above and this gives us the opportunity to reconstruct Ancient Egyptian culture and thereby also discover the source of many modern cultures and religions.

# Chapter 7: Problems in Comparative Mythology, Cultural and Social Studies

## EXAMPLE: Contacts Between Ancient Egypt and Ancient India and How the evidences demonstrating interaction can be overlooked

While the Indologists (Feuerstein, Frawley and Kak)[209] acknowledge the role of Ancient Egypt in the development of Ancient Greece, they nevertheless as if appropriate the legacy of Ancient Egyptian culture and civilization as an Indian extraction. The authors acknowledge that there are "curious parallels" between Ancient Egyptian and Indian myth and symbolism that "deserve careful investigation," but go on nevertheless to question Egypt as being the source of culture and civilization. They turn their attention towards India as the source from which the Ancient Egyptians derived their wisdom, which they conferred upon early Greek philosophers.

> "But where did the Egyptians themselves get their wisdom? We know that they owed a great debt to the learned men and sages of India. There was a colony of Indic people in Memphis as long ago as 500 B.C. But Egypt's connection with India may go back much farther in time. Indeed, there are many curious parallels between Egyptian and Indic mythology and symbolism, which deserve careful investigation."[210]

The authors seem to acknowledge a connection between Ancient Egypt and India and even state that the possibility deserves more "careful investigation," but then seem to digress to the theory that India is the "Cradle" of world civilization, including the Mesopotamian and Ancient Egyptian civilizations. The statement seems to be used as a means to establish a connection but for the purpose of saying or implying that the connection is one in which the Ancient Egyptians drew from Indian civilization. Note that the statement is provided as a scholarly opinion without support (evidence), and yet it is used to raise the specter of

---

[209] *In Search of the Cradle of Civilization,* 1995, co-authored by Georg Feuerstein, David Frawley, and Subhash Kak

[210] Ibid.

dubious indigenous Ancient Egyptian origins of civilization as if the scholarship ascertaining that civilization originated in Africa, by Africans, is unfounded or questionable. The very idea that Ancient Egyptian culture and civilization can be derived from Indian culture and civilization shows that the authors recognize a connection between the two nations. Thus, if the flow of culture can be viewed in one direction, it can also be viewed in the opposite as well. This means the possibility exists that Indian culture and civilization could have been derived from Ancient Egyptian culture and civilization. However, to arrive at such a conclusion requires a thorough investigation and review of the archeological and anthropological evidences at hand. If it can be demonstrated which culture emerged anterior, pioneered civilization, and then had contact with the other and if correlations of factors of cultural expression between the two can be demonstrated, then could be possible to have a basis to ascertain that there was contact and which culture derived from the other.

Many who are interested in Ancient Egypt from a cultural as well as a spiritual point of view feel that 20th century Western Egyptologists have not been reporting all of the discoveries in the ancient histories and accounts or modern Egyptian excavations, nor applying the correct dating of objects and historical events. Some scholars cite the apparent confusion in dating events in Ancient Egypt as a sufficient cause to consider Ancient Egyptian history as *"bedeviled with difficulties"* and therefore they feel justified in reaching the presumptuous[211] conclusions such as were stated in the book *In Search of the Cradle of Civilization*: (*Highlighted text by Ashby)

"There can be little question that the Vedas are the most impressive literary achievement of antiquity. <u>In extent,</u> they far surpass the Bible, and they dwarf Homer's epics as they do the sacred canon of the ancient Chinese civilization." p.17

"Most of the "first time ever" claims made for the Sumerians have in recent years been exposed as exaggerated or absurd. <u>There is mounting evidence that neither Sumer nor Egypt quite deserve the pride of place among the ancient civilizations. Rather the cradle of civilization appears to lie beyond the fertile valleys of the Nile, Tigris, and Euphrates Rivers.</u>" p.xviii

---

[211] the use of the term *"the most impressive"* could be construed as a presumptuous or even arrogant attempt to elevate Indian culture above others on the basis of volume of writings alone, not considering quality or other factors or criteria of evaluation if such evaluations are useful at all.

The statements above have been cited by some readers as self-important, and seeming to impugn the research of scholars who have brought forth evidences of contact and cultural exchange between Ancient Egypt and India, characterizing these as spurious theories, lacking authenticity and validity in essence or origin, in favor of an "Indian Cradle of Civilization" theory. The authors seem to say that a voluminous collection of writings[212] automatically deserves a high placement on the ancient literary and civilization scale. The modern publishing industry of Western Culture puts out more books, magazines, etc., than at any other time in history. Can we automatically say that this means we live in a high culture and civilization? This argument would overlook the fringe writings, writings directed at frivolous entertainment or to prurient interests, and other negative writings which are injurious to society or have no value to society. In any case, the vast literature of Ancient Egypt, considered collectively, constitutes a staggering compilation, and is mostly dedicated to spiritual matters and philosophy. It can only be dismissed as "undeserving the pride of place among ancient civilizations" if it is approached by ignorance and languorous scholarship or biased research. In the view of the authors, early India would seem to have had no significant contact with other ancient civilizations and received little from them, or that the contact was in a one way direction with other countries receiving the benefit which led to civilization arising outside of India. Also, they seem to exclude the possibility of new information coming to light, which may in turn lead them, like so many Eurocentrists, to make statements that later need to be upheld by precluding the evidence and concepts of others. Therefore, conclusions should be based on information on hand, logical interpretation, intuition, prudence and freedom from cultural bias. Again, the *"classical writers themselves"* who gave *"testimony"* (above) seem to contradict the apparently "Indocentric" view contained in the statement of the authors.

The Indologists Rajaram and Frawley[213] introduce trapezoidal shapes which he has discovered in both Ancient Egyptian and Indian culture.

> "There is another connection, quite apart from unit fractions and the value of л (pie). Trapezoidal figures shaped like Vedic altars are found on Egyptian monuments. Two of them, taken from Prisse d'Avennes' *Histoire de l'art egyptien d'apres les monuments* (1878-79) are reproduced in figure 2.

---

[212] Note that in the quote above, the words "in extent" were used to refer to the literary works of the Vedas. Thus, this specific reference is to quantity, not quality or content of the works.

[213] "Vedic Aryans and the Origins of Civilization" by Navaratne S. Rajaram and David Frawley

It is not merely [the] ... trapezoidal shapes which impress us, but their subdivisions. The subdivision of the first figure occurs in the *Sulvasutras,* and the second calls to mind the computation of the area [and its proof] in the Apastamba *Sulvasutra.* . . . If these figures occur-red on Indian monuments, we could understand the Indian interest in them: all the hopes of the Indian for health and wealth were tied up with a trapezoid (Seidenberg 1962: 519). (underlined text is by Ashby)

## Figure 25: "Egyptian" figures found in the Sulbas

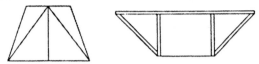

"How are we to explain the presence of trapezoidal figures on Egyptian monuments, particularly when they would have been cumbersome to construct or even to draw using the arithmetical techniques so favored by the Egyptians and Babylonians? I have argued that the Egyptians used mathematical methods derived from the Sulbas. Could the links go further back in time? One other remarkable connection suggests that the practice of building pyramids as funerary structures could have originated in the *Baudhayana Sulba."* P. 86-89[214]

"On mathematical, archaeological, and religious grounds, I consider it very likely that Egypt was in contact with post-Vedic India by 2700. It is not yet advisable, however, to establish chronological markers based on this connection." P. 88-89 [215]

It is Rajaram and Frawley's contention that these similarities and others stem from the Egyptians borrowing from the Ancient Indians. However, in view of the earlier origins of Ancient Egyptian culture and civilization it is impossible for that assertion to be correct considering the available evidence. A common sense approach dictates that if two cultures can be shown to have something in common, as Rajaram and Frawley believe they have in the case of Ancient Egypt and India, then it follows logically that if there is any dissemination of something already existing in the earlier culture, it proceeds TO the later culture and not the other way

---

[214] *Vedic Aryans and The Origins of Civilization* by David Frawley
[215] ibid

around. In this case the similarities have been demonstrated between Ancient Egyptian and Indian mathematics and geometric figures. It has been established that these existed in the early antiquity of Ancient Egyptian civilization which predates that of India by several thousands of years. Therefore, it follows that since there was contact between the two countries, there was likely diffusion from Ancient Egyptian culture to Ancient Indian culture.

In the book *India and Egypt: Influences and Interactions, 1993,* Lutfi A. W. Yehya notes the archeological discoveries, in Ancient Egypt of the Ptolemaic era, which conclusively prove contact between the Ancient Egyptians and Indians of that time as well as a blending of Ancient Egyptian and Indian religion as evidenced by the artifacts found in Memphis, Egypt.

"There seems to be sufficient evidence to indicate that Indians in good number had started visiting Egypt in the Ptolemaic period and even before it-from the third century, BC onwards. Athenaeus refers to the presence of Indian women, Indian cows and camels, and Indian hunting dogs in the royal processions of Ptolemy Philadelphus in Egypt.[216] An Indian colony probably existed in Egypt even earlier at Memphis. The excavations at Memphis have yielded some terracotta fragments and figurines[217] which from their facial features and costume, appear to be Indian.[218] Some of them have been identified as the representations of Panchika, a Buddhist divinity.[219]

Again, indicative of the close contact during Ptolemaic times is a gravestone which bears an Indian symbol of the trident and wheel, and the infant deity Horus is shown sitting in Indian attitude on a lotus."[220]

It is well known that Emperor Ashoka of India, upon becoming a Buddhist convert, was instrumental in the dissemination of the Buddhist teachings throughout the known ancient world. He sent Buddhist missionaries throughout India and to various countries. There are also

---

[216] H.G. Rawlison, *Intercourse Between India and the Western World,* Cambridge, 1916, pp. 93-94

[217] Now at the Petrie Museum in London (UC nos. 8816, 8931, 8788)

[218] Flinders Petrie, *Memphis,* vol. 1, London 1909, pp. 16-17 pl. XXXIX.

[219] J.C.Harke, "The Indian Terracottas from Ancient Memphis: Are they really Indian?", *Dr. Debala Mitra Volume,* Delhi, 1991, pp. 55-61

[220] Charles Elliot, *Hinduism and Buddhism,* vol. III, London, 1954, pp. 93-94

several iconographical evidences that link Buddhism with Neterianism (Ancient Egyptian Religion) and especially with the Temple of Het-ka-Ptah (*Menefer*-Memphis) in Egypt.

> "Asoka (c. 291-232 BC), emperor of India. He sent missionaries to countries as remote as Greece and Egypt. His reign is known from engravings on rocks and from traditions in Sanskrit literature. He was the most celebrated ruler of ancient India, known for his benevolent rule and for making Buddhism the official religion of his empire. Despite Asoka's vigorous exertions in behalf of his faith, he was tolerant of other religions, and India enjoyed marked prosperity during his reign."[221]

In the chapter of the book *India and Egypt: Influences and Interactions*, 1993, entitled "Transmission of Ideas and Imagery," the scholar M. C. Joshi reports on ancient written documents attesting to the communications and cultural exchanges between Ancient Egypt and India during the time of the Indian emperor Ashoka. This record shows not only economic exchanges but social and humanitarian exchanges, pointing to the compatibility of the two country's cultures. Just as two people who are of opposite character cannot get along, so too countries cannot get along if their peoples are of an opposite nature.

What follows is a portion of the research contributed by Indian scholars based on archeological excavations, working in India and Egypt on the question of contact and interaction between Ancient Egypt and India. The maritime trade between Ancient Egypt and India is known to have lasted longer and to have been more reliable than the over-land route through Asia Minor (Afghanistan, Iran, Iraq and Syria.). Therefore, during the periods when Egyptian rule over Asia Minor waned, due to wars and the influx of Indo-European peoples from the North of Asia, the contact between Ancient Egypt and India was maintained by sea.

> "Direct contact between the two countries (India and Egypt) during this period (Pharaonic Egypt 3400-525 B.C.) is suggested by some highly specialized artifacts which are found in India as well as in Egypt but which,

---

[221] "Asoka," Microsoft (R) Encarta Copyright (c) 1994 Funk & Wagnall's Corporation.
"Ashoka," Random House Encyclopedia Copyright (C) 1983,1990 by Random House Inc.

surprisingly, are absent in the vast West Asian region between-Afghanistan, Iran, Iraq and Syria."[222]

The material evidence of such contact includes:

"HEAD-RESTS: Indian head-rests found at some Neolithic sites such as T. Narsipur, Hemmige, and Hallur-all in Karnataka in south India-may be consigned to dates in the first half of the second millennium B.C. on the basis of radio-carbon tests. Curiously, they occur only in south India[223] and have no parallels elsewhere in entire subcontinent except for a solitary contemporaneous specimen from Chanudaro assigned to Jhukar levels[224] of circa 1800 B.C.

In Egypt, similar head-rests belonging to a period spanning the pre-Dynasty Period to Roman times have been discovered. A number of them are made of wood but in some, intended for royalty and the aristocracy, costlier materials such as ivory and lapis lazuli are employed. Egyptian headrests occur in a variety of forms. Incidentally, certain tribes of Africa[225] and India use wooden head-rests even today.[226] Strikingly identical head-rests have also been carved in rock bruisings at Piklilial in Karnataka (India), which site has, interestingly also yielded specimens in pottery belonging to the Neolithic period."

---

[222] *Doshi, Saryu, Editor-Indian Council for Cultural Relations India and Egypt: Influences and Interactions 1993*

[223] *Pottery Headrests from Narsipur Sangam,* F.R. Allchin, *Studies in Indian Prehistory*, D. Sen and A.K. Ghosh, eds., Calcutta, 1966, pp. 58-63

[224] *Chanudaro Excavations, 1935-36* E.J.H. Mackay, American Oriental Society, New Heaven, 19443, pp. 25 and 220, pl. XCII, 38

[225] Nagaraja Rao, op. Cit., p. 144; also Allchin, op. Cit.

[226] Ibid.

**Figure 26: Picture of a display at the Brooklyn Museum (1999-2000) demonstrating the similarity between the headrest of Ancient Egypt (foreground) and those used in other parts of Africa (background). (Photo by M. Ashby)**

## The Far Reaching Implications of the New Evidence Concerning the Sphinx and Other New Archeological Evidences in Egypt and the Rest of Africa

In the last 20 years traditional Egyptologists, archeologists and others have been taking note of recent studies performed on the Ancient Egyptian Sphinx which sits at Giza in Egypt. Beginning with such students of Ancient Egyptian culture and architecture as symbolist R. A. Schwaller de Lubicz in the 1950's, and most recently, John Anthony West, with his book *Serpent In the Sky*, many researchers have used modern technology to study the ancient monument and their discoveries have startled the world. Since the deterioration of the Great Sphinx was caused by water erosion, we now understand that the erosion damage on the Sphinx could not have occurred after the period 10,000-7,000 B.C.E. because this was the last period in which there would have been enough rainfall in the area to cause such damage. This means that most of the damage which the Sphinx displays itself, which would have taken thousands of years to occur, would have happened prior to that time (10,000 B.C.E.).

Many scholars have downplayed or misunderstood the new geological evidences related to the Great Sphinx. One example are the authors of the book *In Search of the Cradle of Civilization,* Georg Feuerstein, David Frawley (prominent western Indologists), and Subhash Kak, in which the authors state the following: (highlighted text is by Ashby)

> In seeking to refute current archeological thinking about the Sphinx, West relies on a *single geological feature.* Understandably, most Egyptologists have been less than accepting of his redating of this monument, *hoping* that some other explanation can be found for the *strange* marks of erosion. P. 6

The characterization of the evidence as a "single geological feature" implies it stands alone as an anomaly that does not fit into the greater picture of Ancient Egyptian history and is completely without basis. In support of orthodox Egyptologists, the authors agree with them, stating that their attitude is understandable. Now, even if there were only a single form of evidence, does this mean that it is or should be considered suspect especially when considering the fact that Egyptology and archeology are not exact sciences and geology is an exact science? Further, the authors mention the wishful thinking of the orthodox Egyptologists as they (the authors) search in vein (wishing) for some other way to explain the evidence (strange marks). Yet, the authors seem to agree with the orthodox Egyptological view and thereby pass over this evidence as an inconsistency that need not be dealt with further.

> The following evidences must also be taken into account when examining the geology of the Sphinx and the Giza plateau.
>
> ➢ The surrounding Sphinx Temple architecture is similarly affected.
>
> ➢ Astronomical evidence agrees with the geological findings.
>
> ➢ Ancient Egyptian historical documents concur with the evidence.

It is important to understand that what we have in the Sphinx is not just a monument now dated as one of the earliest monuments in history (based on irrefutable geological evidence). Its existence signifies the earliest practice not only of high-art and architecture, but it is also the first monumental statue in history dedicated to religion. This massive project including the Sphinx and its attendant Temple required intensive planning and engineering skill. Despite its deteriorated state, the Sphinx stands not only as the most ancient mystical symbol in human history, but also as the most ancient architectural monument, and a testament to the presence of Ancient African (Egyptian) culture and religion in the earliest period of antiquity, long before others. Further, this means that while the two other emerging civilizations of antiquity (Sumer and Indus) were in their Neolithic period (characterized by the development of agriculture, pottery and the making of polished stone implements), Ancient Egypt had already achieved mastery over monumental art, architecture and religion as an adjunct to social order, as the Sphinx is a symbol of the Pharaoh (leader and upholder of Maat-order, justice and truth) as the god Heru. The iconography of the Sphinx is typical of that which is seen throughout Ancient Egyptian history and signals the achievement of the a culture of high morals which governs the entire civilization to the period of Persian and Greek conquest.

**Figure 27:** The Great Sphinx of Ancient Egypt-showing the classical Pharaonic headdress popularized in Dynastic times. Also, the water damage can be seen in the form of vertical indentations in the sides of the monument.

The water erosion of the Sphinx is to history what the convertibility of matter into energy is to physics.
                                        -John Anthony West *Serpent In the Sky*

254

Many people have heard of the new evidence concerning the water damage on the Sphinx and how it has been shown to be much older than previously thought. However, as we saw earlier, detractors usually claim that this is only one piece of evidence that is inconclusive. This is the usual opinion of the uninformed. The findings have been confirmed by seismographic tests[227] as well as examination of the water damage on the structures related to the Sphinx and the Sphinx Temple, as compared to the rest of the structures surrounding it which display the typical decay due to wind and sand. It has been conclusively determined that the Sphinx and its adjacent structures (Sphinx Temple) were built in a different era and that the surrounding structures do not display the same water damage. Therefore, the wind and sand damaged structures belong to the Dynastic Era and the Sphinx belongs to the Pre-Dynastic Era. Therefore, the evidence supporting the older dating of the Sphinx is well founded and confirmed.

**Figure 28:** Sphinx rump and Sphinx enclosure show detail of the water damage (vertical damage).

The new evidence related to the Sphinx affects many other forms of evidence which traditional Egyptologists have also sought to dismiss. Therefore, it is a momentous discovery on the same order the discernment of the Ancient Egyptian Hieroglyphic texts. It requires an opening up of the closely held chronologies and timelines of ancient cultures for revision,

---

[227] *Traveler's Key to Ancient Egypt*, John Anthony West

thereby allowing the deeper study of the human experience on this earth and making the discovery of our collective past history possible. Thus, it is clear to see that the problem in assigning dates to events in Ancient Egypt arises when there is an unwillingness to let go of closely held notions based on biased information that is accepted as truth and passed on from one generation of orthodox Egyptologists to the next generation, rather than on authentic scholarship (constant search for truth). This deficiency led to the exclusion of the ancient historical writings of Ancient Egypt (*Palermo Stone, Royal Tablets at Abydos, Royal Papyrus of Turin*, the *Dynastic List* of Manetho). However, now, with the irrefutable evidence of the antiquity of the Sphinx, and the excavations at Abydos and Hierakonpolis, the mounting archeological evidence and the loosening grip of Western scholars on the field of Egyptology, it is no longer possible to ignore the far reaching implications of the Ancient Egyptian historical documents.

## How Some Western and Arab Scholars Distort Evidence Pointing to the Older Age of Ancient Egyptian Culture

After examining the writings of many Western scholars, the feeling of many Africentrists (view of Africa as a central perspective in cultural studies) and Africologists (researchers into African culture) of African descent and some non-African Western scholars is that traditional Egyptologists, a group comprised almost entirely of people of European descent or who have been trained by Western scholars, have over the years sought to bring down the estimated date for the commencement of the Dynastic Period in Egypt in order to show that Ancient Egyptian culture was at most contemporary with or emerged after Mesopotamian culture. Presumably, this was done because Mesopotamia is held by many Western scholars to be their (Western Culture's) own, if not genetic, cultural ancestral homeland. The reader should understand the context of this issue that goes to the heart of cultural relations between Western Culture and Eastern and African cultures. From the perspective of many people of non-European descent, Western Culture has sought to establish its socio-economic supremacy by suppressing and undermining the capacity of indigenous peoples worldwide, to govern themselves and control their own resources. This is verified by the documented evidence of the African slave trade,[228] military and covert intervention to destabilize governments, distortion of history,[229\230] colonial and neocolonial systems,[231] etc., either

---

[228] *The Middle Passage: White Ships Black Cargo* by Tom Feelings, John Henrik, Dr Clarke

[229] *Stolen Legacy*, George James

[230] *Black Athena, The Afroasiatic Origins of Classical Civilization* by Martin Bernal

[231] *Destruction of Black Civilization: Great Issues of a Race from 4500bc to 2000ad* by Chancellor Williams

set up or supported by Western countries in the past 500 years. In order to perpetuate this control, the image of superiority demands that Western Culture should be able to project an ancestral right, as it were, to control other countries. Therefore, twisting evidence in order to make Western Culture appear ancient, wise, beneficial, etc., necessitates a denial that there is any civilization that is older or possibly better than Western civilization, or that there could be any genetic or cultural relation with the non-Western Cultures which are being subjugated, or a common ancestry with the rest of humanity. An example of this twisting of history by Western scholars is the well known and documented deliberate misinterpretation of the Biblical story of Noah, so as to make it appear that the Bible advocated and condoned the enslavement of the children (descendants) of Ham (all Hamitic peoples- people of African descent) by the children (descendants) of Japheth (all peoples of Germanic {European} descent).

Along with the natural stubbornness of ordinary human beings to accept change due to the their identification with the prestige of their culture and heritage as a source of self-worth instead of truth and virtue, two methods of discrediting the early achievements of Ancient Egypt have been used.

Some non-western scholars reason that the desire of Western Culture to envision their own history as a civilized culture stretching back into antiquity, having realized that Greek culture is too late in history to establish this claim, and not wanting to acknowledge that Ancient Greece essentially owes[232] its civilization to Ancient Egypt,[233] have promoted a process of downplaying the importance of Ancient Egypt in history, by means of reducing the chronology in which history took place. How could this obfuscation of the record occur?

In addition to the resistance by some Western scholars to accept information, which they fear, will change the prestige of their culture and heritage with which they identify as a source of their self-worth, instead of defining themselves by the standards of truth and ethics, other methods of discrediting the early achievements of Ancient Egypt have been used. Two ways of invalidating Ancient Egyptian history are prominent: 1- misunderstanding or 2- supporting erroneous theories.

One method used by Western Egyptologists to contradict Ancient Egyptian history was to examine surviving[234] Ancient Egyptian mummies

---

[232] *Stolen Legacy,* George G.M. James
[233] *From Egypt to Greece,* M. Ashby C. M. Books 1997
[234] Many mummies have been destroyed throughout history by the early Christians and Muslims who wanted to eradicate all records of religions existing prior to their own, and also early European explorers who sold the mummies for

and apply undetermined forensic techniques in order to assign "causes of death" to the entire Ancient Egyptian culture. From this they concluded that the Ancient Egyptians had a short life span due to "primitive living conditions," and that the average life expectancy of a Pharaoh was no more than 20 years or so. However, since the cause of death can often not be determined even in modern times, how can the results derived from any technique(s) being applied to a 3,000 + years old mummified body be conclusive? When such rationales are not considered, and the erroneous pronouncements are repeated over and over again, they become "accepted" as truth by scholars and lay persons for a variety of reasons, some of which we have already touched on above. Through television channels such as The Discovery Channel and The Learning Channel, such distortions are routinely disseminated and they then become "common knowledge" over time. The problem becomes compounded because many scholars and lay people alike do not do their own research or look at the evidence themselves and draw their own conclusions. Rather, they are comfortable accepting the information being provided, without questioning its validity. Some don't want to know, because they do not want to risk their positions by disrupting the status quo. Others may be unwilling, or unable due to blind faith and mental weakness, to examine the evidences. In addition, there are other factors to be considered such as socio-economic obstacles, physical barriers preventing access to information, training, etc.

Another method used to revise the history of the Dynastic Period in Ancient Egypt is to say that the kings or queens were ruling concurrently in certain periods as opposed to subsequently. In certain periods such as the invasion of the Hyksos and the Assyrians, Persians, etc. who conquered part of the country, Egyptian leaders ruled in their part of the country while the conquerors temporarily ruled the conquered territory that they captured. Also, this is possible in the Intermediate period when there was a partial breakdown of social order. Further, due to the destruction of records, there are many Ancient Egyptian rulers (kings and queens) mentioned whose names are no longer recorded.

Since we have lists of the Pharaohs of the Dynastic Period, we can easily count the number of Pharaohs and use this figure to estimate what the average life span of each Pharaoh would have to be to cover the time span of the Dynastic Period, which lasted approximately 3,000 + years. Doing the math by multiplying this number by the life expectancy proposed by scholars (20 years), one arrives at a figure that is less than 3,000 years, the duration of the Dynastic period. Also, as to the conclusion drawn from the above methodology used to estimate the life span of the Ancient Egyptian peoples from mummified bodies (of the average life span of 20 years), even if it were accurate, does not make sense if we

---

experimentation as well as other Europeans who created a fad of pulverizing the mummies and using them in potions as medicinal supplements.

consider the ample documentation showing that Ancient Egypt was reputed to have the "best doctors" in the ancient world. Further, even if it were true that ordinary people existed in "primitive living conditions," does it make sense that the kings and queens would get the worst health care out of the entire population? Thus, as a scholar, is it prudent to apply this number to the royalty? Also, there is documented evidence to show that kings and queens, as well as other members of the society, lived normal healthy lives by modern standards. There are surviving records and statues, as well as illustrations, of kings, mummies and other royalty who lived well into their 80's and 90's such as Amunhotep Son of Hapu and Ramses II and others. One might also envision the wretchedness of such a life where members of a society die at such an early age. No sooner would they realize the potential of life, only to hasten on to death, as a mere immature youth. Life would hardly be worth living. Also, since spiritual evolution requires maturity in ordinary human terms, that is, sufficient time to grow up and discover the meaning of life, a short life-span would make the vast number of extant Ancient Egyptian texts treating the subject of spiritual enlightenment impossible to create, and useless because there would not be sufficient time to take advantage of them.

Another method used to discredit the Ancient Egyptian history is to arbitrarily claim that when the Ancient Egyptians spoke of "years," they were actually referring to "months".[235] This practice is predicated on baseless supposition, and is therefore patently false and demeaning since there is no precedent for this practice in Ancient Egyptian culture. It is an imaginary notion introduced by some Egyptologists who prefer to fabricate convenient chronologies rather than face the magnitude of the meaning of their discoveries. Thus, the corrupt nature of the historians, scholars and those who perpetuate such iniquitous misrepresentations is evident.

Still another motivation has been to try to synchronize the events such as those described in Ancient Egyptian texts or the Greek histories with those of the Bible. An example of this kind of writing can be found in a book by W. G. Waddell, called *Manetho*. Some historians feel this kind of distortion was done to establish the prestige of the Judeo-Christian tradition, the reasoning being similar to that discussed above. They believe that Judeo-Christian view was that having other traditions that are recognized as older and having more honor, heritage and prominence would undermine the perception that the Bible is ancient and infallible.

Others feel the reason was out of an effort to prove that Ancient Egyptian culture existed within the timeframe that the Bible has posed for

---

[235] *Manetho*, W. G. Waddell

the Creation of the world. The Creation was dated by the 17th-century[236] Irish archbishop James Ussher to have occurred in the year 4004 B.C.E.[237] this dating is presumed to be based on the varied chronologies given in the Judeo-Christian Bible, which is held by many Christians as the factual and historical word of God. If the world, according to the Bible, was approximately 6,005[238] years old, as postulated by the archbishop, that would support the teaching presented in the church and invalidate the existence of culture, philosophy, and most of all, religion, prior to the emergence of Christianity and would accord prominence as well as supremacy of Christianity over all other religious traditions. However, the evidence of the existence of more ancient civilizations as well as the evidence of the existence of dinosaurs and other discoveries about the eons and ages of the world, the sun, the galaxies, etc. invalidates the biblical tradition so completely that only the most blindly faithful to this tradition and those who ignore the scientific evidences can deny it.

The work of Darwin (theory of evolution) and other scientists caused major controversies in western society. A case in point is the attempt to correlate the events of the Biblical story of Exodus with those of Ancient Egyptian Pharaoh, Ramses II. First, there are no accounts of any conflict between the Jews and the Egyptians in any Ancient Egyptian records yet discovered, beyond an inscription at the Karnak Temple in Egypt, that may refer to the Jews of the Bible, stating that the Jews were one of the tribes under Egyptian rule in Palestine. Secondly, there are no corroborating records of the events chronicled in the Bible in any of the contemporary writings from countries that had contact with the Jews and the Ancient Egyptians. Thirdly, there were at least eleven kings who went by the title Ramses (Ramses I, II, III, III, etc.), spanning a period dated by traditional Egyptologists from 1,307 B.C.E. to 1,070 B.C.E. Further, some localities were also referred to as Ramses.

The oldest scholarly dating for the existence of Moses, if he did exist, is c. 1,200 B.C.E. However, most Bible scholars agree that the earliest texts of the Bible were composed around 1,000 B.C.E or later, and were developed over the next millennia. Also, most scholars are now beginning to accept the Ancient Egyptian and therefore, African ethnicity of the original Jewish peoples. An example of modern scholarship on the question of the origins of the Jews occurs in the book *Bible Myth: The*

---

[236] 17th century refers to the time period from 1,600-1,699 A.C.E.

[237] Encarta Encyclopedia, Copyright (c) 1994

[238] 4,004 + 1,600 to1,699 gives a range of time span from 4,604-5,703; this has been conservatively rounded to 6,000.

*African Origins of the Jewish People.* In a section entitled "Contradictory Biblical Evidence," the author, Gary Greenberg states:

> Dating the Exodus is problematic because evidence of its occurrence appears exclusively in the Bible, and what little it tells is contradictory. Exodus 12:40-41, for example, places the Exodus 430 years after the start of Israel's sojourn in Egypt (i.e., beginning with Jacob's arrival), whereas Genesis 15:13-14 indicates that four hundred years transpired from the birth of Isaac to the end of the bondage. Both claims cannot be true. Jacob was born in Isaac's 60th year,[239] and he didn't arrive in Egypt until his 130th year.[240] If the sojourn lasted 430 years, then the Exodus would have to have occurred 620 years after Isaac's birth.[241] On the other hand, if the Exodus occurred 400 years after Isaac was born, then the sojourn could only have been 210 years long.[242] Other biblical passages raise additional problems.[243]

The story of Sargon I points to another source and purpose for the Moses story, in the context of our present study. According to the Biblical tradition, at about 1200? B.C.E., the Hebrews were in Egypt, serving as slaves. A Jewish woman placed her son in a basket and allowed it to float downstream where the Egyptian queen found it, and then adopted the child. The child was Moses, the chosen one of God, who would lead the Jews out of bondage in Egypt. Moses was taken in by the royal family and taught the wisdom related to rulership of the nation as well as to the Egyptian religion and the Egyptian Temples (Bible: Acts 7:22). He was being groomed to be king and high priest of Egypt. This is why the Bible says he was knowledgeable in the wisdom of the Egyptians (Bible: Acts 7:22 and Koran C.144: Verses 37 to 76).

A story similar to the birth of Moses, about a child being placed in a basket and put in a stream which was later found by a queen, can be found in Zoroastrian mythology as well.[58] Sargon I reined about 2,335-2,279 B.C.E. He was called "Sargon, The Great." He was one of the first known major Semitic conquerors in history. He was successful in conquering the entire country of Sumer, an ancient country of southwestern Asia, which corresponds approximately to the biblical land known as Babylonia (Babylon). Babylon was an ancient city of Mesopotamia, which was

---

[239] Gen. 25:26
[240] Gen. 47:9
[241] 60+130+430=620.
[242] 400-130-60=210.
[243] *Bible Myth: The African Origins of the Jewish People* Gary Greenberg

located on the Euphrates River about 55mi (89km) South of present-day Baghdad. Sargon I created an empire stretching from the Mediterranean to the Persian Gulf in c.2,350 B.C.E. The adoption of the child into royalty and rulership motif was apparently a popular theme in ancient times for those who wanted to legitimize their ascendancy to power by creating the perception that it was divinely ordained.[244]

Despite the myriad of ongoing excavations that have been conducted, many sponsored by Christian or Jewish groups, no substantial evidence has been unearthed that supports the historicity of the Bible. However, new discoveries have been brought forth that corroborate Herodotus' statements and the histories relating to the fact that the land that is now called Palestine, was once part of Ancient Egypt.

> An approximately 5,000-year-old settlement discovered in southern Israel was built and ruled by Egyptians during the formative period of Egyptian civilization, a team of archaeologists announced last week.
>
> The new find, which includes the first Egyptian-style tomb known to have existed in Israel at that time, suggests that ancient Egypt exerted more control over neighboring regions than investigators have often assumed, contends project director Thomas E. Levy of the University of California, San Diego.
>
> Source: Science News, Oct 5, 1996 v150 n14 p215(1).
> Title: Ancient Egyptian outpost found in Israel.
> (Halif Terrace site in southern Israel upsets
> previous estimates of Egyptian imperialism) Author: Bruce
> Bower

## The Contradictions in the Historicity of the Exodus and its Effect on Comparative Myth, Cultural and Social Studies

If we are to understand the story Genesis as a mythic announcement of a societal philosophy, a worldview and the book of Exodus as the social establishment the that worldview in the form of a culture, of the Jewish tradition, and if we were to see the Jewish teaching of the Pentateuch as a mythic metaphor, we may think of it as an archetypal *psychomythic* journey using Jewish Category-Factors of Cultural Expression; in this journey the personality finds itself captive and pledges to have faith in a divinity that will set it free from its bondage once the personality has undergone certain trials that test its faith in the divinity. But why must the story be historical instead of metaphorical? That issue has already been

---

[244] *The Power of Myth*, Joseph Campbell

discussed elsewhere in this volume. However, if the story never occurred as a historical fact, why was it necessary to place Egypt, a real place, and the Ancient Egyptians, a real people with a historical culture, in the position of a cultural villain? In India, the emergence of Hinduism saw a similar situation as with the one that occurred between the Jewish tradition and Ancient Egyptian Religion. In a later period (c. 800 B.C.E.-600 B.C.E.), the earlier Vedic-Aryan religious teachings related to the God Indra (c. 1,000 B.C.E.) were supplanted by the teachings related to the Upanishadic Vaishnava tradition. The Vedic god Indra (ruler of heaven, great god of storms, thunder and lightning, regulator of the days, months, and seasons.) was cast in the position as a "villain" who was overpowered and surpassed by the Hindu god Vishnu (sustainer of Creation) of the Upanishadic era of Indian culture. Vishnu, especially through his avatars, Rama and Krishna, took over the duty of fighting and destroying demons in order to protect and show human beings the way to spiritual enlightenment. As Ancient Egyptian culture was legendary, even after it was conquered by the Greeks and later the Romans, the prestige of having the Jewish God defeat the Egyptian Gods would have elevated the Jewish tradition to major prominence. Thus, the Jewish writers were co-opting their relationship with Ancient Egypt, which was by the available accounts, unremarkable, to create a position of status for their tradition.

A cursory review of encyclopedic entries related to the origins and significance of the Passover tradition reveals inconsistencies and changes in the tradition, transforming it into a commemoration related to deliverance from Ancient Egypt. (Highlighted text by Ashby)

> **Passover**, in Judaism, one of the most important and elaborate of religious festivals. Its celebration begins on the evening of the 14th of Nisan (first month of the religious calendar, corresponding to March-April) and lasts seven days in Israel, eight days in the Diaspora (although Reform Jews observe a seven-day period). Numerous theories have been advanced in explanation of its original significance, which has become obscured by the association it later acquired with the Exodus. In pre-Mosaic times it may have been a spring festival only, but in its present observance as a celebration of deliverance from the yoke of Egypt, that significance has been practically forgotten. See T. H. Gaster, Passover: Its History and Traditions (1949, repr. 1962); P. Goodman, ed., The Passover Anthology (1961).[245]

---

[245] Passover. (n.d.). *Columbia Electronic Encyclopedia.* Retrieved April 09, 2007, from Reference.com website: http://www.reference.com/browse/columbia/Passover

From the encyclopedic entry above we learned that there was a pre-Mosaic practice of a ritual that later became associated with the deliverance from Egypt. In the next entry (below) we find no mention of a pre-Mosaic tradition of the ritual, which may have been associated with a "spring festival only", originally having nothing to do with Ancient Egypt. Thus, the association became so complete that today it is assumed to be true.

> **Passover-**An annual Jewish festival, occurring in March or April (15–22 Nisan), commemorating the exodus of the Israelites from Egypt; named from God's passing over the houses of the Israelites when he killed the first-born children of the Egyptians (Ex 13); also known as Pesach [paysakh]. It is marked by a special meal including unleavened bread and bitter herbs. [246]

The English term "Passover" was introduced to the English language by way of William Tyndale's Bible translation, it later was used in the King James Version. If we are to see the Bible as a historical document then we must be able to see how the dates of the Bible correlate or do not correlate with other historical evidences. If we assume that the first five books of the Bible Old Testament are the Pentateuch, which are Genesis, Exodus, Leviticus, Numbers, and Deuteronomy, and if we assume that the book of Exodus contains the first record of a Passover related to deliverance from bondage in Ancient Egypt, we should be able to find evidences of the existence of the book and the bondage at the time they are claimed to have existed. In the Documentary Hypothesis of Julius Wellhausen (1844-1918 A.C.E.), the Pentateuch was supposed to be composed of four identifiable and separate texts which have been dated "roughly" from Solomon's period up to the time of the exilic scribes and priests. It was those various texts which were brought together in the form of one document (referred to as the Pentateuch, or Torah) after the exile by scribes. The texts are, The Jahwist (or J) - written circa 850 BCE., The Elohist (or E) - written circa 750 BCE., The Deuteronomist (or D) - written circa 621 BCE., and The Priestly source (or P) - written during or after the exile. There is scholarly debate as to the exact dates and documents that compose the Pentateuch. The earliest fragment of any book or passage from the Pentateuch is a piece of an amulet referred to as "The Priestly Benediction on a Silver Amulet." Ca. 600 B.C. (Israelite period). It is inscribed on a silver leaf

---

[246] Passover. (n.d.). *Crystal Reference Encyclopedia.* Retrieved April 09, 2007, from Reference.com website: http://www.reference.com/browse/crystal/24338

measuring in width about 7/8 of an inch before it is unrolled; it contains a passage from the Priestly Benediction of the Book of Numbers, 6:24-26, which begins, "The Lord bless thee and keep thee. .. ." [247]

Thus, while scholars assign dates to the earliest writings of what later came to be known as the Pentateuch to dates between 850 and 621 B.C.E. the only tangible artifact we have that is considered as the earliest fragment of what later writers compiled into what was called the Pentateuch is dated at 600 B.C.E. This also points out the fact that the writings were created at different times and by different writers and later collected into a collection of 5 books later to be called Pentateuch and even later the "Old Testament". Therefore, no single person called Moses wrote all the books. The scholarly debate over the historicity and dating of the texts is revealed in the following reference.

> Current debate concerning the historicity of the Old Testament can be divided into several camps. One group has been labeled "biblical minimalists" by its critics. Minimalists (e.g., Philip Davies, Thompson, Seters) see very little reliable history in any of the Old Testament. Conservative Old Testament scholars, "biblical maximalists," generally accept the historicity of most Old Testament narratives (save the accounts in Gen 1–11) on confessional grounds, and noted Egyptologists (e.g., Kenneth Kitchen) argue that such a belief is not incompatible with the external evidence. Other scholars (e.g., William Dever) are somewhere in between: they see clear signs of evidence for the monarchy and much of Israel's later history, though they doubt the Exodus and Conquest. The vast majority of scholars at American universities are somewhere between biblical minimalism and maximalism; there are still many maximalists at conservative/evangelical seminaries, while there are very few biblical minimalists at any American universities. Interestingly, both Kitchen and archaeologist Israel Finkelstein of Tel Aviv University are not the only scholars from the maximalist and minimalist camps who are sufficiently trained to address these questions with the necessary sophistication but both are experts in their fields—and both come to different conclusions. ..
> … There are many different reasons for these difficulties. Firstly there is great dispute over the date of the composition of the texts themselves. Both sides would agree that the date of most of the component books was in place by sometimes shortly after the end of the Babylonian exile in about 539 BCE. For the historical books, the Bible itself refers to the use of pre-existing

---

[247] Jerusalem, Ketef Hinnom, Israel Museum, Jerusalem.

materials, chronicles and annals of the states involved, but we have no idea of how these materials were reworked, and none of them have survived to the modern day.[248]

The historicity of the earliest books of the Bible cannot be independently verified by corroboration with other sources. The texts themselves provide contradictory information that confounds scholars to the present day. What is known about the books is that they were written over a period of time many hundreds of years after the period they were supposed to be writing about. Neither the events recounted in Exodus nor the existence of Moses can be established. So it would appear that the historicity and literalism of the texts cannot be established or is contradictory and therefore erroneous and they are unusable as historical documents. Lastly, what was going on in Ancient Egypt during the time that the events in the book of Exodus were supposed to have occurred and what was going on in Ancient Egypt during the time when the book of Exodus was supposedly written?

If as some scholars suppose, Moses existed at around the year c.1200 B.C.E. he would have experienced the 19th Dynasty (1292-1190 B.C.E. (Thebes) Dynasty) in Egypt, which was founded by Ramses I. Ramses' son was named Seti I. Ramses II, who later become known as "the Great" continued on with Seti's struggle against the Hittites. This period was a revival of the ancient glory and power of Egypt. Ramses II (1279-1213 Ramses II "Ramses The Great") was perhaps the most powerful Pharaoh of Egypt. There are records of his battles with the Hittites but the only record that may possibly be ascribed to Isrealites is an inscription (c.1209/1208 B.CE.) commissioned by the son of Ramses II, Merneptah. The inscription refers to people living in Palestine who were called 𓈎𓏤𓈙𓂋𓇋𓏏𓀀 *Ysyriar* + symbol ("foreigner" and symbol "people") and it states that " *Ysyriar is laid waste; his seed is not"*. Thus, if the *Ysyriar* were the ancient Israelites of that time the only record if of their conquest and subjugation and not of a conflict between their god and the gods of the Egyptians. If we are to accept the scholarly assertions of the *Documentary Hypothesis* (explained above), or similar, and the idea that the texts from the source "Jahwist" (or J) were written circa 850 BCE. And that those texts were combined by a Judaean some time after the fall of the northern kingdom and are to be found inextricably associated in Genesis, Exodus, Numbers, Joshua, Judges, First and Second Samuel, and First and

---

[248] Wikipedia Encyclopedia http://en.wikipedia.org/wiki/Old_Testament

Second Kings,[249] then we should expect to find some corroborating evidence(s) in that time period.

During the years 1075-656 B.C.E. Egypt experienced what is referred to by Egyptologists as a *Third Intermediate Period*. This period was characterized by political instability and fracture. In the 21st Dynasty there were rival Pharaohs based at Tanis and at Thebes, but the two sets of rulers coexisted amicably, united by marriage ties, until the last high priest reunited Egypt as Pharaoh Psusennes II. When he died 945 B.C.E. the rule of Thebes came to an end. Sheshonq I (945–924), a member of a powerful family of Libyans based at Herakleopolis, took the throne founding the 22nd Dynasty. He asserted his authority in Upper Egypt, and it was probably then that some priests of Amun left Thebes for Napata, the future seat of the 25th Dynasty. Peraah (Pharaoh) Sheshonq (perhaps the Shishak of the Bible) attacked Palestine after the death of Solomon[250], and sacked Jerusalem, refilling his treasury and temporarily increasing the prestige of Egypt. Then followed 150 years of increasing anarchy, during which rival Libyan chieftains and the priests of Amun at Thebes vied for power. During the years 874 - 835 B.C.E., when, according to Biblical scholars, the Exodus text was supposed to have been written, the Pharaoh of Egypt was Osorkon II.

Egypt was reunited by Shoshenq I who founded the Twenty-Second Dynasty in 945 BC (or 943 BC). This reunification brought stability to Egypt for more than a hundred years. After the reign of Pharaoh Osorkon II, Egypt again had splintered into two states. Assyria, which was growing in power, began encroaching on the lands known as Canaan and Syria which were territories under Egypt's control. In 853 BC, Osorkon's forces, in a coalition with those of the peoples of Canaan (which included Israel) and Byblos, fought against the army of Shalmaneser III at the Battle of Qarqar. That battle ended in a stalemate and that halted the Assyrian expansion in Canaan, at least for some time.

Thus, during the time of the events of the Bible where Egypt was supposedly defeated by the Jews with the help of their god, the Egyptians were at the hight of their power in that period of history and there are no records of losses to the Isrealites, but only the reverse. Why would the

---

[249] *According to scholars, this combined JE narrative is the bulk of the earlier Old Testament. The Columbia Electronic Encyclopedia Copyright © 2004, Columbia University Press.*
*Licensed from Columbia University Press*
[250] third king of Israel (c. 961-922 BC), son of David and Bathsheba.

Isrealites have a great victory against the greatest power of the ancient world and then not announce it or celebrate it until 350 years later ($1200^{251}$-$850^{252}$=350)? At the time of the writing of the book of Exodus, there was stability in Egypt and there is also a reversed record, that the Isrealites were soldiers in the Egyptian army, fighting against the Assyrians. If indeed, as scholars have found, there are indications that the "passover" ritual was practiced as a spring festival only and that it was only associated with an Exodus from Egypt at the time of the creation of the Book of Exodus in the Pantateuch, this means that during the intervening years, between 1200 and 850 B.C.E., after the supposed Exodus in 1200 B.C.E. there was no observance or mention of and Exodus from Egypt. This suggests that the ritual was co-opted by the writers of the book of Exodus in a deliberate attempt to create a ritual and tradition, for their new religion, with grander import.

This short exploration of the movements in two traditions to supplant the greater culture they are trying to emerge out of (Jews from Ancient Egypt, Vaishnavism from Aryan Tradition) points to some areas in the study of cultural interactions and possible biases that researchers need to look out for. The assumption that the events recounted in Exodus about the Egyptian gods or in the Hindu texts about the Aryan gods are true by virtue of the fact that they are widely accepted is not a scholarly perspective. In order to arrive at correct understanding and reconstruction of factors of cultural expression as well as cultural interactions there must be great care taken in applying historical knowledge correctly and logically along with the maintenance of vigilance over personal or professional agendas.

## The Eurocentric and American Control Over Egyptology and its Effect on Comparative Myth, Cultural and Social Studies

Ancient Egyptian Studies (Egyptology) is very important not only to those interested in Ancient Egypt but to those interested in any culture that came into contact with Ancient Egypt. That is because there are many examples that demonstrate how the interactions were fruitful for varied developments in other cultures from art, to religion and social order systems. Many researchers have noticed and written about a problem in the field of Egyptology wherein orthodoxy and bias has distorted the new knowledge about Ancient Egypt or suppressed and or prevented it from being released widely and accepted broadly throughout the world.

---

[251] Date given for the existence of Moses
[252] Date of the supposed writing of the book of Exodus by the Documentary Hypothesis

Speaking out against the stronghold, which modern European and American Egyptologists have created, the Egyptologist, scholar and author, John Anthony West, detailed his experiences and those of others attempting to study the Ancient Egyptian monuments and artifacts who are not part of the "accepted" Egyptological clique. He describes the situation as a kind of "Fortress Egypt." He describes the manner in which, not only are the Ancient Egyptian artifacts closely protected from the examination by anyone outside this group, but also the interpretation of them as well. It is as if there is a propaganda machine, which, like the orthodox medical establishment, has set itself up as sole purveyors of the "correct" knowledge in the field, and thereby invalidates the findings of other scholars or scientists. In discussing the way in which mistakes made by scholars are treated, mister West says the following:

> In academia, the rules vis-à-vis mistakes change according to location. Only those within the establishment are allowed to 'make mistakes.' Everyone else is a 'crank' 'crackpot' or 'charlatan,' and entire lifetimes of work are discredited or dismissed on the basis of minor errors.

Also, the treatment of any scholar who reads metaphysical import in the teachings, literature or iconography of Ancient Egypt is generally ridiculed by orthodox Egyptologists. For instance, anyone suggesting that the Great pyramids were not used as burial chambers (mummies or remnants of mummies have never been discovered in them), but rather as temples, is openly called a "Pyramidiot,"[253] West describes the ominous power that orthodox Egyptologists have taken to themselves and the danger this power poses to humanity:

> A tacit territorial agreement prevails throughout all Academia. Biochemists steer clear of sociology; Shakespearean scholars do not disparage radio astronomy. It's taken for granted that each discipline, scientific, scholarly or humanistic, has its own valid self-policing system, and that academic credentials ensure expertise in a given field.
>
> With its jealous monopoly on the impenetrable hieroglyphs,± its closed ranks, restricted membership, landlocked philosophical vistas, empty coffers, and its lack of impact upon virtually every other academic, scientific or humanistic field, Egyptology has prepared a near-impregnable strategic position for itself - an academic Switzerland but without chocolate, cuckoo clocks, scenery or ski slopes, and cannily concealing its banks. Not only is it indescribably boring and difficult to attack, who'd want to?
>
> But if Swiss financiers suddenly decided to jam the world's banking system, Swiss neutrality and impregnability might

---

[253] *Traveler's Key to Ancient Egypt*, John Anthony West

suddenly be at risk. That is partially analogous to the situation of Egyptology. The gold is there, but its existence is denied, and no one is allowed to inspect the vaults except those whose credentials make them privy to the conspiracy and guarantee their silence. To date, only a handful of astute but powerless outsiders have recognized that the situation poses real danger. But it's not easy to generate a widespread awareness or appreciation of that danger.

If you think of Egyptologists at all, the chances are you conjure up a bunch of harmless pedants, supervising remote desert digs or sequestered away in libraries, up to their elbows in old papyrus. You don't think of them as sinister, or dangerous. The illuminati responsible for the hydrogen bomb, nerve gas and Agent Orange are dangerous; if you reflect upon it you see that the advanced beings who have given us striped toothpaste and disposable diapers are also dangerous ... but Egyptologists?

Possibly they are the most dangerous of all; dangerous because false ideas are dangerous. At any rate *some* false ideas are dangerous. Belief in the flat earth never hurt anyone though it made navigation problematic. Belief in a geocentric universe held back advances in astronomy but otherwise had certain metaphysical advantages. Academic Egyptology is dangerous because it maintains, in spite of Schwaller de Lubicz's documented scholarly evidence, and the obvious evidence of our own eyes and hearts when we go there, that the race responsible for the pyramids and the temples of Karnak and Luxor was less, 'advanced' than ourselves. As long as academic Egyptology prevails, children will be brought up with a totally distorted view of our human past, and by extension, of our human present. And millions of tourists will continue to visit Egypt every year, and have the experience of a lifetime vitiated and subverted by a banal explanation that the greatest art and architecture in the world to superstitious primitives.

So the fabulous metaphysical gold of Egypt remains hidden; it's existence stridently denied. For orthodox Egyptology is really little more than a covert operation within the Church of Progress. Its unspoken agenda is to maintain the faith; not to study or debate the truth about Egypt.[254]

±NOTE (by West): Who will claim authority to challenge the accepted translations of the texts, even when these read as nonsense? Actually, a number of independent scholars have learned the hieroglyphs for themselves and produced alternative less insulting translations of some of the texts. But since these are either ignored or dismissed out of hand by orthodox Egyptologists, there is no way to know if these

---

[254] *Serpent in the Sky,* John Anthony West, p. 239

> translations come closer to the real thinking of the ancients or if they are themselves no more than figments of the translators' imaginations, and in consequence no more representative and satisfactory than the standard translations.

Noting further difficulties of sustaining independent or "alternative" Egyptology studies, West remains hopeful that the pressure to revise their unsupportable findings, not just from alternative Egyptologists, but also from geologists who bring to bear an irrefutable and exacting science to the dating of Ancient Egyptian monuments as opposed to the methods which other reputable sociologists and historians have found to be unreliable. Of the major methods accepted for establishing a chronology to understand the origins of civilization and the history of the world such as Astronomical Time, Geological Time, Archaeological Time and Political or Historical Time, the use of Scriptural chronology is recognized as being "extremely uncertain because various local chronologies were used at different times by scriptural writers, and different systems were used by contemporaneous writers."[255]

> An alternative Egyptology is less easily managed. Almost no one can earn a living from it. Serious research is difficult to accomplish on a spare-time basis, and research requires access to the few major Egyptological libraries scattered around the world. In Egypt itself, excavation and all work on or in the pyramids, temples and tombs are controlled by the Egyptian Antiquities Organizations. No one without academic credentials can expect to obtain permission to carry out original work.[256]

---

[255] "Chronology," Microsoft (R) Encarta Encyclopedia. Copyright (c) 1994

[256] West adds the following footnote: Prior to the development of modern day Egyptology by the western nations, native Egyptians showed little regard or respect for their distant dynastic ancestors; the temples were quarried for stone, anything movable was cheerfully sold to antiquities dealers. Islam, along with Christianity and Judaism, tended to regard ancient Egypt as pagan and idolatrous. But today, at least in private, Egyptian Egyptologists often display a much higher degree of understanding and sensitivity toward the Pharaonic achievement than their European and American colleagues. It would not surprise me to find some closet symbolists among them. Egyptian licensed tour guides (a much coveted job) must have degrees in academic Egyptology and pass an exacting test to qualify. Over the course of years of research and leading tours myself, at least a few dozen have approached me, eager to learn more about symbolist Egypt. But within the closed ranks of practicing, professional Egyptology, academic prestige (such as it is) is still wielded by the major European and American Universities. So even though all ancient Egyptian sites are now entirely under Egyptian control, an Egyptian Egyptologist would be as unlikely to try to break the "common front of silence" as anyone else, whatever his or her private convictions."

Infiltration from within is also peculiarly difficult. At least a few people I know personally have set out to acquire degrees in Egyptology, hoping to devote themselves full time to Egypt and ultimately to legitimize the symbolist interpretation. So far, none have been able to stick out the boredom or dutifully parrot the party line for the years necessary to get the diploma, knowing better from the onset.

It seems unlikely that symbolist Egypt will ever establish itself from within its own ranks. But pressure from outside Egyptology but within academia could force a change. Academics with an interest but no personal stake in the matter must sooner or later realize that the support of highly qualified geologists (of a fundamentally geological theory) must overrule either the clamor or the silence of the Egyptological/archeological establishment. At some point they must express those views.[257]

Thus, the Evidence of Contact analysis is very important in the determination of cultural relations and comparative studies. It is also important to be aware of logical arguments based on the indirect evidences such as geometric forms or geological evidences that may have an impact on the determination of primacy in the contact. Finally it is important to be aware of biases that scholars may have in putting forth their theories of contact or lack thereof due to any personal or cultural agendas that may be present. Nevertheless, Evidence of Contact remains a foundational aspect of cultural relations studies since without it we would not be able to say with a high degree of certainty that cultural correlations exist or even if there is a strong likelihood that a correlation exists between two cultures, that is, a cultural category or a cultural factor is the same or has the same origin in two seemingly separate cultures.

## Ethnicity, Race as Culture Factors

Modern scientists and scholars say that race distinctions based on genetics is unscientific and wrong. The animosity and hatred of modern times, caused by the distorting of religious scriptures when being rewritten or reinterpreted by various groups or ignorance of the true intent of the teachings of the religious holy books, has led to a situation where social problems have rendered practitioners of religion incapable of reaching a higher level of spiritual understanding. Many people in modern society are caught up in the degraded level of disputes and wars in an attempt to support ideas, which are in reality absurd and destructive in reference to the authentic doctrines of religion. Ironically, the inability of leaders in the

---

[257] *Serpent in the Sky,* John Anthony West, p. 241

church, synagogue or secular society to accept the truth about the origins of humanity comes from their desire to gain and maintain control over and the fear of losing control over their followers and the financial income they derive from them. Now that modern science is showing that all human beings originated from the same source, in Africa, and that racial distinctions are at least questionable and misleading and at worst, malicious lies and race baiting, it means that those who have perpetrated and sustained racism can no longer use science or religious teachings to support their iniquity and ignorant designs. They have no leg to stand on. The following excerpt was taken from Encarta Encyclopedia, and is typical of the modern scientific understanding of the question of human genetics and race issues.

"The concept of race has often been misapplied. One of the most telling arguments against classifying people into races is that persons in various cultures have often mistakenly acted as if one race were superior to another. Although, with social disadvantages eliminated, it is possible that one human group or another might have some genetic advantages in response to such factors as climate, altitude, and specific food availability, these differences are small. There are no differences in native intelligence or mental capacity that cannot be explained by environmental circumstances. Rather than using racial classifications to study human variability, anthropologists today define geographic or social groups by geographic or social criteria. They then study the nature of the genetic attributes of these groups and seek to understand the causes of changes in their genetic makeup. Contributed by: Gabriel W. Laser, "Races, Classification of," Encarta." Copyright (c) 1994

It should be noted here that there is no evidence that racial classifications for the purpose of supporting racist views existed in Ancient Egypt. However, the concept of ethnicity, which is often erroneously confused with the modern concept of race, was acknowledged in ancient times. That is to say, the Ancient Egyptians recognized that some of the physical features, mannerisms, traditions and other characteristics of the Asiatics, Europeans, and other groups were different from themselves and the Nubians. However, they din not ascribe those differences to substantive human dissimilarity; all human beings are alike. They recognized themselves as looking like the Nubians, but as possessing differences in culture. The Ancient Egyptian's depictions of themselves and their neighbors shows us beyond reasonable doubt, that they were dark skinned people like all other Africans, before the influx of Asiatics and Europeans to the country. Since genetics is increasingly being recognized as a false method of differentiating people the concept of phenotype has progressively more been used.

**phe·no·type** (fē/nə-tīp') *n.* **1.a.** The observable physical or biochemical characteristics of an organism, as determined by both genetic makeup and environmental influences. **b.** The expression of a specific trait, such as stature or blood type, based on genetic and environmental influences. **2.** An individual or group of organisms exhibiting a particular phenotype.[258]

It has been shown that climactic conditions, geography, solar exposure, vegetation, etc., have the effect of changing the appearance of people. This means that while people (human beings) remain equally human internally, their physiognomy and shade of skin adapt to the conditions where they live. This means that the external differences in people have little to do with their internal humanity and therefore are illusory. The concept of social typing is therefore based on ignorance about the race issue and its misconceptions, and cannot be supported by the scientific evidences. Further, an advancing society cannot hold such erroneous notions without engendering strife, and confusion, within the society. An advancing society will not be able to attain the status of "civilization" while holding on to such spurious concepts.

One of the major problems for society and non-secular groups is that the teachings and scientific evidence presented here has not been taught to the world population at large as part of the public or private education system. Even if it were, it would take time for people to adjust to their new understanding. Most people grow up accepting the ignorance of their parents who received the erroneous information from their own parents, and so on. Racism, sexism and other scourges of society are not genetically transmitted. They are transmitted by ignorant family members or the leaders of the culture (parents of the culture) who pass on their ignorance, prejudices and bigotries to their children (society), and so on down through the generations.

---

[258] American Heritage Dictionary

# Conclusion

Culture is the means by which human beings interact with and make sense of their world and their place in it as well as the meaning of life. Culture is composed of several component parts which may be referred to as *Categories of Cultural Expression*. Those categories can be further broken down into their constituent parts, *Factors of Cultural Expression*. Those factors can be classified and compared with the factors of other aspects of the same culture or with that of other cultures. This is the fundamental concept behind *The Cultural Category- Factor Correlation Method* for comparative mythology, religious cultural and social studies work.

The factors of cultural expression can be used by a society to express individual as well as collective ways of interacting with the world based on varied perspectives or viewpoints about the world. If a sufficient number of those ways were found to exhibit parallel or compatible formats beyond simple chance and if contact between the agents (actors) can be established, it is possible to discern and ascertain the probability of matching cultural expressions either between peoples in varied parts of the same culture, in the same or in different periods of time or between peoples of apparently different cultures. Such findings could enlighten us and the actors themselves about the deeper nature, history and meaning of their own actions or traditions as well as their possible hitherto unknown connections with other traditions; that could lead to better understanding through the realization of the deeper connections between apparently different traditions. These studies could also assist educators in alleviating the problems of social strife either through individual or group misunderstandings about their own history and that of others due to the deficiencies of the normal enculturation process.

Human beings have some aspects that are similar to animals, their instincts and desires. Like other animals, human beings have certain instinctual behaviors like suckling at the mother's breast. However, unlike animals, human beings have the capacity to exercise reason by means of their intellects. However, through the study of history and the observation of society it becomes apparent that human beings must go through the process of enculturation in order to learn the social values and traditions of the culture they grow up in; these are not instinctual. This means that the accumulated knowledge or wisdom of a society is not all learned cumulatively or even progressively since each new individual that enters (by being born into it) does not bring with it the knowledge previously learned by its parents. Each generation must learn the information again but it is not exactly the same as the old information, but the new and improved version. The incapacity to transfer cultural knowledge genetically or instinctually can be a benefit because a society can more easily leave behind detrimental cultural factors but it can also have deleterious effects. A potential danger for a society and its culture can arise if a society is sufficiently disrupted, either through wars, disease, acculturation, through pressures from a more powerful culture, etc. A society may lose its myth, traditions, its values, the elements that compose its culture and it can become lost in the struggle for survival and the loss of its firm identity or concept of self.

However, human beings are not a "clean slate" when they are born. There are some individuals who exhibit extraordinary abilities to perform certain tasks they did not learn previously, such as spontaneous musical ability. Others seem to have certain skills or wisdom without training or studying philosophy, etc. In Ancient Egyptian, Indian and Chinese religion this is explained as an effect of Karma and Reincarnation. Nevertheless, the masses, the vast majority of society, are relatively in the dark as they grow up and must be guided to the knowledge they need to make their way in life in a society and discover the culture and the meaning of life. This feature of human existence opens the possibility of acculturation, or the misleading (changing of a person's proper culture, traditions, values, etc.) of people through their own ignorance and desires or through outside manipulation and deception.

Therefore, the role of the leaders of a society, those who pass on the cultural values and wisdom is extremely important for the continued survival and well being of a society. Thus, cultural studies, especially its mythic and other *Fundamental Cultural Category-Factors of Cultural Expression,* are of extreme importance for understanding the enculturation process beyond the parochial and/or folkloric aspects of cultural expression that appear to offer so much diversity but really do not represent the essence of the human experience that is more common to all human beings that can easily become corrupted. In this way teachers and scholars may apply a technique of enculturation, based on the understanding of the universal categories of cultural expression, the purpose of culture and how to relate apparently different cultures so as to honor diversity while demonstrating the common shared process of cultural expression as well as the common struggle of life which the varied methods of cultural expression can offer insights into. This may allow people in a society to better equip themselves to handle the complexities of their personal human quest and the intricacies of human interaction through better understanding among peoples and consequently better understanding among the cultures those peoples operate through when their cultures interact.

## INDEX

# SEMA INSTITUTE

Cruzian Mystic P.O.Box 570459, Miami, Florida. 33257 (305) 378-6253, Fax. (305) 378-6253

WWW.Egyptianyoga.com

# Other Books From C M Books

**P.O.Box 570459**
**Miami, Florida, 33257**
**(305) 378-6253 Fax: (305) 378-6253**

This book is part of a series on the study and practice of Ancient Egyptian Yoga and Mystical Spirituality based on the writings of Dr. Muata Abhaya Ashby. They are also part of the Egyptian Yoga Course provided by the Sema Institute of Yoga. Below you will find a listing of the other books in this series. For more information send for the Egyptian Yoga Book-Audio-Video Catalog or the Egyptian Yoga Course Catalog.

Now you can study the teachings of Egyptian and Indian Yoga wisdom and Spirituality with the Egyptian Yoga Mystical Spirituality Series. The Egyptian Yoga Series takes you through the Initiation process and lead you to understand the mysteries of the soul and the Divine and to attain the highest goal of life: ENLIGHTENMENT. The *Egyptian Yoga Series*, takes you on an in depth study of Ancient Egyptian mythology and their inner mystical meaning. Each Book is prepared for the serious student of the mystical sciences and provides a study of the teachings along with exercises, assignments and projects to make the teachings understood and effective in real life. The Series is part of the Egyptian Yoga course but may be purchased even if you are not taking the course. The series is ideal for study groups.

**Prices subject to change.**

1.    *EGYPTIAN YOGA:  THE PHILOSOPHY OF ENLIGHTENMENT*
     An original, fully illustrated work, including hieroglyphs, detailing the meaning of the Egyptian mysteries, tantric yoga, psycho-spiritual and physical exercises. Egyptian Yoga is a guide to the practice of the highest spiritual philosophy which leads to absolute freedom from human misery and to immortality. It is well known by scholars that Egyptian philosophy is the basis of Western and Middle Eastern religious philosophies such as *Christianity, Islam, Judaism,* the

*Kabala*, and Greek philosophy, but what about Indian philosophy, Yoga and Taoism? What were the original teachings? How can they be practiced today? What is the source of pain and suffering in the world and what is the solution? Discover the deepest mysteries of the mind and universe within and outside of your self. 8.5" X 11" ISBN: 1-884564-01-1 Soft $19.95

2.   *EGYPTIAN YOGA: African Religion Volume 2-* Theban Theology U.S. In this long awaited sequel to *Egyptian Yoga: The Philosophy of Enlightenment* you will take a fascinating and enlightening journey back in time and discover the teachings which constituted the epitome of Ancient Egyptian spiritual wisdom. What are the disciplines which lead to the fulfillment of all desires? Delve into the three states of consciousness (waking, dream and deep sleep) and the fourth state which transcends them all, Neberdjer, "The Absolute." These teachings of the city of Waset (Thebes) were the crowning achievement of the Sages of Ancient Egypt. They establish the standard mystical keys for understanding the profound mystical symbolism of the Triad of human consciousness. ISBN 1-884564-39-9 $23.95

3.   *THE KEMETIC DIET: GUIDE TO HEALTH, DIET AND FASTING* Health issues have always been important to human beings since the beginning of time. The earliest records of history show that the art of healing was held in high esteem since the time of Ancient Egypt. In the early 20th century, medical doctors had almost attained the status of sainthood by the promotion of the idea that they alone were "scientists" while other healing modalities and traditional healers who did not follow the "scientific method' were nothing but superstitious, ignorant charlatans who at best would take the money of their clients and at worst kill them with the unscientific "snake oils" and "irrational theories". In the late 20th century, the failure of the modern medical establishment's ability to lead the general public to good health, promoted the move by many in society towards "alternative medicine". Alternative medicine disciplines are those healing modalities which do not adhere to the philosophy of allopathic medicine. Allopathic medicine is what medical doctors practice by an large. It is the theory that disease is caused by agencies outside the body such as bacteria, viruses or physical means which affect the body. These can therefore be treated by medicines and therapies  The natural healing method began in the absence of extensive technologies with the idea that all the answers for health may be found in nature or rather, the deviation from nature. Therefore, the health of the body can be restored by correcting the aberration and thereby restoring balance. This is the area that will be covered in this volume. Allopathic techniques have their place in the art of healing. However, we should not forget that the body is a grand achievement of the spirit and built into it is the capacity to maintain itself and heal itself. Ashby, Muata ISBN: 1-884564-49-6 $28.95

4.   INITIATION INTO EGYPTIAN YOGA Shedy: Spiritual discipline or program, to go deeply into the mysteries, to study the mystery teachings and literature profoundly, to penetrate the mysteries. You will learn about the mysteries of

initiation into the teachings and practice of Yoga and how to become an Initiate of the mystical sciences. This insightful manual is the first in a series which introduces you to the goals of daily spiritual and yoga practices: Meditation, Diet, Words of Power and the ancient wisdom teachings. 8.5" X 11" ISBN 1-884564-02-X Soft Cover $24.95 U.S.

5.   *THE AFRICAN ORIGINS OF CIVILIZATION, RELIGION AND YOGA SPIRITUALITY AND ETHICS PHILOSOPHY* HARD COVER EDITION Part 1, Part 2, Part 3 in one volume 683 Pages Hard Cover First Edition Three volumes in one. Over the past several years I have been asked to put together in one volume the most important evidences showing the correlations and common teachings between Ancient Egyptian (Ancient Egyptian) culture and religion and that of India. The questions of the history of Ancient Egypt, and the latest archeological evidences showing civilization and culture in Ancient Egypt and its spread to other countries, has intrigued many scholars as well as mystics over the years. Also, the possibility that Ancient Egyptian Priests and Priestesses migrated to Greece, India and other countries to carry on the traditions of the Ancient Egyptian Mysteries, has been speculated over the years as well. In chapter 1 of the book *Egyptian Yoga The Philosophy of Enlightenment,* 1995, I first introduced the deepest comparison between Ancient Egypt and India that had been brought forth up to that time. Now, in the year 2001 this new book, *THE AFRICAN ORIGINS OF CIVILIZATION, MYSTICAL RELIGION AND YOGA PHILOSOPHY,* more fully explores the motifs, symbols and philosophical correlations between Ancient Egyptian and Indian mysticism and clearly shows not only that Ancient Egypt and India were connected culturally but also spiritually. How does this knowledge help the spiritual aspirant? This discovery has great importance for the Yogis and mystics who follow the philosophy of Ancient Egypt and the mysticism of India. It means that India has a longer history and heritage than was previously understood. It shows that the mysteries of Ancient Egypt were essentially a yoga tradition which did not die but rather developed into the modern day systems of Yoga technology of India. It further shows that African culture developed Yoga Mysticism earlier than any other civilization in history. All of this expands our understanding of the unity of culture and the deep legacy of Yoga, which stretches into the distant past, beyond the Indus Valley civilization, the earliest known high culture in India as well as the Vedic tradition of Aryan culture. Therefore, Yoga culture and mysticism is the oldest known tradition of spiritual development and Indian mysticism is an extension of the Ancient Egyptian mysticism. By understanding the legacy which Ancient Egypt gave to India the mysticism of India is better understood and by comprehending the heritage of Indian Yoga, which is rooted in Ancient Egypt the Mysticism of Ancient Egypt is also better understood. This expanded understanding allows us to prove the underlying kinship of humanity, through the common symbols, motifs and philosophies which are not disparate and confusing teachings but in reality expressions of the same study of truth through metaphysics and mystical realization of Self. (HARD COVER) ISBN: 1-884564-50-X   $45.00 U.S.   81/2" X 11"

6. *AFRICAN ORIGINS BOOK 1 PART 1* African Origins of African Civilization, Religion, Yoga Mysticism and Ethics Philosophy-Soft Cover $24.95 ISBN: 1-884564-55-0

7. *AFRICAN ORIGINS BOOK 2 PART 2* African Origins of Western Civilization, Religion and Philosophy (Soft) -Soft Cover $24.95 ISBN: 1-884564-56-9

8. *EGYPT AND INDIA AFRICAN ORIGINS OF Eastern Civilization, Religion, Yoga Mysticism and Philosophy*-Soft Cover $29.95 (Soft) ISBN: 1-884564-57-7

9. *THE MYSTERIES OF ISIS: **The Ancient Egyptian Philosophy of Self-Realization*** - There are several paths to discover the Divine and the mysteries of the higher Self. This volume details the mystery teachings of the goddess Aset (Isis) from Ancient Egypt- the path of wisdom. It includes the teachings of her temple and the disciplines that are enjoined for the initiates of the temple of Aset as they were given in ancient times. Also, this book includes the teachings of the main myths of Aset that lead a human being to spiritual enlightenment and immortality. Through the study of ancient myth and the illumination of initiatic understanding the idea of God is expanded from the mythological comprehension to the metaphysical. Then this metaphysical understanding is related to you, the student, so as to begin understanding your true divine nature. ISBN 1-884564-24-0 $22.99

10. *EGYPTIAN PROVERBS:* collection of —Ancient Egyptian Proverbs and Wisdom Teachings -How to live according to MAAT Philosophy. Beginning Meditation. All proverbs are indexed for easy searches. For the first time in one volume, ——Ancient Egyptian Proverbs, wisdom teachings and meditations, fully illustrated with hieroglyphic text and symbols. EGYPTIAN PROVERBS is a unique collection of knowledge and wisdom which you can put into practice today and transform your life. $14.95 U.S        ISBN: 1-884564-00-3

11. *GOD OF LOVE: THE PATH OF DIVINE LOVE The Process of Mystical Transformation and The Path of Divine Love*        This Volume focuses on the ancient wisdom teachings of "Neter Merri" –the Ancient Egyptian philosophy of Divine Love and how to use them in a scientific process for self-transformation. Love is one of the most powerful human emotions. It is also the source of Divine feeling that unifies God and the individual human being. When love is fragmented and diminished by egoism the Divine connection is lost. The Ancient tradition of Neter Merri leads human beings back to their Divine connection, allowing them to discover their innate glorious self that is actually Divine and immortal. This volume will detail the process of transformation from ordinary consciousness to cosmic consciousness through the

integrated practice of the teachings and the path of Devotional Love toward the Divine. 5.5"x 8.5" ISBN 1-884564-11-9 $22.95

12. *INTRODUCTION TO MAAT PHILOSOPHY: Spiritual Enlightenment Through the Path of Virtue* Known as Karma Yoga in India, the teachings of MAAT for living virtuously and with orderly wisdom are explained and the student is to begin practicing the precepts of Maat in daily life so as to promote the process of purification of the heart in preparation for the judgment of the soul. This judgment will be understood not as an event that will occur at the time of death but as an event that occurs continuously, at every moment in the life of the individual. The student will learn how to become allied with the forces of the Higher Self and to thereby begin cleansing the mind (heart) of impurities so as to attain a higher vision of reality. ISBN 1-884564-20-8 $22.99

13. *MEDITATION The Ancient Egyptian Path to Enlightenment* Many people do not know about the rich history of meditation practice in Ancient Egypt. This volume outlines the theory of meditation and presents the Ancient Egyptian Hieroglyphic text which give instruction as to the nature of the mind and its three modes of expression. It also presents the texts which give instruction on the practice of meditation for spiritual Enlightenment and unity with the Divine. This volume allows the reader to begin practicing meditation by explaining, in easy to understand terms, the simplest form of meditation and working up to the most advanced form which was practiced in ancient times and which is still practiced by yogis around the world in modern times. ISBN 1-884564-27-7 $22.99

14. *THE GLORIOUS LIGHT MEDITATION* TECHNIQUE OF ANCIENT EGYPT New for the year 2000. This volume is based on the earliest known instruction in history given for the practice of formal meditation. Discovered by Dr. Muata Ashby, it is inscribed on the walls of the Tomb of Seti I in Thebes Egypt. This volume details the philosophy and practice of this unique system of meditation originated in Ancient Egypt and the earliest practice of meditation known in the world which occurred in the most advanced African Culture. ISBN: 1-884564-15-1 $16.95 (PB)

15. *THE SERPENT POWER: The Ancient Egyptian Mystical Wisdom of the Inner Life Force.* This Volume specifically deals with the latent life Force energy of the universe and in the human body, its control and sublimation. How to develop the Life Force energy of the subtle body. This Volume will introduce the esoteric wisdom of the science of how virtuous living acts in a subtle and mysterious way to cleanse the latent psychic energy conduits and vortices of the spiritual body. ISBN 1-884564-19-4 $22.95

16. *EGYPTIAN YOGA The Postures of The Gods and Goddesses* Discover the physical postures and exercises practiced thousands of years ago in Ancient Egypt which are today known as Yoga exercises. Discover the history of

the postures and how they were transferred from Ancient Egypt in Africa to India through Buddhist Tantrism. Then practice the postures as you discover the mythic teaching that originally gave birth to the postures and was practiced by the Ancient Egyptian priests and priestesses. This work is based on the pictures and teachings from the Creation story of Ra, The Asarian Resurrection Myth and the carvings and reliefs from various Temples in Ancient Egypt 8.5" X 11" ISBN 1-884564-10-0 Soft Cover $21.95    Exercise video  $20

17.   *SACRED SEXUALITY: EGYPTIAN TANTRA YOGA:  The Art of Sex* Sublimation and Universal Consciousness This Volume will expand on the male and female principles within the human body and in the universe and further detail the sublimation of sexual energy into spiritual energy. The student will study the deities Min and Hathor, Asar and Aset, Geb and Nut and discover the mystical implications for a practical spiritual discipline. This Volume will also focus on the Tantric aspects of Ancient Egyptian and Indian mysticism, the purpose of sex and the mystical teachings of sexual sublimation which lead to self-knowledge and Enlightenment.    5.5"x 8.5"    ISBN 1-884564-03-8 $24.95

18.   *AFRICAN RELIGION  Volume  4:  ASARIAN  THEOLOGY: RESURRECTING OSIRIS* The path of Mystical Awakening and the Keys to Immortality NEW REVISED AND EXPANDED EDITION!  The Ancient Sages created stories based on human and superhuman beings whose struggles, aspirations, needs and desires ultimately lead them to discover their true Self. The myth of Aset, Asar and Heru is no exception in this area. While there is no one source where the entire story may be found, pieces of it are inscribed in various ancient Temples walls, tombs, steles and papyri. For the first time available, the complete myth of Asar, Aset and Heru has been compiled from original Ancient Egyptian, Greek and Coptic Texts. This epic myth has been richly illustrated with reliefs from the Temple of Heru at Edfu, the Temple of Aset at Philae, the Temple of Asar at Abydos, the Temple of Hathor at Denderah and various papyri, inscriptions and reliefs.   Discover the myth which inspired the teachings of the *Shetaut Neter* (Egyptian Mystery System - Egyptian Yoga) and the Egyptian Book of Coming Forth By Day. Also, discover the three levels of Ancient Egyptian Religion, how to understand the mysteries of the Duat or Astral World and how to discover the abode of the Supreme in the Amenta,  *The Other World*    The ancient religion of Asar, Aset and Heru, if properly understood, contains all of the elements necessary to lead the sincere aspirant to attain immortality through inner self-discovery. This volume presents the entire myth and explores the main mystical themes and rituals associated with the myth for understating human existence, creation and the way to achieve spiritual emancipation - *Resurrection.* The Asarian myth is so powerful that it influenced and is still having an effect on the major world religions. Discover the origins and mystical meaning of the Christian Trinity, the Eucharist ritual and the ancient origin of the birthday of Jesus Christ. Soft Cover ISBN: 1-884564-27-5 $24.95

19. *THE EGYPTIAN BOOK OF THE DEAD MYSTICISM OF THE PERT EM HERU* " I Know myself, I know myself, I am One With God!– From the Pert Em Heru "The Ru Pert em Heru" or "Ancient Egyptian Book of The Dead," or "Book of Coming Forth By Day" as it is more popularly known, has fascinated the world since the successful translation of Ancient Egyptian hieroglyphic scripture over 150 years ago. The astonishing writings in it reveal that the Ancient Egyptians believed in life after death and in an ultimate destiny to discover the Divine. The elegance and aesthetic beauty of the hieroglyphic text itself has inspired many see it as an art form in and of itself. But is there more to it than that? Did the Ancient Egyptian wisdom contain more than just aphorisms and hopes of eternal life beyond death? In this volume Dr. Muata Ashby, the author of over 25 books on Ancient Egyptian Yoga Philosophy has produced a new translation of the original texts which uncovers a mystical teaching underlying the sayings and rituals instituted by the Ancient Egyptian Sages and Saints. "Once the philosophy of Ancient Egypt is understood as a mystical tradition instead of as a religion or primitive mythology, it reveals its secrets which if practiced today will lead anyone to discover the glory of spiritual self-discovery. The Pert em Heru is in every way comparable to the Indian Upanishads or the Tibetan Book of the Dead." $28.95     ISBN# 1-884564-28-3 Size: 8½" X 11

20. *African Religion VOL. 1- ANUNIAN THEOLOGY THE MYSTERIES OF RA* The Philosophy of Anu and The Mystical Teachings of The Ancient Egyptian   Creation Myth Discover the mystical teachings contained in the Creation Myth and the gods and goddesses who brought creation and human beings into existence. The Creation myth of Anu is the source of Anunian Theology but also of the other main theological systems of Ancient Egypt that also influenced other world religions including Christianity, Hinduism and Buddhism. The Creation Myth holds the key to understanding the universe and for attaining spiritual Enlightenment. ISBN: 1-884564-38-0 $19.95

21. *African Religion VOL  3: Memphite Theology: MYSTERIES OF MIND* Mystical Psychology & Mental Health for Enlightenment and Immortality based on the Ancient Egyptian Philosophy of Menefer -Mysticism of Ptah, Egyptian Physics and Yoga Metaphysics and the Hidden properties of Matter.   This volume uncovers the mystical psychology of the Ancient Egyptian wisdom teachings centering on the philosophy of the Ancient Egyptian city of Menefer (Memphite Theology). How to understand the mind and how to control the senses and lead the mind to health, clarity and mystical self-discovery. This Volume will also go deeper into the philosophy of God as creation and will explore the concepts of modern science and how they correlate with ancient teachings. This Volume will lay the ground work for the understanding of the philosophy of universal consciousness and the initiatic/yogic insight into who or what is God? ISBN 1-884564-07-0     $22.95

22.  *AFRICAN RELIGION VOLUME 5: THE GODDESS AND THE EGYPTIAN MYSTERIESTHE PATH OF THE GODDESS THE GODDESS PATH* The Secret Forms of the Goddess and the Rituals of Resurrection The Supreme Being may be worshipped as father or as mother. *Ushet Rekhat* or *Mother Worship,* is the spiritual process of worshipping the Divine in the form of the Divine Goddess. It celebrates the most important forms of the Goddess including *Nathor, Maat, Aset, Arat, Amentet and Hathor* and explores their mystical meaning as well as the rising of *Sirius,* the star of Aset (Aset) and the new birth of Hor (Heru). The end of the year is a time of reckoning, reflection and engendering a new or renewed positive movement toward attaining spiritual Enlightenment. The Mother Worship devotional meditation ritual, performed on five days during the month of December and on New Year's Eve, is based on the Ushet Rekhit. During the ceremony, the cosmic forces, symbolized by Sirius - and the constellation of Orion ---, are harnessed through the understanding and devotional attitude of the participant. This propitiation draws the light of wisdom and health to all those who share in the ritual, leading to prosperity and wisdom. $14.95 ISBN 1-884564-18-6

23.  *THE MYSTICAL JOURNEY FROM JESUS TO CHRIST* Discover the ancient Egyptian origins of Christianity before the Catholic Church and learn the mystical teachings given by Jesus to assist all humanity in becoming Christlike. Discover the secret meaning of the Gospels that were discovered in Egypt. Also discover how and why so many Christian churches came into being. Discover that the Bible still holds the keys to mystical realization even though its original writings were changed by the church. Discover how to practice the original teachings of Christianity which leads to the Kingdom of Heaven. $24.95 ISBN# 1-884564-05-4 size: 8½" X 11"

24.  *THE STORY OF ASAR, ASET AND HERU:* An Ancient Egyptian Legend (For Children)    Now for the first time, the most ancient myth of Ancient Egypt comes alive for children. Inspired by the books *The Asarian Resurrection: The Ancient Egyptian Bible* and *The Mystical Teachings of The Asarian Resurrection, The Story of Asar, Aset and Heru* is an easy to understand and thrilling tale which inspired the children of Ancient Egypt to aspire to greatness and righteousness.  If you and your child have enjoyed stories like *The Lion King* and *Star Wars you will love The Story of Asar, Aset and Heru.* Also, if you know the story of Jesus and Krishna you will discover than Ancient Egypt had a similar myth and that this myth carries important spiritual teachings for living a fruitful and fulfilling life.  This book may be used along with *The Parents Guide To The Asarian Resurrection Myth: How to Teach Yourself and Your Child the Principles of Universal Mystical Religion.* The guide provides some background to the Asarian Resurrection myth and it also gives insight into the mystical teachings contained in it which you may introduce to

your child. It is designed for parents who wish to grow spiritually with their children and it serves as an introduction for those who would like to study the Asarian Resurrection Myth in depth and to practice its teachings. 8.5" X 11" ISBN: 1-884564-31-3    $12.95

25.    *THE PARENTS GUIDE TO THE AUSARIAN RESURRECTION MYTH:* How to Teach Yourself and Your Child  the Principles of Universal Mystical Religion.   This insightful manual brings for the timeless wisdom of the ancient through the Ancient Egyptian myth of Asar, Aset and Heru and the mystical teachings contained in it for parents who want to guide their children to understand and practice the teachings of mystical spirituality. This manual may be used with the children's storybook *The Story of Asar, Aset and Heru* by Dr. Muata Abhaya Ashby.    ISBN: 1-884564-30-5    $16.95

26.    *HEALING THE CRIMINAL HEART.* Introduction to Maat Philosophy, Yoga and Spiritual Redemption Through the Path of Virtue    Who is a criminal? Is there such a thing as a criminal heart? What is the source of evil and sinfulness and is there any way to rise above it? Is there redemption for those who have committed sins, even the worst crimes?    Ancient Egyptian mystical psychology holds important answers to these questions. Over ten thousand years ago mystical psychologists, the Sages of Ancient Egypt, studied and charted the human mind and spirit and laid out a path which will lead to spiritual redemption, prosperity and Enlightenment.    This introductory volume brings forth the teachings of the Asarian Resurrection, the most important myth of Ancient Egypt, with relation to the faults of human existence: anger, hatred, greed, lust, animosity, discontent, ignorance, egoism jealousy, bitterness, and a myriad of psycho-spiritual ailments which keep a human being in a state of negativity and adversity    ISBN: 1-884564-17-8    $15.95

27.    *TEMPLE RITUAL OF THE ANCIENT EGYPTIAN MYSTERIES-- THEATER & DRAMA OF THE ANCIENT EGYPTIAN MYSTERIES*: Details the practice of the mysteries and ritual program of the temple and the philosophy an practice of the ritual of the mysteries, its purpose and execution. Featuring the Ancient Egyptian stage play-"The Enlightenment of Hathor' Based on an Ancient Egyptian Drama, The original Theater -Mysticism of the Temple of Hetheru 1-884564-14-3 $19.95  By Dr. Muata Ashby

28.    GUIDE TO PRINT ON DEMAND: SELF-PUBLISH FOR PROFIT, SPIRITUAL FULFILLMENT AND SERVICE TO HUMANITY Everyone asks us how we produced so many books in such a short time. Here are the secrets to writing and producing books that uplift humanity and how to get them printed for a fraction of the regular cost. Anyone can become an author even if they have limited funds. All that is necessary is the willingness to learn how the printing and book business work and the desire to follow the special instructions given here for preparing your manuscript format. Then you take your work directly to the non-

traditional companies who can produce your books for less than the traditional book printer can. ISBN: 1-884564-40-2    $16.95 U. S.

29.    *Egyptian Mysteries: Vol. 1,* Shetaut Neter What are the Mysteries? For thousands of years the spiritual tradition of Ancient Egypt, *Shetaut Neter,* "The Egyptian Mysteries," "The Secret Teachings," have fascinated, tantalized and amazed the world. At one time exalted and recognized as the highest culture of the world, by Africans, Europeans, Asiatics, Hindus, Buddhists and other cultures of the ancient world, in time it was shunned by the emerging orthodox world religions. Its temples desecrated, its philosophy maligned, its tradition spurned, its philosophy dormant in the mystical *Medu Neter,* the mysterious hieroglyphic texts which hold the secret symbolic meaning that has scarcely been discerned up to now. What are the secrets of *Nehast* {spiritual awakening and emancipation, resurrection}. More than just a literal translation, this volume is for awakening to the secret code *Shetitu* of the teaching which was not deciphered by Egyptologists, nor could be understood by ordinary spiritualists. This book is a reinstatement of the original science made available for our times, to the reincarnated followers of Ancient Egyptian culture and the prospect of spiritual freedom to break the bonds of *Khemn,* "ignorance," and slavery to evil forces: *Sâaa* . ISBN: 1-884564-41-0    $19.99

30.    *EGYPTIAN MYSTERIES VOL 2:* Dictionary of Gods and Goddesses This book is about the mystery of neteru, the gods and goddesses of Ancient Egypt (Ancient Egypt, Kemet). Neteru means "Gods and Goddesses." But the Neterian teaching of Neteru represents more than the usual limited modern day concept of "divinities" or "spirits." The Neteru of Ancient Egypt are also metaphors, cosmic principles and vehicles for the enlightening teachings of Shetaut Neter (Ancient Egyptian-African Religion). Actually they are the elements for one of the most advanced systems of spirituality ever conceived in human history. Understanding the concept of neteru provides a firm basis for spiritual evolution and the pathway for viable culture, peace on earth and a healthy human society.    Why is it important to have gods and goddesses in our lives? In order for spiritual evolution to be possible, once a human being has accepted that there is existence after death and there is a transcendental being who exists beyond time and space knowledge, human beings need a connection to that which transcends the ordinary experience of human life in time and space and a means to understand the transcendental reality beyond the mundane reality. ISBN: 1-884564-23-2    $21.95

31.    *EGYPTIAN MYSTERIES VOL. 3* The Priests and Priestesses of Ancient Egypt This volume details the path of Neterian priesthood, the joys, challenges and rewards of advanced Neterian life, the teachings that allowed the priests and priestesses to manage the most long lived civilization in human history and how that path can be adopted today; for those who want to tread the path of the Clergy of Shetaut Neter. ISBN: 1-884564-53-4 $24.95

32.   *The War of Heru and Set:* The Struggle of Good and Evil for Control of the World and The Human Soul This volume contains a novelized version of the Asarian Resurrection myth that is based on the actual scriptures presented in the Book Asarian Religion (old name –Resurrecting Osiris). This volume is prepared in the form of a screenplay and can be easily adapted to be used as a stage play. Spiritual seeking is a mythic journey that has many emotional highs and lows, ecstasies and depressions, victories and frustrations. This is the War of Life that is played out in the myth as the struggle of Heru and Set and those are mythic characters that represent the human Higher and Lower self. How to understand the war and emerge victorious in the journey o life? The ultimate victory and fulfillment can be experienced, which is not changeable or lost in time. The purpose of myth is to convey the wisdom of life through the story of divinities who show the way to overcome the challenges and foibles of life. In this volume the feelings and emotions of the characters of the myth have been highlighted to show the deeply rich texture of the Ancient Egyptian myth. This myth contains deep spiritual teachings and insights into the nature of self, of God and the mysteries of life and the means to discover the true meaning of life and thereby achieve the true purpose of life. To become victorious in the battle of life means to become the King (or Queen) of Egypt. Have you seen movies like The Lion King, Hamlet, The Odyssey, or The Little Buddha? These have been some of the most popular movies in modern times. The Sema Institute of Yoga is dedicated to researching and presenting the wisdom and culture of ancient Africa. The Script is designed to be produced as a motion picture but may be addapted for the theater as well. $21.95   copyright 1998 By Dr. Muata Ashby ISBN 1-8840564-44-5

33.   *AFRICAN DIONYSUS: FROM EGYPT TO GREECE:* The Ancient Egyptian Origins of Greek Culture and Religion ISBN: 1-884564-47-X   FROM EGYPT TO GREECE   This insightful manual is a reference to Ancient Egyptian mythology and philosophy and its correlation to what later became known as Greek and Rome mythology and philosophy. It outlines the basic tenets of the mythologies and shoes the ancient origins of Greek culture in Ancient Egypt. This volume also documents the origins of the Greek alphabet in Egypt as well as Greek religion, myth and philosophy of the gods and goddesses from Egypt from the myth of Atlantis and archaic period with the Minoans to the Classical period. This volume also acts as a resource for Colleges students who would like to set up fraternities and sororities based on the original Ancient Egyptian principles of Sheti and Maat philosophy. ISBN: 1-884564-47-X $22.95 U.S.

*34.*   *THE FORTY TWO   PRECEPTS OF MAAT,   THE PHILOSOPHY OF   RIGHTEOUS ACTION AND THE   ANCIENT EGYPTIAN WISDOM TEXTS* ADVANCED STUDIES  This manual is designed for use with the 1998 Maat Philosophy Class conducted by Dr. Muata Ashby. This is a detailed study of Maat Philosophy. It contains a compilation of the 42 laws or precepts of Maat and the corresponding principles which they represent along with the teachings of the ancient Egyptian Sages relating to each. Maat philosophy was the basis of Ancient Egyptian society and government as well as the heart of Ancient Egyptian myth and spirituality. Maat is at once a goddess, a cosmic force and a living social doctrine, which promotes social harmony and thereby paves the way for spiritual evolution in all levels of society. ISBN: 1-884564-48-8   $16.95 U.S.

## 35.    *THE SECRET LOTUS: Poetry of Enlightenment*

Discover the mystical sentiment of the Kemetic teaching as expressed through the poetry of Sebai Muata Ashby. The teaching of spiritual awakening is uniquely experienced when the poetic sensibility is present. This first volume contains the poems written between 1996 and 2003. 1-884564--16 -X  $16.99

### 36.   The Ancient Egyptian Buddha: The Ancient Egyptian Origins of Buddhism

This book is a compilation of several sections of a larger work, a book by the name of African Origins of Civilization, Religion, Yoga Mysticism and Ethics Philosophy. It also contains some additional evidences not contained in the larger work that demonstrate the correlation between Ancient Egyptian Religion and Buddhism. This book is one of several compiled short volumes that has been compiled so as to facilitate access to specific subjects contained in the larger work which is over 680 pages long. These short and small volumes have been specifically designed to cover one subject in a brief and low cost format. This present volume, The Ancient Egyptian Buddha: The Ancient Egyptian Origins of Buddhism, formed one subject in the larger work; actually it was one chapter of the larger work. However, this volume has some new additional evidences and comparisons of Buddhist and Neterian (Ancient Egyptian) philosophies not previously discussed. It was felt that this subject needed to be discussed because even in the early 21st century, the idea persists that Buddhism originated only in India independently. Yet there is ample evidence from ancient writings and perhaps more importantly, iconographical evidences from the Ancient Egyptians and early Buddhists themselves that prove otherwise. This handy volume has been designed to be accessible to young adults and all others who would like to have an easy reference with documentation on this important subject. This is an important subject because the frame of reference with which we look at a culture depends strongly on our conceptions about its origins. in this case, if we look at the Buddhism as an Asiatic religion we would treat it and it's culture in one way. If we id as African [Ancient Egyptian] we not only would see it in a different light but we also must ascribe Africa with a glorious legacy that matches any other culture in human history and gave rise to one of the present day most important religious philosophies. We would also look at the culture and philosophies of the Ancient Egyptians as having African insights that offer us greater depth into the Buddhist philosophies. Those insights inform our knowledge about other African traditions and we can also begin to understand in a deeper way the effect of Ancient Egyptian culture on African culture and also on the Asiatic as well. We would also be able to discover the glorious and wondrous teaching of mystical philosophy that Ancient Egyptian Shetaut Neter religion offers, that is as powerful as any other mystic system of spiritual philosophy in the world today.

### 37.   The Death of American Empire: Neo-conservatism, Theocracy, Economic Imperialism, Environmental Disaster and the Collapse of Civilization

This work is a collection of essays relating to social and economic, leadership, and ethics, ecological and religious issues that are facing the world today in order to understand the course of history that has led humanity to its present condition and then arrive at positive solutions that will lead to better outcomes for all humanity. It surveys the development and decline of major empires throughout history and focuses on the creation of American Empire along with the social, political and economic policies that led to the prominence of the United States of America as a Superpower including the rise of the political control of the neo-con political philosophy including militarism and the military industrial complex in American politics and the rise of the religious right into and American Theocracy movement. This volume details, through historical and current events, the psychology behind the dominance of western culture in world politics through the "Superpower Syndrome Mandatory Conflict Complex" that drives the Superpower culture to establish itself above all others and then act hubristically to dominate world culture through legitimate influences as well as coercion, media censorship and misinformation leading to international hegemony and world conflict. This volume also details the financial policies that gave rise to American prominence in the global economy, especially after World War II, and promoted American preeminence over the world economy through Globalization as well as the environmental policies, including the oil economy, that are promoting degradation of the world ecology and contribute to the decline of America as an Empire culture. This volume finally explores the factors pointing to the decline of the American Empire economy and imperial power and what to expect in the aftermath of American prominence and how to survive the decline while at the same time promoting policies and social-economic-religious-political changes that are needed in order to promote the emergence of a beneficial and sustainable culture.

### 38.  The African Origins of Hatha Yoga: And its Ancient Mystical Teaching
The subject of this present volume, The Ancient Egyptian Origins of Yoga Postures, formed one subject in the larger works, African Origins of Civilization Religion, Yoga Mysticism and Ethics Philosophy and the Book Egypt and India is the section of the book African Origins of Civilization. Those works contain the collection of all correlations between Ancient Egypt and India. This volume also contains some additional information not contained in the previous work. It was felt that this subject needed to be discussed more directly, being treated in one volume, as opposed to being contained in the larger work along with other subjects, because even in the early 21st century, the idea persists that the Yoga and specifically, Yoga Postures, were invented and developed only in India. The Ancient Egyptians were peoples originally from Africa who were, in ancient times, colonists in India. Therefore it is no surprise that many Indian traditions including religious and Yogic, would be found earlier in Ancient Egypt. Yet there is ample evidence from ancient writings and perhaps more importantly, iconographical evidences from the Ancient Egyptians themselves and the Indians themselves that prove the connection between Ancient Egypt and India as well as the existence of a discipline of Yoga Postures in Ancient Egypt long before its practice in India. This handy volume has been designed to be accessible to young adults and all others who would like to have an easy reference with documentation on this important subject. This is an important subject because the frame of reference with which we look at a culture depends strongly on our conceptions about its origins. In this case, if we look at the Ancient Egyptians as Asiatic peoples we would treat them and their culture in one way. If we see them as Africans we not only see them in a different light but we also must ascribe Africa with a glorious legacy that matches any other culture in human history. We would also look at the culture and philosophies of the Ancient Egyptians as having African insights instead of Asiatic ones. Those insights inform our knowledge bout other African traditions and we can also begin to understand in a deeper

way the effect of Ancient Egyptian culture on African culture and also on the Asiatic as well. When we discover the deeper and more ancient practice of the postures system in Ancient Egypt that was called "Hatha Yoga" in India, we are able to find a new and expanded understanding of the practice that constitutes a discipline of spiritual practice that informs and revitalizes the Indian practices as well as all spiritual disciplines.

### 39. The Black Ancient Egyptians

This present volume, The Black Ancient Egyptians: The Black African Ancestry of the Ancient Egyptians, formed one subject in the larger work: The African Origins of Civilization, Religion, Yoga Mysticism and Ethics Philosophy. It was felt that this subject needed to be discussed because even in the early 21st century, the idea persists that the Ancient Egyptians were peoples originally from Asia Minor who came into North-East Africa. Yet there is ample evidence from ancient writings and perhaps more importantly, iconographical evidences from the Ancient Egyptians themselves that proves otherwise. This handy volume has been designed to be accessible to young adults and all others who would like to have an easy reference with documentation on this important subject. This is an important subject because the frame of reference with which we look at a culture depends strongly on our conceptions about its origins. in this case, if we look at the Ancient Egyptians as Asiatic peoples we would treat them and their culture in one way. If we see them as Africans we not only see them in a different light but we also must ascribe Africa with a glorious legacy that matches any other culture in human history. We would also look at the culture and philosophies of the Ancient Egyptians as having African insights instead of Asiatic ones. Those insights inform our knowledge bout other African traditions and we can also begin to understand in a deeper way the effect of Ancient Egyptian culture on African culture and also on the Asiatic as well.

### 40. The Limits of Faith: The Failure of Faith-based Religions and the Solution to the Meaning of Life

Is faith belief in something without proof? And if so is there never to be any proof or discovery? If so what is the need of intellect? If faith is trust in something that is real is that reality historical, literal or metaphorical or philosophical? If knowledge is an essential element in faith why should there by so much emphasis on believing and not on understanding in the modern practice of religion? This volume is a compilation of essays related to the nature of religious faith in the context of its inception in human history as well as its meaning for religious practice and relations between religions in modern times. Faith has come to be regarded as a virtuous goal in life. However, many people have asked how can it be that an endeavor that is supposed to be dedicated to spiritual upliftment has led to more conflict in human history than any other social factor?

## Order Form

Telephone orders: Call Toll Free: 1(305) 378-6253. Have your AMEX, Optima, Visa or MasterCard ready.

    Fax orders: 1-(305) 378-6253    E-MAIL ADDRESS: Semayoga@aol.com

Postal Orders: Sema Institute of Yoga, P.O. Box 570459, Miami, Fl. 33257. USA.

           Please send the following books and / or tapes.

ITEM

_____Cost $_____

_____Cost $_____

_____Cost $_____

_____Cost $_____

_____Cost $_____

                        Total $_____

Name:_____

Physical Address:_____

City:_____ State:_____ Zip:_____

Sales tax: Please add 6.5% for books shipped to Florida addresses

_____Shipping: $6.50 for first book and .50¢ for each additional

_____Shipping: Outside US $5.00 for first book and $3.00 for each additional

_____Payment:_____

_____Check -Include Driver License #:

          _____

_____Credit card: _____ Visa, _____ MasterCard, _____ Optima,

_____ AMEX.

Card number:_____

Name on card:_____ Exp. date:_____/_____

**Copyright 1995-2005 Dr. R. Muata Abhaya Ashby**
**Sema Institute of Yoga**
**P.O.Box 570459, Miami, Florida, 33257**
**(305) 378-6253 Fax: (305) 378-6253**

Printed in the United States
88680LV00003B/23/A